Middle School 2-2
기말고사 완벽대비

적중100

영어 기출 문제집

중**2**

비상 | 김진완

Best Collection

구성과 특징

교과서의 주요 학습 내용을 중심으로 학습 영역별 특성에 맞춰 단계별로 다양한 학습 기회를 제공하여 단원별 학습능력 평가는 물론 중간 및 기말고사 시험 등에 완벽하게 대비할 수 있도록 내용을 구성

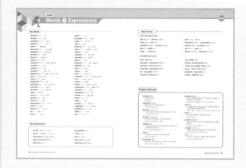

Words & Expressions

Step1 Key Words 단원별 핵심 단어 설명 및 풀이
Key Expression 단원별 핵심 숙어 및 관용어 설명
Word Power 반대 또는 비슷한 뜻 단어 배우기
English Dictionary 영어로 배우는 영어 단어

Step2 실력평가 단원별 수시평가 대비 주관식, 객관식 문제풀이

Step3 서술형 대비 학업성취도 및 수행능력평가 대비 서술형 문제풀이

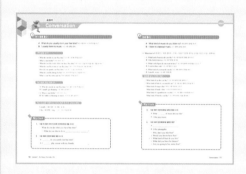

Conversation

Step1 핵심 의사소통 의사소통에 필요한 주요 표현 방법 요약
핵심 Check 기본적인 표현 방법 및 활용능력 확인

Step2 대화문 익히기 상황에 따른 대화문 활용 및 연습

Step3 기본평가 시험대비 기초 학습 능력 평가

Step4 실력평가 단원별 수시평가 대비 주관식, 객관식 문제풀이

Step5 서술형 대비 학업성취도 및 수행능력평가 대비 서술형 문제풀이

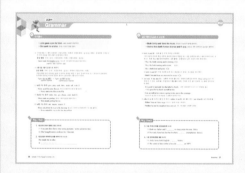

Grammar

Step1 주요 문법 단원별 주요 문법 사항과 예문을 알기 쉽게 설명
핵심 Check 기본 문법사항에 대한 이해 여부 확인

Step2 기본평가 시험대비 기초 학습 능력 평가

Step3 실력평가 단원별 수시평가 대비 주관식, 객관식 문제풀이

Step4 서술형 대비 학업성취도 및 수행능력평가 대비 서술형 문제풀이

Reading

Step1 구문 분석 단원별로 제시된 문장에 대한 구문별 분석과 내용 설명
확인문제 문장에 대한 기본적인 이해와 인지능력 확인

Step2 확인학습A 빈칸 채우기를 통한 문장 완성 능력 확인

Step3 확인학습B 제시된 우리말을 영어로 완성하여 작문 능력 키우기

Step4 실력평가 단원별 수시평가 대비 주관식, 객관식 문제풀이

Step5 서술형 대비 학업성취도 및 수행능력평가 대비 서술형 문제풀이
교과서 구석구석 교과서에 나오는 기타 문장까지 완벽 학습

Composition

|영역별 핵심문제|

단어 및 어휘, 대화문, 문법, 독해 등 각 영역별 기출문제의 출제 유형을 분석하여 실전에 대비하고 연습할 수 있도록 문제를 배열

|서술형 실전 및 창의사고력 문제|

학교 시험에서 점차 늘어나는 서술형 시험에 집중 대비하고 고득점을 취득하는데 만전을 기하기 위한 학습 코너

|단원별 예상문제|

기출문제를 분석한 후 새로운 시험 출제 경향을 더하여 새롭게 출제될 수 있는 문제를 포함하여 시험에 완벽하게 대비할 수 있도록 준비

|단원별 모의고사|

영역별, 단계별 학습을 모두 마친 후 실전 연습을 위한 모의고사

on the textbook ·· 교과서 파헤치기

- 단어Test1~2 영어 단어 우리말 쓰기와 우리말을 영어 단어로 쓰기
- 대화문Test1~2 대화문 빈칸 완성 및 전체 대화문 쓰기
- 본문Test1~5 빈칸 완성, 우리말 쓰기, 문장 배열연습, 영어 작문하기 복습 등 단계별 반복 학습을 통해 교과서 지문에 대한 완벽한 습득
- 구석구석지문Test1~2 지문 빈칸 완성 및 전문 영어로 쓰기

이책의 차례 Contents

Lesson 7

Art around Us

 ### 의사소통 기능

- 구체적인 종류나 장르 묻기
  A: **What Kind of** music are you going to play?
  B: I'm going to play rock music.

- 둘 중에 더 좋아하는 것 말하기
  A: There are two kinds of *Mona Lisas*. Which do you prefer?
  B: I **prefer** Botero's *Mona Lisa* **to** da Vinci's.

언어 형식

- 사역동사
  It will **make** you **wonder** about the painting more.

- 간접의문문
  Do you know **where Icarus is**?

교과서
Words & Expressions

Key Words

- **artist** [ɑ́:rtist] 몡 예술가, 미술가
- **artwork** [ɑ́rtwərk] 몡 예술 작품
- **brush** [brʌʃ] 몡 붓
- **canvas** [kǽnvəs] 몡 화폭, 캔버스
- **classical** [klǽsikəl] 혭 클래식의
- **comedy** [kámədi] 몡 희극, 코미디
- **despite** [dispáit] 젠 ~에도 불구하고
- **detail** [ditéil] 몡 세부 사항
- **direct** [dirékt] 통 ~로 향하다, 겨냥하다
- **direction** [dirékʃən] 몡 방향
- **exhibit** [igzíbit] 통 전시하다
- **feather** [féðər] 몡 깃털
- **flat** [flæt] 혭 납작한
- **frog** [frɔːg] 몡 개구리
- **hip-hop** [híphap] 몡 (음악) 힙합
- **landscape** [lǽndskèip] 몡 풍경
- **maze** [meiz] 몡 미로
- **melt** [melt] 통 녹다
- **modern** [mádərn] 혭 현대의
- **myth** [miθ] 몡 신화
- **notice** [nóutis] 통 ~을 알아차리다

- **novel** [návəl] 몡 소설
- **novelist** [návəlist] 몡 소설가
- **pop** [pɑp] 몡 팝 음악
- **prefer** [prifə́ːr] 통 더 좋아하다
- **prince** [prins] 몡 왕자
- **produce** [prədjúːs] 통 생산하다
- **production** [prədʌ́kʃən] 몡 생산
- **promise** [prámis] 통 약속하다
- **queen** [kwiːn] 몡 왕비, 여왕
- **real** [ríːəl] 혭 진짜의, 현실적인
- **rock** [rɑk] 몡 록 음악
- **seaside** [síːsaid] 몡 해변, 바닷가
- **since** [sins] 접 ~ 때문에, ~이므로
- **stick** [stik] 통 (몸의 일부를) 밀다, 내밀다
- **teen** [tiːn] 몡 십 대
- **tourist** [túərist] 몡 관광객
- **tragedy** [trǽdʒədi] 몡 비극
- **version** [və́ːrʒən] 몡 (어떤 것의) 변형
- **wax** [wæks] 몡 밀랍, 왁스
- **wing** [wiŋ] 몡 날개
- **wonder** [wʌ́ndər] 통 궁금해하다

Key Expressions

- **glance at** ~을 힐끗 보다
- **loot at** ~을 보다
- **move on** ~로 이동하다, 넘어가다
- **prefer A to B** A를 B보다 더 좋아하다

- **right away** 즉시, 바로
- **soap bubble** 비눗방울
- **stay away from** ~을 가까이하지 않다
- **take a look** ~을 보다

Word Power

※ 서로 반대되는 뜻을 가진 어휘

- □ **ancient** 고대의 ↔ **modern** 현대의
- □ **noticed** 알아차려진 ↔ **unnoticed** 눈에 띄지 않는
- □ **melt** 녹다 ↔ **freeze** 얼다
- □ **comedy** 희극 ↔ **tragedy** 비극
- □ **ask** 묻다 ↔ **answer** 대답하다
- □ **cheap** 싼 ↔ **expensive** 비싼

- □ **prince** 왕자 ↔ **princess** 공주
- □ **direct** 직접적인 ↔ **indirect** 간접적인
- □ **king** 왕 ↔ **queen** 왕비, 여왕
- □ **produce** 생산하다 ↔ **consume** 소비하다
- □ **real** 진짜의 ↔ **fake** 가짜의
- □ **entire** 전체의 ↔ **partial** 일부의

English Dictionary

- □ **artist** 예술가
  → someone who produces art
  예술을 만들어 내는 사람

- □ **canvas** 화폭, 캔버스
  → a piece of thick cloth used by artists for painting on, usually with oil paints, or the painting itself
  보통 유성 물감으로 그 위에 그림을 그리기 위해, 또는 그림 자체를 위해 미술가에 의해 사용되는 두꺼운 천 조각

- □ **detail** 세부 사항
  → a single piece of some information of fact about something
  무언가에 관한 사실에 대한 하나의 정보

- □ **direction** 방향
  → the way something or someone moves, faces, or is aimed
  무언가 또는 누군가가 움직이거나 마주하거나 또는 목표로 하는 길

- □ **feather** 깃털
  → one of the light soft things that cover a bird's body
  새의 몸을 덮고 있는 가볍고 부드러운 것들 중 하나

- □ **landscape** 풍경
  → an area of countryside, especially in relation to its appearance
  특히 외관과 관련된 시골 지역

- □ **melt** 녹다
  → to change from a solid to a liquid by applying heat
  열을 가함으로써 고체에서 액체로 변하다

- □ **myth** 신화
  → an ancient story, especially one invented in order to explain natural or historical events
  특히 자연적이거나 역사적인 사건을 설명하기 위해 만들어진 고대의 이야기

- □ **notice** 알아차리다
  → to see or become conscious of something or someone
  무언가 또는 어떤 사람을 보거나 의식하게 되다

- □ **seaside** 해변, 바닷가
  → an area that is close to the sea
  바다에 가까운 지역

- □ **stick** 내밀다
  → to put it in a position where other people can see a part of your body
  다른 사람들이 당신의 신체의 일부를 볼 수 있는 자리에 놓다

- □ **tragedy** 비극
  → a very sad event, especially one involving death
  특히 죽음과 관련된 매우 슬픈 사건

- □ **wing** 날개
  → one of the parts of a bird's or insect's body that it uses for flying
  날기 위해 사용하는 새나 곤충의 신체 부분 중의 하나

- □ **wonder** 궁금해하다
  → to want to know more about something because it interests you
  당신에게 흥미를 불러일으키기 때문에 어떤 것에 대해 더 알고 싶어지다

서답형

01 다음 짝지어진 단어의 관계가 같도록 빈칸에 알맞은 말을 쓰시오.

> increase : decrease = _____ : freeze

02 다음 영영풀이가 가리키는 것을 고르시오.

> an ancient story, especially one invented in order to explain natural or historical events

① myth　　　　② article
③ novel　　　　④ essay
⑤ poem

03 다음 중 밑줄 친 부분의 뜻풀이가 바르지 <u>않은</u> 것은?

① He doesn't use a <u>brush</u> when he draws. 붓
② My boss will tell you about the <u>details</u>. 세부 사항
③ I like to watch the <u>comedy</u> show on Sundays. 희극
④ Our attention <u>directed</u> to the result of the race. 향했다
⑤ Jane looks young and beautiful <u>despite</u> her age. ~ 때문에

서답형

04 다음 우리말에 맞게 빈칸에 알맞은 말을 쓰시오.

(1) 우리는 멈춰서 그 가게를 보았다.
　➡ We stopped and _____ a look at the store.
(2) 그녀는 버스 정류장에서 나를 힐끗 보았다.
　➡ She _____ at me at the bus station.
(3) 나는 종종 미술 작품을 보러 박물관에 간다.
　➡ I often go to the museum to see _____.
(4) 아이들이 비눗방울을 가지고 놀고 있다.
　➡ The kids are playing with _____ _____.

서답형

05 다음 문장의 빈칸에 들어갈 말을 〈보기〉에서 골라 쓰시오.

> ┌─ 보기 ─┐
> wings / details / wax / myth / landscape

(1) A tiger and a bear appear in the _____ of Dangun.
(2) I looked down on the peaceful _____ from the hill.
(3) My boss will tell you about the _____.
(4) They made _____ dolls of many actors.
(5) Airplanes have _____ like birds.

06 다음 주어진 문장의 밑줄 친 notice와 같은 의미로 쓰인 것은?

> I didn't <u>notice</u> the mistakes in this movie.

① I didn't <u>notice</u> whether she was there or not.
② This <u>notice</u> was on my front door.
③ We received the <u>notice</u> two weeks ago.
④ All rules cannot be changed without any <u>notice</u>.
⑤ Will you post up a <u>notice</u> on the board?

01 다음 짝지어진 단어의 관계가 같도록 빈칸에 알맞은 말을 쓰시오.

> king : queen = prince : _____

02 다음 우리말에 맞게 빈칸에 알맞은 말을 쓰시오.

(1) 산꼭대기 위의 눈은 절대 녹지 않는다.
➡ The snow on the top of the mountain never _____.

(2) 나는 당신을 나의 전시회에 초대하고 싶어요.
➡ I'd like to invite you to my _____.

(3) 어떤 새들은 다채로운 깃털을 갖고 있다.
➡ Some birds have colorful _____.

03 다음 문장의 빈칸에 들어갈 말을 〈보기〉에서 골라 쓰시오.

> ┤ 보기 ├
> notice / landscape / seaside / promise / stick

(1) From the hill, she looked down on the peaceful _____.

(2) I didn't _____ that Ted was there.

(3) Don't _____ your arm out of the car window.

(4) My dad _____d to buy me new shoes.

(5) We are going on a picnic at the _____ this Sunday.

04 다음 우리말을 주어진 단어를 이용하여 영작하시오.

(1) 나는 그가 왜 나를 그의 파티에 초대했는지 궁금하다. (invite)
➡ _____

(2) 새 자동차의 생산이 다음 달에 시작될 것이다. (car, start)
➡ _____

(3) 처음에 아무도 나를 알아차리지 못했다. (nobody)
➡ _____

05 다음 영영풀이가 가리키는 말을 쓰시오.

> to change from a solid to a liquid by applying heat

➡ _____

06 다음 우리말과 일치하도록 주어진 단어를 모두 배열하여 영작하시오.

(1) 폭풍우 치는 동안 창문 가까이 가지 마라.
(during / stay / a storm / windows / from / away)
➡ _____

(2) 제가 당신의 영화표를 봐도 될까요?
(take / movie / I / at / your / may / look / a / ticket)
➡ _____

(3) 나는 경찰에 바로 신고했다.
(police / right / called / I / away / the)
➡ _____

Conversation

1 구체적인 종류나 장르 묻기

A What kind of music are you going to play? 어떤 종류의 음악을 연주할 거니?
B I'm going to play rock music. 나는 록 음악을 연주할 거야.

■ "What kind of ~?"는 어떤 대상의 종류나 유형에 대해서 구체적으로 묻고자 할 때 사용된다. 예를 들어, 어떤 식당에서 먹을 수 있는 음식의 종류가 무엇인지 궁금할 때 "What kind of food does the restaurant serve?"와 같이 물을 수 있다.

구체적인 종류나 장르 묻기

• What sort of traditional food do you like? 어떤 종류의 전통 음식을 좋아하니?

• What type of person is the new math teacher? 새로 오신 수학 선생님은 어떤 사람인가요?

• To which category does this game belong? 이 게임은 어느 범주에 속하나요?

핵심 Check

1. 다음 우리말과 일치하도록 빈칸에 알맞은 말을 쓰시오.

(1) A: _____ _____ _____ _____ do you like? (어떤 종류의 콘서트를 좋아하니?)

B: I like a rock concert. (나는 록 콘서트를 좋아해.)

(2) A: What sort of _____ _____ _____ _____ _____ _____?
(어떤 종류의 영화를 보고 싶니?)

B: I want to see a comedy movie. (나는 코미디 영화를 보고 싶어.)

(3) A: What _____ of person is the new English teacher? (새로 오신 영어 선생님은 어떤 분이니?)

B: She is so kind and humorous. (그 선생님은 매우 친절하고 유머가 풍부하셔.)

2 둘 중에 더 좋아하는 것 말하기

A There are two kinds of *Mona Lisas*. Which do you prefer?

두 종류의 모나리자가 있어. 어느 것을 더 좋아하니?

B I prefer Botero's *Mona Lisa* to da Vinci's. 나는 다 빈치의 모나리자보다 보테로의 모나리자를 더 좋아해.

■ "I prefer A to B."는 두 가지 비교되는 사람이나 사물 등에 대하여 자신이 어떤 것을 더 좋아하는지를 표현할 때 사용된다. 예를 들어, 책을 읽는 것보다 영화 보는 것을 더 좋아한다는 것을 표현하고자 할 때는 "I prefer watching movies to reading books."와 같이 말할 수 있다.

둘 중에 더 좋아하는 것 말하기

- I like watching music videos better than listening to music.
  나는 음악을 듣는 것보다 음악 비디오를 보는 것을 더 좋아한다.

- I prefer taking a taxi to the station if possible. 나는 가능하면 역에 택시 타고 가는 것을 더 좋아한다.

- I think sending text messages is better than talking on the phone.
  나는 문자 메시지를 보내는 것이 전화로 이야기하는 것보다 더 낫다고 생각한다.

핵심 Check

2. 다음 우리말과 일치하도록 빈칸에 알맞은 말을 쓰시오.

(1) **A:** _____ _____ _____ _____, listening to music or reading books?

　　(음악 듣는 것과 책을 읽는 것 중에 어느 것을 더 좋아하니?)

　　B: I prefer listening to music to reading books. (나는 책을 읽는 것보다 음악 듣는 것을 더 좋아해.)

(2) **A:** Which do you prefer, taking photos or drawing pictures?

　　(사진 찍는 것과 그림 그리는 것 중에 어느 것을 더 좋아하니?)

　　B: I prefer _____ _____ to _____ _____.

　　(나는 그림을 그리는 것보다 사진 찍는 것을 더 좋아해.)

(3) **A:** Which do you prefer, dogs or cats? (개와 고양이 중에 어느 것을 더 좋아하니?)

　　B: _____ _____ _____ _____ _____. (나는 고양이보다 개를 더 좋아해.)

 Listen & Talk 1-B

W: (*ringing*) Hello, Steve.

M: Hi, Anna. We're meeting at the arts festival tomorrow at 1:30, right?

W: Right. ❶What kind of performance do you want to watch first?

M: I want to watch the hip-hop dance performance first.

W: ❷Sounds good. It's at 2 p.m. at the ❸gym, right?

M: Yeah, and ❹how about watching the play, *Romeo and Juliet*, at 4 p.m.?

W: Oh, the ❺one at the Main Hall near the gym? Sure!

W: (전화벨 소리) 안녕, Steve.

M: 안녕, Anna. 우리 내일 1시 30분에 예술 축제에서 만나는 거 맞지?

W: 맞아. 먼저 어떤 종류의 공연을 보고 싶어?

M: 난 힙합 댄스 공연을 먼저 보고 싶어.

W: 좋은 생각이야. 체육관에서 오후 2시에 하는 거 맞지?

M: 응, 그리고 오후 4시에 '로미오와 줄리엣' 연극을 보는 건 어때?

W: 아, 체육관 근처 대강당에서 하는 연극 말이지? 좋아!

---

❶ 구체적인 종류를 묻는 질문으로 'What sort of performance do you want to watch first?'로 바꾸어 쓸 수 있다.
❷ (That) sounds good. = Good idea.
❸ gym: 체육관
❹ 제안하는 표현으로 What about ~? = Why don't we ~? = Let's ~ 구문으로 바꾸어 쓸 수 있다.
❺ one은 play를 가리킨다.

Check(√) True or False

(1) Anna and Steve are going to visit the arts festival tomorrow. T ☐ F ☐

(2) Anna prefers watching the play to the hip-hop dance performance. T ☐ F ☐

 Communication

M: Hi, we are planning a school festival, so we want to ❶find out students' favorite types of performances. ❷May I ask you a few questions?

W: Sure.

M: What kind of performance do you like best?

W: I like music performances best.

M: Okay. Then, which do you prefer, rock or hip-hop?

W: I ❸prefer rock to hip-hop.

M: Who's your favorite musician?

W: ❹My favorite musician is TJ.

M: Great. Thank you for your answers.

M: 안녕하세요, 저희는 학교 축제를 계획 중이고, 그래서 학생들이 어떤 종류의 공연을 좋아하는지 알고 싶습니다. 몇 가지 질문을 해도 될까요?

W: 물론이죠.

M: 어떤 종류의 공연을 가장 좋아하나요?

W: 저는 음악 공연을 가장 좋아해요.

M: 알겠습니다. 그러면 록과 힙합 중 어느 것을 더 좋아하나요?

W: 저는 힙합보다 록을 더 좋아해요.

M: 가장 좋아하는 뮤지션은 누구인가요?

W: 제가 가장 좋아하는 뮤지션은 TJ입니다.

M: 좋습니다. 답변해 주셔서 감사합니다.

---

❶ find out: ~을 알아내다
❷ 부탁을 나타내는 표현으로 'Can I ask you a few questions?'로 바꾸어 쓸 수 있다.
❸ prefer A to B: A를 B보다 더 좋아하다.
❹ I love TJ. 또는 I like TJ best.로 바꾸어 쓸 수 있다.

Check(√) True or False

(3) The boy is asking some questions to prepare a school festival. T ☐ F ☐

(4) The girl likes rock more than hip-hop. T ☐ F ☐

Listen & Talk 1 A-1

W: Brian, is your band going to play at the Teen Music Festival?

M: Yes, we're practicing ❶almost every day.

W: ❷What kind of music are you going to play ❸this year?

M: Rock music. We'll play songs from the nineties.

❶ almost: 거의
❷ 'What sort of music are you going to play this year?'로 바꾸어 쓸 수 있다.
❸ this year: 올해

Listen & Talk 1 A-2

W: ❶Can you help me? I don't know how to paint clean lines.

M: What kind of ❷brush were you using?

W: This round brush.

M: When you paint lines, a ❸flat brush is better. Try this one.

W: Okay, thank you.

❶ 도움을 요청하는 표현으로 'Can you give me your hand?' = 'Would you help me?' 등으로 바꾸어 쓸 수 있다.
❷ brush: 붓
❸ flat: 평평한

Listen & Talk 2 A-1

M: What are you reading, Jina?

W: The ❶novel, *Life of Pi*. ❷It's a story of a boy and a tiger.

M: ❷It's a great book. I've seen the movie of ❷ it, too. I prefer the movie to the novel.

W: Why do you like ❷it better?

M: The ❸scenes are very beautiful. And the tiger ❹looks so ❺real.

❶ novel: 소설
❷ It[it]은 모두 *Life of Pi*를 가리킨다.
❸ scene: 장면
❹ look+형용사: ～처럼 보이다
❺ real: 진짜의 (↔ fake: 가짜의)

Listen & Talk 2 A-2

W: ❶Have you listened to Jane's new song, *Girl Friend*?

M: Yeah, ❷it's really cool. The guitar part is great.

W: ❸There is also a dance version of the song on the album.

M: I've listened to ❹it, but I prefer the guitar version to the dance version. ❺It matches her voice better.

❶ 현재완료(have+p.p) 구문으로 경험을 묻고 있다.
❷ it은 Jane's new song, *Girl Friend*를 가리킨다.
❸ There is+단수 명사: ～가 있다
❹ it은 a dance version을 가리킨다.
❺ It은 the guitar version을 가리킨다.

Listen & Talk 2 B

W: I saw an interesting painting in an art book. ❶Look at this.

M: Wow, it looks like da Vinci's *Mona Lisa*.

W: ❷Actually, it's *Mona Lisa* by Fernando Botero. Which do you prefer?

M: I prefer da Vinci's to Botero's. Da Vinci's *Mona Lisa* has an interesting smile. ❸How about you?

W: Well, I prefer Botero's to da Vinci's. His *Mona Lisa* is cute, and ❹it looks ❺modern.

❶ look at: ～을 보다
❷ actually: 사실은, 실제로
❸ How about you? = What about you?: 너는 어때?
❹ Botero's *Mona Lisa*를 가리킨다.
❺ modern: 현대적인

Wrap Up 1

M: Can you help me? I want to buy a guitar.

W: ❶There are various kinds of guitars. What kind of music do you want to play?

M: I want to play pop songs.

W: Then you should get a classical guitar.

M: Okay, I will take a classical guitar.

❶ There are+복수 명사

● 다음 우리말과 일치하도록 빈칸에 알맞은 말을 쓰시오.

Listen & Talk 1 A-1

W: Brian, is your band _____ _____ _____ at the Teen Music Festival?

M: Yes, we're practicing _____ _____ _____.

W: _____ _____ _____ _____ are you going to play this year?

M: Rock music. We'll _____ _____ from the nineties.

Listen & Talk 1 A-2

W: Can you help me? I don't know _____ _____ _____ _____ _____.

M: _____ _____ _____ _____ were you using?

W: This round brush.

M: When you paint lines, a _____ brush is _____. _____ this one.

W: Okay, thank you.

Listen & Talk 1 B

W: (*ringing*) Hello, Steve.

M: Hi, Anna. We're _____ at the arts festival tomorrow at 1:30, _____?

W: Right. What kind of performance _____ _____ _____ _____ _____ _____?

M: I _____ _____ watch the hip-hop dance performance first.

W: _____ good. It's at 2 p.m. at the gym, _____?

M: Yeah, and how about _____ _____ _____, *Romeo and Juliet*, at 4 p.m.?

W: Oh, _____ _____ at the Main Hall near the gym? Sure!

Listen & Talk 2 A-1

M: What are you reading, Jina?

W: The novel, *Life of Pi*. It's _____ _____ of a boy and a tiger.

M: It's a great book. I've seen the movie _____ _____, too. I _____ the movie _____ the novel.

W: Why do you _____ it _____?

M: The _____ are very beautiful. And the tiger looks so _____.

W: Brian, 너희 밴드는 '십 대 음악 축제'에서 연주할 거야?
M: 응, 우리는 거의 매일 연습하고 있어.
W: 너희는 올해 어떤 종류의 음악을 연주하려고 해?
M: 록 음악. 우리는 90년대 곡들을 연주할 거야.

W: 나 좀 도와줄래? 나는 선을 깔끔하게 그리는 방법을 모르겠어.
M: 어떤 종류의 붓을 사용하고 있었니?
W: 이 둥근 붓이야.
M: 선을 그릴 때는 납작한 붓이 더 나아. 이것을 써 봐.
W: 알았어, 고마워.

W: (전화벨 소리) 안녕, Steve.
M: 안녕, Anna. 우리 내일 1시 30분에 예술 축제에서 만나는 거 맞지?
W: 맞아. 먼저 어떤 종류의 공연을 보고 싶어?
M: 난 힙합 댄스 공연을 먼저 보고 싶어.
W: 좋은 생각이야. 체육관에서 오후 2시에 하는 거 맞지?
M: 응, 그리고 오후 4시에 '로미오와 줄리엣' 연극을 보는 건 어때?
W: 아, 체육관 근처 대강당에서 하는 연극 말이지? 좋아!

M: 지나야, 너 무엇을 읽고 있니?
W: '파이 이야기'라는 소설이야. 한 소년과 호랑이에 대한 이야기이지.
M: 훌륭한 책이야. 나는 그것을 영화로도 봤어. 나는 소설보다는 영화가 더 좋아.
W: 왜 영화가 더 좋은데?
M: 장면이 매우 아름다워. 그리고 호랑이가 매우 진짜같이 보이거든.

Listen & Talk 2 A-2

W: _____ you _____ to Jane's new song, *Girl Friend*?

M: Yeah, it's really _____. The guitar _____ is great.

W: There is also a _____ _____ of the song on the album.

M: I've listened to it, but _____ _____ _____ _____ _____ to the dance version. It _____ her voice better.

Listen & Talk 2 B

W: I saw an _____ _____ in an art book. Look at this.

M: Wow, it _____ _____ da Vinci's *Mona Lisa*.

W: Actually, it's *Mona Lisa* by Fernando Botero. _____ _____ _____ _____?

M: I _____ da Vinci's _____ Botero's. Da Vinci's *Mona Lisa* has an interesting smile. _____ _____ _____?

W: Well, I _____ Botero's _____ da Vinci's. His *Mona Lisa* is cute, and it looks _____.

Communication

M: Hi, we are planning a school festival, _____ we want to _____ _____ students' favorite types of performances. _____ I _____ you a few questions?

W: Sure.

M: _____ _____ _____ _____ _____ do you like best?

W: I like music performances best.

M: Okay. Then, which _____ you _____, rock or hip-hop?

W: I _____ _____ _____ _____.

M: Who's your _____ _____?

W: My favorite musician is TJ.

M: Great. _____ you _____ your answers.

Wrap Up 1

M: _____ you _____ me? I want to buy a guitar.

W: There are _____ _____ of guitars. _____ _____ _____ _____ do you want to play?

M: I _____ _____ play pop songs.

W: Then you _____ _____ a classical guitar.

M: Okay, I will take a classical guitar.

해석

W: 너는 Jane의 새 노래인 '여자 친구'를 들어 봤니?

M: 응, 정말 멋져. 기타 부분이 굉장하지.

W: 앨범에는 그 노래의 댄스 버전도 있어.

M: 나는 그것을 들었는데 댄스 버전보다는 기타 버전이 더 좋아. 그 버전이 그녀의 목소리와 더 잘 어울리거든.

W: 나 미술 책에서 흥미로운 그림을 봤어. 이것 봐.

M: 와, 그것은 다빈치의 '모나리자'처럼 보이는데.

W: 사실 이 그림은 페르난도 보테로의 '모나리자'야. 넌 어느 것이 더 마음에 드니?

M: 나는 보테로의 그림보다 다빈치의 모나리자가 더 좋아. 다빈치의 '모나리자'에는 흥미로운 미소가 있어. 너는 어때?

W: 음, 나는 다빈치의 모나리자보다는 보테로의 모나리자가 더 좋아. 그의 '모나리자'는 귀엽고 현대적으로 보여.

M: 안녕하세요, 저희는 학교 축제를 계획 중이고, 그래서 학생들이 어떤 종류의 공연을 좋아하는지 알고 싶습니다. 몇 가지 질문을 해도 될까요?

W: 물론이죠.

M: 어떤 종류의 공연을 가장 좋아하나요?

W: 저는 음악 공연을 가장 좋아해요.

M: 알겠습니다. 그러면 록과 힙합 중 어떤 것을 더 좋아하나요?

W: 저는 힙합보다 록을 더 좋아해요.

M: 가장 좋아하는 뮤지션은 누구인가요?

W: 제가 가장 좋아하는 뮤지션은 TJ입니다.

M: 좋습니다. 답변해 주셔서 감사합니다.

M: 저 좀 도와주시겠어요? 저는 기타를 하나 사고 싶어요.

W: 다양한 종류의 기타가 있어요. 어떤 종류의 음악을 연주하고 싶으신가요?

M: 저는 팝송을 연주하려고 해요.

W: 그럼 클래식 기타를 사셔야 해요.

M: 알겠습니다, 클래식 기타로 살게요.

[01~02] 다음 대화를 읽고 물음에 답하시오.

> Sora: (A)Can you help me? I don't know how to paint clean lines.
>
> Mike: _____(B)_____
>
> Sora: This round brush.
>
> Mike: When you paint lines, a flat brush is better. Try this one.
>
> Sora: Okay, thank you.

01 위 대화의 밑줄 친 (A)와 바꾸어 쓸 수 있는 것을 <u>모두</u> 고르시오.

① Can you give me a hand? ② Do you need any help?

③ What can I do for you?   ④ Would you do me a favor?

⑤ Can I give you a hand?

02 위 대화의 빈칸 (B)에 들어갈 말을 <보기>에 주어진 단어를 배열하여 완성하시오.

> ┤ 보기 ├
>
> of / brush / you / what / using / were / kind

➡ _____

[03~04] 다음 대화를 읽고 물음에 답하시오.

> Minsu: What are you reading, Jina?
>
> Jina: The novel, *Life of Pi*. It's a story of a boy and a tiger.
>
> Minsu: It's a great book. I've seen the movie of (A)it, too. I prefer the movie to the novel.
>
> Jina: Why do you like (B)it better?
>
> Minsu: The scenes are very beautiful. And the tiger looks so real.

03 위 대화의 밑줄 친 (A)와 (B)의 it이 각각 가리키는 것을 찾아 쓰시오.

(A) _____   (B) _____

04 위 대화의 내용과 일치하지 <u>않는</u> 것은?

① Jina is reading *Life of Pi*.

② *Life of Pi* is the novel about a boy and a tiger.

③ Minsu has seen the movie of *Life of Pi*.

④ Minsu likes the novel more than the movie.

⑤ The scenes are very beautiful in the movie.

01 다음 대화의 내용과 일치하지 <u>않는</u> 것은?

> Susan: Brian, is your band going to play at the Teen Music Festival?
>
> Brian: Yes, we're practicing almost every day.
>
> Susan: What kind of music are you going to play this year?
>
> Brian: Rock music. We'll play songs from the nineties.

① Brian의 밴드는 '십 대 음악 축제'에서 연주할 것이다.

② Brian의 밴드는 거의 매일 연습하고 있다.

③ Brian의 밴드는 올해 록 음악을 연주할 것이다.

④ Brian의 밴드는 90년대 곡들을 연주할 것이다.

⑤ Brian의 밴드는 90분 동안 연주할 것이다.

[02~03] 다음 대화를 읽고 물음에 답하시오.

> Sue: Have you listened to Jane's new song, *Girl Friend*?
>
> Tony: Yeah, (A)<u>it</u>'s really cool. The guitar part is great.
>
> Sue: There is also a dance version of the song on the album.
>
> Tony: I've listened to (B)<u>it</u>, but I prefer the guitar version to the dance version. (C)<u>It</u> matches her voice better.

서답형

02 위 대화의 밑줄 친 (A)~(C)의 it이 가리키는 것을 각각 찾아 쓰시오.

(A) _____

(B) _____

(C) _____

03 위 대화의 내용과 일치하지 <u>않는</u> 것은?

① Jane released her new song, *Girl Friend*.

② Tony likes the guitar part of *Girl Friend*.

③ There are both a dance version and the guitar version of *Girl Friend* on the album,

④ Tony thought that Jane's voice matches the dance version.

⑤ Tony likes the guitar version more than the dance version.

04 다음 대화를 읽고 대답할 수 <u>없는</u> 질문은?

> Anna: (*ringing*) Hello, Steve.
>
> Steve: Hi, Anna. We're meeting at the arts festival tomorrow at 1:30, right?
>
> Anna: Right. What kind of performance do you want to watch first?
>
> Steve: I want to watch the hip-hop dance performance first.
>
> Anna: Sounds good. It's at 2 p.m. at the gym, right?
>
> Steve: Yeah, and how about watching the play, *Romeo and Juliet*, at 4 p.m.?
>
> Anna: Oh, the one at the Main Hall near the gym? Sure!

① What is Anna going to do with Steve tomorrow?

② What kind of performance does Steve want to watch first?

③ When is the hip-hop dance performance?

④ Where can Anna and Steve watch the play, *Romeo and Juliet*?

⑤ Why does Steve suggest watching the play, *Romeo and Juliet*?

서답형

05 다음 대화의 내용과 일치하도록 주어진 표를 완성하시오.

Mina: I saw an interesting painting in an art book. Look at this.

Jack: Wow, it looks like da Vinci's *Mona Lisa*.

Mina: Actually, it's *Mona Lisa* by Fernando Botero. Which do you prefer?

Jack: I prefer da Vinci's to Botero's. Da Vinci's *Mona Lisa* has an interesting smile. How about you?

Mina: Well, I prefer Botero's to da Vinci's. His *Mona Lisa* is cute, and it looks modern.

Title	*Mona Lisa*	
Painter	Leonardo da Vinci	Fernando Botero
Who prefers	(A)	(B)
opinion	(C)	(D)

(A) _____ (B) _____

(C) _____

(D) _____

[06~08] 다음 대화를 읽고 물음에 답하시오.

Jason: Hi, we are planning a school festival, so we want to find out students' favorite types of performances. (A) May I ask you a few questions?

Emily: Sure.

Jason: What kind of performance do you like best?

Emily: I like music performances best.

Jason: Okay. Then, (B)어느 것을 더 좋아하나요, rock or hip-hop?

Emily: I prefer rock to hip-hop.

Jason: Who's your favorite musician?

Emily: My favorite musician is TJ.

Jason: Great. Thank you for your answers.

06 위 대화의 밑줄 친 (A)와 바꾸어 쓸 수 있는 것은?

① Do you have any questions?

② Do you want to ask any questions?

③ Would you answer a few questions?

④ How can I ask a few questions of you?

⑤ Did you answer a few questions?

서답형

07 위 대화의 밑줄 친 (B)의 우리말을 4단어를 사용하여 영작하시오.

➡ _____

서답형

08 What kind of music does Emily like better?

➡ _____

서답형

09 다음 주어진 문장 뒤에 이어지는 대화가 자연스럽게 이어지도록 순서대로 배열하시오.

Can you help me? I want to buy a guitar.

(A) Okay, I will take a classical guitar.

(B) I want to play pop songs.

(C) There are various kinds of guitars. What kind of music do you want to play?

(D) Then you should get a classical guitar.

➡ _____

01 다음 대화의 빈칸 (A)~(C)에 들어갈 알맞은 대답을 〈보기〉에서 찾아 쓰시오.

> Jason: Hi, we are planning a school festival, so we want to find out students' favorite types of performances. May I ask you a few questions?
>
> Emily: Sure.
>
> Jason: What kind of performance do you like best?
>
> Emily: (A)_____
>
> Jason: Okay. Then, which do you prefer, rock or hip-hop?
>
> Emily: (B)_____
>
> Jason: Who's your favorite musician?
>
> Emily: (C)_____
>
> Jason: Great. Thank you for your answers.

┌─── 보기 ───┐
ⓐ My favorite musician is TJ.
ⓑ I like music performances best.
ⓒ I prefer rock to hip-hop.
└─────────────┘

(A) _____ (B) _____ (C) _____

[02~03] 다음 대화를 읽고 물음에 답하시오.

Sue: Have you listened to Jane's new song, *Girl Friend*?

Tony: Yeah, it's really cool. The guitar part is great.

Sue: There is also a dance version of the song on the album.

Tony: I've listened to it, but I prefer the guitar version to the dance version. It matches her voice better.

02 What song have Tony and Sue listened to in Jane's album?

➡ _____

03 Why does Tony prefer the guitar version to the dance version?

➡ _____

_____

[04~06] 다음 대화를 읽고 물음에 답하시오.

Minsu: What are you reading, Jina?

Jina: The novel, *Life of Pi*. It's a story of a boy and a tiger.

Minsu: It's a great book. I've seen the movie of it, too. (A)나는 소설보다는 영화가 더 좋아. (prefer)

Jina: Why do you like it better?

Minsu: The scenes are very beautiful. And the tiger looks so real.

04 위 대화의 밑줄 친 (A)의 우리말을 주어진 단어를 사용하여 영작하시오.

➡ _____

05 What is the novel, *Life of Pi*, about?

➡ _____

06 Why does Minsu prefer the movie to the novel?

➡ _____

_____

Grammar

1 사역동사

- He **made** me **do** the laundry. 그는 내가 빨래를 하도록 시켰다.
- Alicia **had** her son **park** her car. Alicia는 그녀의 아들이 그녀의 차를 주차하게 했다.

■ 사역동사는 문장의 주어가 목적어에게 어떠한 행동을 하도록 시키는 동사로 make, have, let 등이 이에 속한다.

- Gloria **let** me **go** home early. Gloria는 내가 집에 일찍 가도록 허락해 주었다.
- Paul **had** my sister **sing** in front of many people. Paul은 내 여동생이 많은 사람들 앞에서 노래하게 했다.
- They **make** us **do** our best. 그들은 우리가 최선을 다하게 만든다.

■ 사역동사는 5형식에 속하여 목적격 보어를 갖는데, 사역동사의 목적격 보어는 동사원형의 형태를 취하며, '~에게 …하게 하다'라고 해석하는 것에 유의한다.

- The teacher **made** us **find** the dog. 선생님은 우리가 그 개를 찾도록 시키셨다.
- She **had** me **do** the job instead of her. 그녀는 그녀 대신에 내가 그 일을 하도록 시켰다.
- The sisters **made** me buy the car. 그 자매들은 내가 그 차를 사게 했다.
- I **had** my sister **fix** dinner. 나는 내 여동생이 저녁 식사를 차리게 했다.

■ 준사역동사에 해당하는 help는 목적격 보어로 to부정사나 동사원형 형태를 취한다.

- We **helped** the man **stand[to stand]** on his own. 우리는 그 남자가 혼자 힘으로 설 수 있도록 도왔다.

핵심 Check

1. 다음 우리말과 일치하도록 빈칸에 알맞은 말을 쓰시오.

(1) Mike는 내가 그의 가방을 지켜보게 했다.

➡ Mike had _____ _____ his bag.

(2) 나는 그가 내 스마트폰을 사용하게 한다.

➡ I let _____ _____ my smartphone.

(3) 엄마는 아빠가 일찍 집에 오게 하셨다.

➡ My mom made _____ _____ _____ home early.

---

② 간접의문문

- Do you know **who he is**? 너는 그가 누구인지 아니?
- I wonder **what her name is**. 나는 그녀의 이름이 무엇인지 궁금해.

■ 의문문이 문장 내에서 주어, 목적어, 보어 역할을 할 때 이를 간접의문문이라고 한다. 간접의문문의 어순은 '의문사+주어+동사'임에 유의한다.

- I don't know **how you came here**. 나는 네가 어떻게 이곳에 왔는지 모르겠어.
- He doesn't remember **what her name is**. 그는 그녀의 이름이 무엇인지 기억하지 못한다.
- Jane wants to know **where her mother is**. Jane은 그녀의 엄마가 어디에 있는지 알고 싶다.

■ 의문사가 주어로 쓰인 경우 의문사가 동시에 주어 역할을 하므로 의문사 뒤에 동사가 바로 이어서 나올 수 있다.

- Do you know **who invented the light bulb**? 누가 전구를 발명했는지 아니?
- Can you tell me **what made her upset**? 무엇이 그녀를 화나게 했는지 말해줄 수 있니?

■ think, believe, guess, imagine, suppose 등과 같은 동사가 주절에 있을 경우 간접의문문의 의문사를 문장 맨 앞으로 배치한다.

- Do you think what it is? (X)

  What do you think **it is**? (○) 너는 그것이 무엇이라고 생각하니?

- Do you guess who he is? (X)

  Who do you guess **he is**? (○) 너는 그가 누구라고 생각하는 거야?

■ 의문사가 없는 경우 간접의문문의 어순은 'if/whether+주어+동사'로 쓴다.

- Can you tell me? + Is he hungry?
  → Can you tell me **if[whether] he is hungry**? 그가 배가 고픈지 내게 말해줄래?
- I wonder **whether Kevin wants to come**. Kevin이 오기를 원하는지 궁금하다.
- I want to know **whether they will accept the job**. 그들이 그 일을 받아들일지 알고 싶어.

핵심 Check

2. 다음 두 문장을 하나의 문장으로 연결할 때 빈칸에 알맞은 말을 쓰시오.

(1) Do you know? Who is she?

➡ Do you know _____ _____ _____?

(2) Can you tell me? Why do you study English?

➡ Can you tell me _____ _____ _____ English?

(3) I wonder. Where did you go yesterday?

➡ I wonder _____ _____ _____ yesterday.

01 다음 문장에서 어법상 <u>어색한</u> 부분을 바르게 고쳐 쓰시오.

(1) My teacher made me to read this book.

    _____ ➡ _____

(2) I wonder how was the weather yesterday.

    _____ ➡ _____

(3) My father let me buying the laptop computer.

    _____ ➡ _____

(4) I didn't know who were you at first.

    _____ ➡ _____

02 다음 두 문장을 간접의문문을 이용하여 하나의 문장으로 쓰시오.

(1) Oliver wanted to ask. Was she satisfied with his service?

  ➡ _____

(2) Can you tell me? Where are we going?

  ➡ _____

(3) I'd like to know. What do you do during your free time?

  ➡ _____

(4) I wonder. How often do you water the plant?

  ➡ _____

03 주어진 어구를 바르게 배열하여 다음 우리말을 영어로 쓰시오. 필요하다면 어형을 바꾸시오.

(1) 그 상사는 그가 사무실에 머무르게 시켰다.

(the office / make / stay / him / in / the boss)

  ➡ _____

(2) 너는 네 친구가 네 자전거를 빌려가도록 허락했니?

(bicycle / did / your / you / borrow / let / friend / your)

  ➡ _____

(3) 우리는 그가 밀짚모자를 쓰게 했어요.

(have / wear / we / him / a straw hat)

  ➡ _____

(4) 제가 답을 보게 해 주세요.

(the answer / me / please / see / let)

  ➡ _____

☆ 중요
01 다음 빈칸에 들어갈 말로 적절하지 <u>않은</u> 것은?

> Mary _____ us play the computer game.

① made   ② saw   ③ let
④ had   ⑤ wanted

02 다음 우리말을 영어로 바르게 옮긴 것은?

> 나는 그 남자가 내 차를 세차하게 만들었다.

① I wanted the man to wash my car.
② I wondered whether the man washed my car.
③ I made the man wash my car.
④ I asked the man to wash my car.
⑤ I saw the man wash my car.

 중요
03 다음 중 빈칸에 들어갈 수 <u>없는</u> 말은?

> Who do you _____ has this car?

① guess   ② imagine   ③ think
④ wonder   ⑤ suppose

04 다음 중 빈칸에 들어갈 단어 'do'의 형태가 <u>다른</u> 하나는?

① Julie made me _____ my best.
② Clara saw me _____ aerobics.
③ They let me _____ the flowers.
④ Paul had me _____ some research.
⑤ June allowed me _____ the cooking with her brother.

서답형
05 다음 빈칸에 알맞은 말을 쓰시오.

> 그들은 내가 이곳에 일찍 오게 했습니다.
> ➡ They made me _____ here early.

서답형
06 다음 우리말을 영어로 옮길 때 다섯 번째로 오는 단어를 쓰시오.

> 나는 네가 이곳에 언제 도착할 것인지 궁금해.

➡ _____

07 다음 중 어법상 올바른 문장의 개수는?

> ⓐ Susan had them finish the homework until that night.
> ⓑ I want to know when will they call me again.
> ⓒ My brother let me wearing this new T-shirt.
> ⓓ Tell me who told you the secret.
> ⓔ Could you tell me what Jason is doing in his room?

① 1개   ② 2개   ③ 3개
④ 4개   ⑤ 5개

☆ 중요
08 다음 중 빈칸에 들어갈 말로 가장 적절한 것은?

> I wonder. Why is he running?
> = I wonder _____.

① why he running
② whether he is running
③ why he is running
④ why is he running
⑤ whether he running

09 주어진 단어를 활용하여 다음 우리말을 영어로 쓰시오.

> 너는 그 창문을 누가 깼다고 생각하니?
> (suppose / break)

➡ _____

10 다음 중 밑줄 친 부분이 어색한 것은?

① Can you tell me <u>where he is from</u>?
② Do you know <u>who Hanguel made</u>?
③ I wonder <u>how often you visit your grandparents</u>.
④ Tell me <u>when she sent the email to me</u>.
⑤ Do you understand <u>what he is trying to say</u>?

11 다음 중 빈칸에 들어갈 말이 바르게 짝지어진 것은?

> • Mr. Davidson made the children _____ their hands before dinner.
> • Tell me _____ while your parents are not at home.

① to wash – who do you take care of
② to wash – who you will take care of
③ wash – who will take care of you
④ wash – whom you take care of
⑤ washing – whom you take care of

12 주어진 어구를 바르게 배열하여 대화를 완성하시오.

> A: My teacher made me do my paper again.
> B: _____
> (do you think / you / why / made / she / it / again / do)

13 주어진 단어를 활용하여 다음 우리말을 영어로 쓰시오.

> 나는 그가 내 시계를 고치게 했어.
> (make / repair)

➡ _____

14 다음 우리말을 영어로 옮길 때 다섯 번째로 오는 단어는?

> 지금 몇 시라고 생각하세요?

① time   ② you   ③ it
④ think   ⑤ is

15 다음 빈칸에 들어갈 말로 적절하지 <u>않은</u> 것은?

> Did you _____ them study together for the exam?

① have   ② make   ③ let
④ allow   ⑤ help

16 다음 빈칸에 들어갈 말로 가장 적절한 것은?

> A: Do you know _____ now?
> B: Oh, she is making some cookies in the kitchen.

① what is Molly doing
② what Molly doing
③ what Molly is doing
④ Molly is doing what
⑤ Molly is doing

17 다음 빈칸에 들어갈 말로 가장 적절한 것은?

> Lily always makes him _____.

① laughing   ② to laugh   ③ laugh
④ laughs   ⑤ to laughing

18 다음 빈칸에 공통으로 들어갈 말로 가장 적절한 것은?

- Karl _____ her son a tennis player.
- Jina _____ me some delicious cookies.
- He _____ us jump the rope.
- June _____ the paper robot very well.

① had   ② let   ③ went
④ made   ⑤ want

19 다음 중 영어로 옮긴 것이 바르지 <u>않은</u> 것은?

① 나는 그 아이들이 벽에 페인트칠을 하도록 허락했다.
   → I let the children paint on the wall.
② 누가 올 것이라고 생각해?
   → Who do you think will come?
③ 우리 선생님은 가끔 우리에게 무엇을 하라고 시키시니?
   → What does our teacher sometimes make us do?
④ 나는 그가 그녀에게서 무엇을 빌렸는지 몰라요.
   → I don't know what he borrowed from her.
⑤ 누가 그 건물을 지었다고 생각하니?
   → Who do you guess the building built?

20 다음 빈칸에 들어갈 말로 가장 적절한 것은?

A: I'd like to know _____.
B: I'm in the 8th grade.

① where you are now
② which grade are you
③ which grade you are in
④ who you are
⑤ which you are in the grade

21 빈칸에 들어갈 말로 가장 적절한 것은?

Did you _____ the students ride the bikes?

① want   ② force   ③ allow
④ have   ⑤ enable

22 주어진 단어를 활용하여 빈칸에 알맞은 말을 쓰시오. (7단어)

Jason: I would like to know _____.
           (what / do / when / free)
Kelly: I write songs when I am free.

➡ _____

23 다음 중 어법상 <u>어색한</u> 것은?

① He made me stand on the street for an hour.
② They helped me to finish the project very well.
③ Do you think who you are?
④ Tell me when your birthday is.
⑤ Julian had her say sorry again.

24 주어진 문장과 같은 의미의 문장은?

Mom tells me to do something.

① Mom enables me to do something.
② Mom makes me do something.
③ Mom sees me do something.
④ Mom thinks I do something.
⑤ Mom wants to know when I do something.

25 다음 두 문장을 하나의 문장으로 쓰시오.

I want to know. Did she like the present?

➡ _____

01 주어진 단어를 활용하여 다음 우리말을 영어로 바르게 옮기시오.

> 엄마는 나와 내 여동생이 집을 청소하게 시키셨다.
> (make, clean)

➡ _____

02 주어진 단어를 활용하여 다음 우리말을 영어로 쓰시오.

> 누가 그 돈을 훔쳤다고 생각하니?
> (think / steal)

➡ _____

03 주어진 단어를 바르게 배열하여 다음 우리말을 영어로 쓰시오.

> 그들이 언제 너를 집에 가게 했는지 말해 줄 수 있니? (home / can / go / tell / when / you / me / they / you / let)

➡ _____

04 다음 빈칸에 알맞은 말을 쓰시오.

(1) 아빠는 내가 그의 차를 운전하게 허락하신다.
➡ My father lets _____ _____
_____ _____.

(2) Jane은 그가 자기에게 물 한 잔을 가져오게 했다.
➡ Jane had _____ _____ _____
a glass of water.

(3) 그녀는 내가 그녀를 쳐다보게 만들었다.
➡ She made _____ _____ _____
her.

05 주어진 단어를 활용하여 다음 문장과 같은 의미의 문장을 쓰시오.

> Brad forced me to accept the job.
> (make)

➡ _____

06 〈보기〉와 같이 다음 두 문장을 하나의 문장으로 쓰시오.

> ┤ 보기 ├
> Can you tell me? Who is she?
> ➡ Can you tell me who she is?

(1) I don't know. Where does he live?
➡ _____

(2) Do you guess? How old is he?
➡ _____

(3) Can you tell me? Why were you absent from school?
➡ _____

(4) I want to know. When did you meet him for the first time?
➡ _____
_____

(5) Do you think? When does the concert start?
➡ _____

(6) Do you imagine? Why is the baby crying?
➡ _____

(7) Do you know? Was Charley sleeping at that time?
➡ _____
_____

07 주어진 단어를 활용하여 다음 우리말을 영어로 쓰시오.

> 나는 나의 사촌이 숙제하는 것을 도와줬습니다.
> (help / his)

➡ _____

⭐ 중요

08 주어진 단어를 어법이나 내용에 맞게 빈칸에 쓰시오.

┌─── 보기 ────
take / publish / report / work / play
└──────────────

(1) Don't let the children _____ with matches.
(2) Do you know who _____ these books last year?
(3) Julia made the professional photographer _____ pictures of her.
(4) The boss had the employees _____ harder.
(5) What do you think the scientist _____ _____ tomorrow?

09 다음 상황을 읽고 빈칸에 알맞은 말을 쓰시오.

> Andy: How much are the oranges?
> Paul: How many oranges do you want to buy?

➡ Andy wants to know how much _____ _____. So Paul asks Andy _____.

⭐ 중요

10 주어진 단어를 활용하여 다음 우리말을 영어로 쓰시오.

> 여자는 남자가 물을 마시게 한다.
> (the woman / the man / let)

➡ _____

11 주어진 단어를 바르게 배열하여 다음 우리말을 영어로 쓰시오. 필요하다면 어형을 변환하시오.

> 그 정장은 나를 멋지게 보이도록 만들어.
> (fancy / the suit / look / make / me)

➡ _____

🏠 고난이도

12 주어진 단어를 활용하여 다음 대화를 영어로 쓰시오.

> A: 그 영화가 어땠다고 생각하니? (how / think / be)
> B: It was so boring. 그것은 나를 졸리게 만들었어. (make / feel)

A: _____
B: _____

13 다음 우리말을 영어로 쓰시오.

> 어제 그 차를 누가 운전했는지 아니?

➡ _____

14 다음 중 어법상 틀린 것을 바르게 고쳐 올바른 문장으로 다시 쓰시오.

(1) Can you tell me when did she write this book?
➡ _____
(2) You can lead a horse to water, but you can't make him to drink.
➡ _____
(3) I wonder that he is full or not.
➡ _____

The More You See, The More You Know

Welcome to the World Art Museum tour. When you go to an art museum, how much time do you spend looking at each painting?

Many visitors glance at one painting for only a few seconds before they move on. But you might miss the important details of paintings since it is hard to notice them right away.

Today, we'll look at two paintings closely and I'll help you see interesting details.

Look at this painting first. The seaside landscape is so peaceful and beautiful, isn't it? The title of this painting is *Landscape with the Fall of Icarus*. So, can you see where Icarus is? Do you see two legs that are sticking out of the water near the ship? This is Icarus in the famous myth in Greece. In the myth, Icarus' father made wings for him with feathers and wax and told him to stay away from the sun.

---

detail 세부 사항
since ~ 때문에
notice ~을 알아차리다
glance at ~을 힐끗 보다
right away 즉시, 바로
seaside 해변, 바닷가
landscape 풍경
stick 내밀다
myth 신화
wing 날개
feather 깃털
wax 밀랍
stay away from ~을 가까이 하지 않다

 확인문제

- 다음 문장이 본문의 내용과 일치하면 T, 일치하지 <u>않으면</u> F를 쓰시오.

1 It is enough to spend a few minutes looking at a painting. ☐

2 It is hard to notice the important details of paintings right away. ☐

3 We can see peaceful and beautiful landscape in the first painting. ☐

4 Icarus is waving his hands in the painting. ☐

5 Icarus made his wings without any help. ☐

However, Icarus didn't listen. He flew too close to the sun. So, the
fly-flew-flown

wax melted and he fell into the water. Now, look at the entire painting

again. Despite the tragedy of Icarus, people are going on with their
전치사(~에도 불구하고)

everyday activities. Does the painting still look peaceful?
일상의   감각동사+형용사: 평화스럽게 보이다

What do you think the artist is trying to tell us?
간접의문문: think. imagine. guess 등이 동사로 쓰인 문장에서 간접의문문의 의문사를 문장 맨 앞으로 보냄

Now, let's move on to the next painting. Do you see the artist behind
~으로 옮겨가다   ~ 뒤에

the large canvas? He is Diego Velázquez, and he actually painted this

picture. Who do you think he is painting? Take a quick look. The
Do you think? + Who is he painting?

young princess seems to be the main person because she is in the center
~인 것처럼 보이다

of the painting. But the title of the painting is *The Maids of Honour*.

Then, is the artist drawing the two women beside the princess? Take
~ 옆에 있는

a close look. It will make you wonder about the painting more. Try to
앞 문장 'Take a close look.'을 가리킴 사역동사+목적어+동사원형: 목적어가 ~하게 하다   ~하려고 애쓰다

see which direction the artist is looking at. Can you see the king and
Try to see. + Which direction is the artist looking at?

the queen in the mirror in the background of the painting? Who do you
형용사구   the mirror를 수식하는 형용사구   = Do you think? +

think he is painting now?
Who is he painting now?

---

melt 녹다

despite ~에도 불구하고

tragedy 비극

artist 예술가, 미술가

canvas 화폭, 캔버스

wonder 궁금해 하다

direction 방향

take a look 보다

beside ~옆에

background 배경

📎 **확인문제**

● 다음 문장이 본문의 내용과 일치하면 T, 일치하지 <u>않으면</u> F를 쓰시오.

1 Icarus followed what his father had said. ☐

2 Icarus fell into the water because the wax melted. ☐

3 Diego Velázquez is in the painting. ☐

4 There are two women beside the princess. ☐

5 There is a mirror in the background of the painting. ☐

6 Diego Velázquez drew himself in the mirror of the painting. ☐

● 우리말을 참고하여 빈칸에 알맞은 말을 쓰시오.

1 _____ _____ the World Art Museum tour.

2 _____ you _____ _____ an art museum, _____ _____ _____ do you spend _____ at each painting?

3 Many visitors _____ _____ one painting _____ only _____ _____ seconds before they move _____.

4 But you _____ _____ the important details of paintings _____ it is hard _____ _____ _____ right away.

5 Today, we'll _____ _____ two paintings _____ and I'll _____ _____ _____ interesting details.

6 Look _____ this painting _____.

7 The _____ _____ is so _____ and beautiful, _____ _____?

8 The _____ of this painting _____ *Landscape with the Fall of Icarus*.

9 So, can you see _____ _____ _____?

10 Do you see two legs that _____ _____ _____ _____ _____ _____ near the ship?

11 This is Icarus _____ _____ _____ _____ _____ in Greece.

12 In the myth, Icarus' father _____ _____ _____ _____ with feathers and wax and told him _____ _____ _____ the sun.

13 _____, Icarus didn't _____.

14 He _____ _____ _____ _____ to the sun.

15 So, the wax _____ and he _____ _____ the water.

16 Now, look _____ the _____ painting again.

17 _____ the tragedy of Icarus, people are _____ _____ _____ their everyday activities.

18 Does the painting _____ _____ _____?

19 _____ _____ _____ _____ the artist is trying to tell us?

20 Now, let's _____ _____ _____ the next painting.

21 Do you _____ the artist _____ the large canvas?

22 He is Diego Velázquez, and he _____ _____ this picture.

23 _____ _____ _____ _____ _____ _____ painting?

24 _____ a quick look.

25 The young princess _____ _____ _____ the main person _____ she is in the center of the painting.

26 But the _____ of the _____ is *The Maids of Honour*.

27 Then, is the artist _____ the two women _____ the princess?

28 _____ a close look.

29 It will _____ _____ _____ about the painting more.

30 Try to see _____ _____ _____ _____ _____ looking at.

31 Can you _____ the king and the queen _____ _____ _____ in the _____ of the painting?

32 _____ _____ _____ _____ _____ _____ painting now?

16 이제, 그림 전체를 다시 보세요.

17 이카루스의 비극에도 불구하고 사람들은 일상의 활동을 계속하고 있습니다.

18 그림이 여전히 평화로워 보이나요?

19 화가가 우리에게 무엇을 말하려 한다고 생각하나요?

20 이제, 다음 그림으로 넘어갑시다.

21 커다란 캔버스 뒤에 있는 화가가 보이나요?

22 그는 Diego Velázquez이고, 그가 실제로 이 그림을 그렸습니다.

23 그가 누구를 그리고 있다고 생각하나요?

24 재빨리 봅시다.

25 어린 공주가 그림의 중앙에 있기 때문에 주인공처럼 보입니다.

26 하지만 그림의 제목은 '시녀들' 입니다.

27 그렇다면 화가는 공주 옆에 있는 두 여인을 그리고 있나요?

28 자세히 보세요.

29 그림에 대해 더 궁금해하게 될 겁니다.

30 화가가 바라보고 있는 방향을 보려고 노력해 보세요.

31 그림의 배경에 있는 거울 속 왕과 왕비가 보이나요?

32 이제 여러분은 그가 누구를 그리고 있다고 생각하나요?

● 우리말을 참고하여 본문을 영작하시오.

1 세계 미술관(the World Art Museum)에 오신 것을 환영합니다.

➡ _____

2 미술관에 갈 때 여러분은 각각의 그림을 보는 데 얼마나 많은 시간을 보내나요?

➡ _____

3 많은 방문객들은 이동하기 전에 하나의 그림을 몇 초간만 힐끗 봅니다.

➡ _____

4 하지만 그림의 중요한 세부 사항들을 즉시 알아채는 것은 어렵기 때문에 여러분들은 그것들을 놓칠 수 있습니다.

➡ _____

5 오늘 우리는 두 개의 그림을 자세히 살펴볼 것이고, 여러분이 흥미로운 세부 사항들을 볼 수 있도록 제가 도와드리겠습니다.

➡ _____

6 먼저 이 그림을 보세요.

➡ _____

7 바닷가 풍경이 매우 평화롭고 아름답죠, 그렇지 않나요?

➡ _____

8 이 그림의 제목은 '추락하는 이카루스가 있는 풍경'입니다.

➡ _____

9 그러면 이카루스가 어디에 있는지 보이나요?

➡ _____

10 배 근처에 물 밖으로 나와 있는 두 다리가 보이죠?

➡ _____

11 이것이 그리스의 유명한 신화에 나오는 이카루스입니다.

➡ _____

12 신화에서 이카루스의 아버지는 그를 위해 깃털과 밀랍으로 날개를 만들어 주었고 그에게 태양을 가까이 하지 말라고 말했습니다.

➡ _____

_____

13 하지만 이카루스는 듣지 않았습니다.

➡ _____

14 그는 태양에 너무 가깝게 날았습니다.

➡ _____

15 그래서 밀랍이 녹았고 그는 물에 빠졌습니다.

➡ _____

16 이제, 그림 전체를 다시 보세요.

➡ _____

17 이카루스의 비극에도 불구하고 사람들은 일상의 활동을 계속하고 있습니다.

➡ _____

18 그림이 여전히 평화로워 보이나요?

➡ _____

19 화가가 우리에게 무엇을 말하려 한다고 생각하나요?

➡ _____

20 이제, 다음 그림으로 넘어갑시다.

➡ _____

21 커다란 캔버스 뒤에 있는 화가가 보이나요?

➡ _____

22 그는 Diego Velázquez이고, 그가 실제로 이 그림을 그렸습니다.

➡ _____

23 그가 누구를 그리고 있다고 생각하나요?

➡ _____

24 재빨리 봅시다.

➡ _____

25 어린 공주가 그림의 중앙에 있기 때문에 주인공처럼 보입니다.

➡ _____

26 하지만 그림의 제목은 '시녀들'입니다.

➡ _____

27 그렇다면 화가는 공주 옆에 있는 두 여인을 그리고 있나요?

➡ _____

28 자세히 보세요.

➡ _____

29 그림에 대해 더 궁금해하게 될 겁니다.

➡ _____

30 화가가 바라보고 있는 방향을 보려고 노력해 보세요.

➡ _____

31 그림의 배경에 있는 거울 속 왕과 왕비가 보이나요?

➡ _____

32 이제 여러분은 그가 누구를 그리고 있다고 생각하나요?

➡ _____

[01~04] 다음 글을 읽고 물음에 답하시오.

Welcome to the World Art Museum tour. When you go to an art museum, how much time do you spend looking at each painting? Many visitors glance at one painting for only a few seconds before they move on. But you might miss the important details of paintings (A)since it is hard (B)to notice them right away. Today, we'll look at two paintings closely and I'll help you see interesting details.

01 다음 중 밑줄 친 (A)를 대신하여 쓰일 수 있는 것은?

① because　② when　③ if
④ because of　⑤ while

서답형

02 다음과 같이 풀이되는 단어를 위 글에서 찾아 쓰시오.

> to see or become conscious of something or someone

➡ _____

중요

03 다음 중 밑줄 친 (B)와 쓰임이 같은 것은?

① They hoped to meet again someday.
② Are you happy to see me again?
③ It is necessary to keep your promise.
④ Is there anything to drink?
⑤ His hobby is to make something.

서답형

04 According to the writer, how many paintings will we look at closely? Answer in English with a full sentence.

➡ _____

[05~10] 다음 글을 읽고 물음에 답하시오.

Look at this painting first. The seaside landscape is so peaceful and beautiful, isn't it? The title of this painting is *Landscape with the Fall of Icarus*. So, _____(A)_____? Do you see two legs that are sticking out of the water near the ship? This is Icarus in the famous myth in Greece. ① In the myth, Icarus' father made wings for him with feathers and wax and told him to stay away from the sun. ② He flew too close to the sun. ③ So, the wax melted and he fell into the water. ④ Now, look at the entire painting again. ⑤ _____(B)_____ the tragedy of Icarus, people are going on with their everyday activities. Does the painting still look peaceful? What do you think the artist is trying to tell us?

서답형

05 다음 두 문장을 하나의 문장으로 연결하여 빈칸 (A)에 알맞게 쓰시오.

> • Can you see?
> • Where is Icarus?

➡ _____

06 다음 중 빈칸 (B)에 들어갈 말로 가장 적절한 것은?

① In spite of　② Due to
③ In addition to　④ Thanks to
⑤ Along with

서답형

07 다음 중 주어진 문장이 들어가기에 가장 적절한 곳은?

> However, Icarus didn't listen.

①　　②　　③　　④　　⑤

서답형

08 위 글을 읽고 다음 질문에 완전한 문장의 영어로 답하시오.

> Q: What is the title of the painting?

➡ _____

09 첫 번째 그림에서 찾아볼 수 없는 것은?

① peaceful landscape
② people doing their everyday activities
③ Icarus flying to the sun
④ a ship on the water
⑤ two legs sticking out of the water

중요

10 위 글의 내용과 일치하지 않는 것은?

① The landscape of the first painting looks peaceful and beautiful.
② We can see only two legs of Icarus in the painting.
③ Icarus can be seen near the ship in the painting.
④ Icarus made his wings by himself.
⑤ Icarus flew close to the sun and fell into water.

[11~15] 다음 글을 읽고 물음에 답하시오.

Now, let's move on to the next painting. Do you see the artist behind the large canvas? He is Diego Velázquez, and he actually painted this picture. Who do you think he is painting? Take a quick look. ⓐ어린 공주가 그림의 중앙에 있기 때문에 주인공처럼 보입니다. But the title of the painting is *The Maids of Honour*. Then, is the artist drawing the two women beside the princess? Take a close look. It will make you ___(A)___ about the painting more. Try to see which direction the artist is looking at. Can you see the king and the queen in the mirror in the background of the painting? Who do you think he is (B)painting now?

서답형

11 단어 'wonder'를 어법에 맞게 빈칸 (A)에 쓰시오.

➡ _____

12 다음 중 밑줄 친 (B)와 쓰임이 같은 것은?

① Are you interested in writing a poem?
② His job is delivering mails.
③ Jason was doing his laundry.
④ Mina enjoyed watching movies with me.
⑤ David didn't mind asking about it.

서답형

13 위 글의 밑줄 친 우리말 ⓐ를 주어진 어휘를 이용하여 18 단어로 영작하시오. (the young princess로 시작할 것.)

> the young princess, the painting, the main person, the center, because, be

➡ _____

_____

서답형

14 Where can we find the artist of the next painting? Answer in English with a full sentence. Use the word 'him,'

➡ _____

중요

15 다음 중 위 글을 읽고 답할 수 없는 질문은?

① What is the name of the artist of the second painting?
② What makes the young princess seem to be the main person?
③ What is the title of the painting?
④ How many women are there beside the princess?
⑤ How large is the painting?

[16~18] 다음 글을 읽고 물음에 답하시오.

Welcome to the World Art Museum tour. When you go to an art museum, (A)[how many / how much] time do you spend looking at each painting? Many visitors glance at one painting for only a few seconds before they move on. But you might miss the important details of paintings since it is hard to notice (B)[it / them] right away. Today, we'll look at two paintings closely and I'll help you (C)[seeing / to see] interesting details.

16 (A)~(C)에서 어법상 옳은 것끼리 바르게 짝지은 것은?

① how much – them – seeing
② how much – them – to see
③ how many – it – to see
④ how many – it – seeing
⑤ how many – them – to see

서답형

17 According to the writer, how long does it take many visitors to see one painting? Answer in English with a full sentence. Use the words 'it', 'them' and 'to.'

➡ _____

18 다음 중 위 글 다음에 이어질 내용으로 가장 적절한 것은?

① the problem of the museum tour
② a request for donating good paintings
③ how to see the details of paintings
④ bad behaviors of people in the museum
⑤ how to be friendly with the curator

[19~23] 다음 글을 읽고 물음에 답하시오.

Look at this painting first. The seaside landscape is so peaceful and beautiful, ①isn't it? The title of this painting is *Landscape with the Fall of Icarus*. So, can you see ②where is Icarus?
(A) So, the wax melted and he fell into the water. Now, look at the entire painting again. Despite the tragedy of Icarus, people are going on with their everyday activities.
(B) In the myth, Icarus' father made wings ③ for him with feathers and wax and told him ④to stay away from the sun. ⓐ , Icarus didn't listen. He flew too close to the sun.
(C) Do you see two legs that ⑤are sticking out of the water near the ship? This is Icarus in the famous myth in Greece.
Does the painting still look peaceful? What do you think the artist is trying to tell us?

19 다음 중 빈칸 ⓐ에 들어갈 말로 가장 적절한 것은?

① Moreover   ② Therefore
③ However   ④ For example
⑤ Thus

20 자연스러운 내용이 되도록 (A)~(C)를 바르게 나열한 것은?

① (A) – (B) – (C)   ② (B) – (A) – (C)
③ (B) – (C) – (A)   ④ (C) – (A) – (B)
⑤ (C) – (B) – (A)

21 ①~⑤ 중 어법상 바르지 않은 것은?

①   ②   ③   ④   ⑤

22 Which is NOT true about Icarus?

① He is in the famous myth in Greece.

② His father made wings for him.

③ He had wings made of feathers and wax.

④ He flew close to the sun.

⑤ He listened to his father very well.

23 According to the passage, what did Icarus' father tell Icarus? Answer in English with a full sentence.

➡ _____

[24~25] 다음 글을 읽고 물음에 답하시오.

Today, I went to the Amazing Art exhibition. At the exhibition, I saw many interesting pieces of art. Among them, I liked the piece called *Moon Tree*. It was made by French artist, David Myriam. Interestingly, sand was used in this painting. I like it because a tree in the moon makes me ___(A)___ . Now I know that anything can be used to make art. Anything is possible!

24 다음 중 빈칸 (A)에 들어갈 말로 적절한 것은?

① feels calm   ② feel calmly

③ feel calm   ④ feeling calm

⑤ feeling calmly

25 Which is NOT true about the passage?

① There were many interesting pieces of art at the Amazing Art exhibition.

② What the writer liked was *Moon Tree*.

③ *Moon Tree* was made by David Myriam.

④ David Myriam used a tree in his painting.

⑤ David Myriam is French.

[26~28] 다음 글을 읽고 물음에 답하시오.

Now, let's move on to the next painting. Do you see the artist behind the large canvas? He is Diego Velázquez, and he actually painted this picture. Who do you ___(A)___ he is painting? Take a quick look. The young princess seems to be the main person because she is in the center of the painting. But the title of the painting is *The Maids of Honour*. Then, is the artist drawing the two women beside the princess? Take a close look. It will make you wonder about the painting more. Try to see which direction the artist is looking at. Can you see the king and the queen in the mirror in the background of the painting? Who do you think he is painting now?

26 다음 중 빈칸 (A)에 들어갈 말로 적절하지 않은 것은?

① think   ② guess   ③ believe

④ know   ⑤ imagine

27 According to the passage, who is in the middle of the painting? Answer in English with a full sentence.

➡ _____

28 위 글의 내용과 일치하지 않는 것은?

① Diego Velázquez drew *The Maids of Hornour*.

② Diego Velázquez doesn't appear in the painting.

③ Both the king and the queen can be found in the painting.

④ There are two women beside the princess in the painting.

⑤ A mirror was drawn in the background of the painting.

[01~03] 다음 글을 읽고 물음에 답하시오.

Welcome to the World Art Museum tour. (A) When you go to an art museum, how much time do you spend looking at each painting? Many visitors glance at one painting for only a few seconds before they move on. But you might miss the important details of paintings since it is hard to notice (B)them right away. Today, we'll look at two paintings closely and (C)여러분이 흥미로운 세부 사항들을 볼 수 있도록 제가 도와드리겠습니다.

01 다음은 밑줄 친 (A)와 같은 의미의 문장이다. 빈칸을 알맞게 채우시오.

I wonder _____ when you go to an art museum.

➡ _____

02 위 글의 밑줄 친 (B)가 의미하는 것을 위 글에서 찾아 쓰시오.

➡ _____

03 주어진 단어를 활용하여 밑줄 친 우리말 (C)를 영어로 쓰시오.

(help / see)

➡ _____

[04~08] 다음 글을 읽고 물음에 답하시오.

Look at this painting first. The seaside landscape is so peaceful and beautiful, isn't it? The title of this painting is *Landscape with the Fall of Icarus*. So, can you see where Icarus is? Do you see two legs that are sticking out of the water near the ship? This is Icarus in the famous myth in Greece.

In the myth, Icarus' father made wings for him with feathers and wax and told him to stay away from the sun. However, Icarus didn't listen. He flew too close to the sun. So, the wax melted and he fell into the water. Now, look at the entire painting again. Despite the tragedy of Icarus, people are going on with their everyday activities. Does the painting still look peaceful?
_____(A)_____

04 다음 두 문장을 하나의 문장으로 만들어 빈칸 (A)에 쓰시오.

• Do you think?
• What is the artist trying to tell us?

➡ _____

05 다음은 화가가 위 그림을 통해 말하려는 것이다. 빈칸에 적절한 말을 위 글에서 찾아 쓰시오.

The artist is trying to tell us that we do not know other people's _____.

➡ _____

06 What did Icarus' father make for Icarus? Answer in English with five words.

➡ _____

07 위 글의 내용에 맞게 빈칸에 알맞은 말을 쓰시오.

A: What made the wax _____?
B: Flying too close to the sun made it so.

➡ _____

08 다음은 '추락하는 이카루스가 있는 풍경'을 감상하고 있는 두 학생의 대화이다. 빈칸에 알맞은 말을 쓰시오.

> **A:** Can you tell me _____? I can't find him.
> **B:** Oh, he is near the ship.
> **A:** The two legs that _____? Is that him?
> **B:** Yes, he is.

➡ _____, _____

[09~13] 다음 글을 읽고 물음에 답하시오.

Now, let's move on to the next painting. Do you see the artist behind the large canvas? He is Diego Velázquez, and he (A)actual painted this picture. Who do you think he is painting? Take a quick look. The young princess seems to be the main person because she is in the center of the painting. But the title of the painting is *The Maids of Honour*. Then, is the artist drawing the two women beside the princess? Take a close look. (B)It will make you wonder about the painting more. Try to see which direction the artist is looking at. Can you see the king and the queen in the mirror in the background of the painting? Who do you think he is painting now?

09 밑줄 친 (A)를 알맞은 형으로 고치시오.

➡ _____

10 Who painted the picture, *The Maids of Honour*? Answer in English with a full sentence.

➡ _____

11 밑줄 친 (B)가 의미하는 것을 우리말로 쓰시오.

➡ _____

12 Who are the people in the mirror in the background of the painting? Answer in English with a full sentence.

➡ _____

13 위 글의 표현을 이용하여 다음 우리말을 영어로 쓰시오.

> 나는 누가 실제로 이 그림을 그렸는지 궁금해.

➡ _____

[14~15] 다음 글을 읽고 물음에 답하시오.

Today, I went to the Amazing Art exhibition. At the exhibition, I saw many interesting pieces of art. Among them, I liked the piece called *Moon Tree*. It was made by French artist, David Myriam. Interestingly, sand was used in this painting. I like it because a tree in the moon makes me feel calm. Now I know that anything can be used to make art. Anything is possible!

14 위 글의 내용에 맞게 빈칸에 알맞은 말을 쓰시오.

> **A:** Do you know _____ in this painting?
> **B:** Yes, I do. He used sand.

15 Write the reason why the writer likes *Moon Tree*. Use the word 'because.'

➡ _____

해석

Listen & Talk

M: What are you reading, Sally?

W: I'm reading *The Maze Runner*. It's about boys who are put in a maze.
　　　　　　　　　　　　　　= The Maze Runner　　　주격 관계대명사

M: It's a great story. I've seen the movie of it, too. I prefer the novel to the
　　　　　　　　현재완료　　　　　　　　　　prefer A to B: B보다 더 A가 좋다

　　movie.

W: Why do you like it better?
　　　= the novel

M: The novel has various stories. But the movie didn't show some important

　　parts of the story.

구문해설　• maze: 미로　• novel: 소설

M: Sally, 너는 무엇을 읽고 있니?

W: 나는 '미로를 달리는 사람'을 읽고 있어. 미로에 갇힌 소년들에 관한 내용 이야.

M: 그건 대단한 이야기이지. 나는 그것을 영화로도 봤어. 나는 영화보다는 소설이 더 좋아.

W: 왜 소설이 더 좋은데?

M: 소설에는 다양한 이야기가 담겨 있어. 하지만 영화에서는 이야기의 중요한 몇 부분이 나오지 않았어.

Grammar in Real Life

1. Princess, please let me in.
　　　　　　　　let A in: A를 들어가게 하다
2. Who are you?
3. The princess promised me, "If you help me, I'll let you enter the palace and
　　　　　　　　　　　　　　　　　사역동사+목적어+동사원형: 목적어가 ～하게 하다
　　be my friend."
　(let you) be my friend
4. Come here. I'll have people serve you some cookies and tea.
　　　　　　　　　　사역동사　　　　4형식 동사(～에게 …을 내어주다)
5. No! Never let him in. I don't like him.
　　　　부정 명령문
6. Don't worry, Frog. I'll make the princess keep her promise.
　　　　　　　　　　　사역동사+목적어+동사원형: 목적어가 ～하게 하다

구문해설　• promise: 약속하다　• enter: ～로 들어가다　• serve: ～을 내어주다

　　　　　• keep one's promise: ～의 약속을 지키다

1. 공주님, 저를 들어가게 해 주세요.
2. 그대는 누군가?
3. 공주님은 제게 "네가 날 도와준다면, 나는 너를 궁전에 들어오게 하고 내 친구가 되게 해 주겠어."라고 약속하셨어요.
4. 이쪽으로 오게. 내가 사람들을 시켜 자네에게 과자와 차를 가져다 주게 하겠네.
5. 안 돼요! 그를 들어오게 하지 마세요. 저는 그를 좋아하지 않아요.
6. 걱정 말게, 개구리. 나는 공주가 그녀의 약속을 지키게 하겠네.

Think and Write C

Today, I went to the Amazing Art exhibition. At the exhibition, I saw many

interesting pieces of art. Among them, I liked the piece called *Moon Tree*. It
흥미를 유발하는　　　　　　　　　many interesting pieces of art　　= which was called

was made by French artist, David Myriam. Interestingly, sand was used in this
　　　　　　　　　　　　　　　　　　　　　　　　　　　　　　　수동태

painting. I like it because a tree in the moon makes me feel calm. Now I know
　　　　　　　　이유를 나타내는 접속사　　　　　　　　사역동사+목적어+동사원형

that anything can be used to make art. Anything is possible!
명사절을 이끄는 접속사　　　　부사적 용법

구문해설　• exhibition: 전시회　• interesting: 흥미로운　• called: ～라고 불리는

　　　　　• be made by: ～에 의해 만들어지다　• calm: 고요한

오늘 나는 놀라운 미술 전시회에 갔다. 전시회에서, 나는 많은 흥미로운 미술 작품들을 보았다. 그 중에서, 나는 *Moon Tree*라고 불리는 작품이 좋았다. 그것은 프랑스 미술가 **David Myriam**에 의해 만들어졌다. 흥미롭게도, 모래가 이 미술품에 사용되었다. 달 속에 있는 나무 한 그루가 내 마음을 고요하게 만들기 때문에 나는 그것이 좋다. 이제 나는 어떠한 것이든 미술을 만들기 위해 사용될 수 있다는 사실을 안다. 무엇이든 가능하다!

영역별 핵심문제

Words & Expressions

01 다음 짝지어진 단어의 관계가 같도록 빈칸에 알맞은 말을 쓰시오.

> prince: princess = comedy : _____

02 다음 영영풀이가 가리키는 것을 고르시오.

> a very sad event, especially one involving death

① comedy   ② artwork   ③ detail
④ tear   ⑤ tragedy

03 다음 중 밑줄 친 부분의 뜻풀이가 바르지 <u>않은</u> 것은?

① Some birds have colorful <u>feathers</u>. 깃털
② I will <u>exhibit</u> my pictures someday. 전시하다
③ <u>Frogs</u> sleep during winter. 개구리
④ We need <u>flat</u> ground to build a house. 울퉁불퉁한
⑤ I looked down on the peaceful <u>landscape</u> from the hill. 풍경

04 다음 우리말에 맞게 빈칸에 알맞은 말을 쓰시오.

(1) 이탈리아에는 항상 많은 관광객들이 있다.
➡ There are always many _____ in Italy.

(2) 네 친구에게 혀를 내밀지 마라.
➡ Don't _____ your tongue at your friend.

(3) Tom은 정말 소설가를 만나고 싶어 한다.
➡ Tom really wants to meet the _____.

05 다음 우리말에 맞게 주어진 단어를 사용하여 영작하시오.

(1) 나는 시보다 소설을 더 좋아한다. (prefer)
➡ _____

(2) 우리 가족은 해변으로 여행갈 것이다.
(trip, take, seaside)
➡ _____

(3) 그 전쟁은 전 세계에 비극이었다. (whole)
➡ _____

06 다음 주어진 문장의 밑줄 친 stick과 같은 의미로 쓰인 것은?

> Don't <u>stick</u> your head out of the window.

① Did your brother <u>stick</u> a stamp on the letter?
② Would you <u>stick</u> your arms out of your sleeves?
③ Brian is using a <u>stick</u> to find something.
④ Will you <u>stick</u> a note on the door?
⑤ He is striking the tree with a <u>stick</u>.

07 다음 문장에 공통으로 들어갈 말을 고르시오.

> • We need to _____ our attention to our mistakes.
> • Can you _____ me to Seoul Station?
> • Is there a _____ flight to San Francisco?

① direct   ② prefer
③ melt   ④ notice
⑤ promise

[08~09] 다음 대화를 읽고 물음에 답하시오.

Jean: (A) What are you reading, Sally?

Sally: (B) I'm reading *The Maze Runner*. It's about boys who are put in a maze.

Jean: (C) It's a great story. I've seen the movie of it, too. I prefer the novel to the movie.

Sally: (D) Why do you like it better?

Jean: (E) But the movie didn't show some important parts of the story.

08 위 대화의 (A)~(E) 중 주어진 문장이 들어가기에 적절한 곳은?

> The novel has various stories.

① (A) ② (B) ③ (C) ④ (D) ⑤ (E)

09 위 대화의 내용과 일치하지 <u>않는</u> 것은?

① Sally is reading *The Maze Runner*.

② *The Maze Runner* is about boys who are put in a maze.

③ Jean saw the movie of *The Maze Runner* with Sally.

④ Jean prefers the novel to the movie because the novel has various stories.

⑤ Jean thinks that the movie missed some important parts of the story.

[10~11] 다음 대화를 읽고 물음에 답하시오.

Anna: (*ringing*) Hello, Steve.

Steve: Hi, Anna. We're meeting at the arts festival tomorrow at 1:30, right?

Anna: Right. ＿＿＿＿＿＿＿＿＿ (A)

Steve: I want to watch the hip-hop dance performance first.

Anna: Sounds good. It's at 2 p.m. at the gym, right?

Steve: Yeah, and how about watching the play, *Romeo and Juliet*, at 4 p.m.?

Anna: Oh, the one at the Main Hall near the gym? Sure!

10 위 대화의 빈칸 (A)에 들어갈 말을 〈보기〉에 주어진 단어를 모두 배열하여 완성하시오.

┌─ 보기 ┤
kind / do / to / of / watch / you / what / performance/ want / first
└─

➡ ＿＿＿＿＿＿＿＿＿＿＿＿＿＿＿＿＿

11 위 대화의 내용과 일치하지 <u>않는</u> 것은?

① Anna와 Steve는 내일 1시 30분에 예술 축제에서 만나기로 했다.

② Steve는 먼저 힙합 댄스 공연을 보고 싶어 한다.

③ 힙합 댄스 공연은 체육관에서 2시에 열린다.

④ '로미오와 줄리엣' 연극이 오후 4시에 공연된다.

⑤ Anna와 Steve는 연극을 보기 위해 대강당에서 체육관으로 이동할 것이다.

12 다음 짝지어진 대화가 <u>어색한</u> 것은?

① A: What kind of music do you like most?

  B: I love hip-hop.

② A: There are two kinds of guitars. Which do you prefer?

  B: I prefer the classic guitar.

③ A: What kind of brush were you using?

  B: I don't know how to paint clean lines.

④ A: I prefer the movie to the novel.

  B: Why do you like it better?

⑤ A: What kind of movie do you like?

  B: I like horror movies.

[13~14] 다음 대화를 읽고 물음에 답하시오.

> Minsu: What are you reading, Jina? (A)
> Jina: The novel, *Life of Pi*. It's a story of a boy and a tiger. (B)
> Minsu: It's a great book. I've seen the movie of it, too. (C)
> Jina: Why do you like it better? (D)
> Minsu: The scenes are very beautiful. And the tiger looks so real. (E)

13 위 대화의 (A)~(E) 중 주어진 문장이 들어가기에 적절한 곳은?

> I prefer the movie to the novel.

① (A)　② (B)　③ (C)　④ (D)　⑤ (E)

14 위 대화를 읽고 대답할 수 <u>없는</u> 것은?

① What is Jina doing now?
② What is *Life of Pi* about?
③ Which one does Minsu prefer, the novel or the movie?
④ How does the tiger look in the movie?
⑤ When did Minsu see the movie?

[15~16] 다음 대화를 읽고 물음에 답하시오.

> Sora: Can you help me? I don't know how to paint clean lines.
> Mike: What kind of brush were you using?
> Sora: This round brush.
> Mike: When you paint lines, a flat brush is better. Try this one.
> Sora: Okay, thank you.

15 What's the matter with Sora?

➡ _____

16 After talking with Mike, what will Sora use to paint lines?

➡ _____

Grammar

17 다음 우리말을 영어로 바르게 옮긴 것은?

> 누가 너를 이 파티에 초대했는지 말해 줘.

① Tell me who you invited to this party.
② Tell me whom you will invite to this party.
③ Tell me who invited you to this party.
④ I wonder how you were invited to this party.
⑤ I wonder whom you came with.

18 다음 빈칸에 공통으로 들어갈 말로 적절한 것은?

> • _____ he comes late, there will be no food.
> • Do you want to know _____ Jane swims every Sunday?

① that　② who　③ what
④ whether　⑤ if

19 다음 중 어법상 <u>틀린</u> 것은?

① Kelly made me do her homework.
② Julia wondered who brought the book.
③ Jerry asked me what I ate for lunch.
④ Olivia let him to use her computer.
⑤ Tell me whether Tom is tired now.

20 주어진 단어를 활용하여 다음 우리말을 영어로 쓰시오.

> 그녀가 지금 어디에 있다고 생각하시나요?
> (think / where)

➡ _____

21 다음 우리말을 영어로 쓸 때 세 번째 오는 단어와 일곱 번째 오는 단어를 바르게 묶은 것은?

> 당신이 내게 이 꽃을 보내도록 누가 시켰는지 궁금해요.

① wonder – made   ② who – me
③ who – send   ④ made – this
⑤ made – flower

22 다음 두 문장을 하나의 문장으로 바르게 쓴 것은?

> Can you tell me? Who kicked the ball?

① Can you tell me who the ball kicked?
② Can you tell me if who kicked the ball?
③ Can you tell me who kicked the ball?
④ Can you tell me who is kicking the ball?
⑤ Can you tell me who the ball is kicking?

23 다음 중 빈칸에 들어갈 말로 적절하지 <u>않은</u> 것은?

> Thomson _____ us carry the boxes.

① had   ② made   ③ helped
④ let   ⑤ told

24 다음 빈칸에 알맞은 말을 쓰시오. 한 칸에 하나의 단어만 쓰시오.

> 나는 그들이 집안일을 하는 것을 돕습니다.
> ➡ I _____ them _____ the chores.
>
>   * chore: 집안일

25 다음 중 어법상 올바른 문장의 개수는?

> ⓐ Can you tell me who are you talking with?
> ⓑ Their parents always have them to go to school early in the morning.
> ⓒ I want to know what they are doing now.
> ⓓ Can you tell me what does Jason do for a living?
> ⓔ May I ask that you have brothers or sisters?

① 1개   ② 2개   ③ 3개   ④ 4개   ⑤ 5개

26 주어진 단어를 활용하여 다음 우리말을 영어로 쓰시오.

> 그 괴물은 아이들이 비명을 지르게 했다.
> (monster, make, scream)

➡ _____

27 간접의문문을 이용하여 다음 두 문장을 하나의 문장으로 쓰시오.

(1) I didn't hear. What did you say?
➡ _____

(2) I'd like to know. Are you friends with Jina?
➡ _____

28 다음 중 빈칸에 들어갈 말로 적절한 것을 <u>모두</u> 고르시오.

> May I ask _____ Brady is here?

① whether   ② if   ③ where
④ what   ⑤ who

Reading

[29~33] 다음 글을 읽고 물음에 답하시오.

Look at this painting first. The seaside landscape is so peaceful and beautiful, isn't it? The title of this painting is *Landscape with the Fall of Icarus*. So, can you see where Icarus is? Do you see two legs that are sticking out of the water near the ship? This is Icarus in the famous myth in Greece. In the myth, Icarus' father made wings for ①him with feathers and wax and told ②him to stay away from the sun. However, Icarus didn't listen to ③him. ④He flew too close to the sun. So, the wax melted and ⑤he fell into the water. Now, look at the entire painting again. Despite the tragedy of Icarus, people are going on with their everyday activities. (A)Does the painting still look peaceful? What do you think the artist is trying to tell us?

29 위 글의 밑줄 친 ①~⑤ 중 지칭하는 바가 다른 하나는?

①   ②   ③   ④   ⑤

30 What were Icarus' wings made of? Use the word 'they.'

➡ _____

31 다음 중 위 글의 내용과 일치하지 <u>않는</u> 것은?

① You can see the seaside landscape in the painting.
② There is a story behind the painting.
③ Icarus' father made Icarus wings.
④ Icarus didn't listen to what his father said.
⑤ Icarus flew close to the sun without wings.

32 위 글의 밑줄 친 (A)를 어법에 맞게 다음 빈칸에 쓰시오.

I wonder _____ .

➡ _____

33 다음과 같이 풀이되는 단어를 위 글에서 찾아 쓰시오.

a very sad event, especially one involving death

➡ _____

[34~36] 다음 글을 읽고 물음에 답하시오.

Welcome to the World Art Museum tour. When you go to an art museum, how much time do you spend (A)[looking / to look] at each painting? Many visitors glance at one painting for only (B)[a few / a little] seconds before they move on. But you might miss the important details of paintings since ⓐit is hard to notice them right away. Today, we'll look at two paintings (C)[close / closely] and I'll help you see interesting details.

34 (A)~(C)에서 어법상 옳은 것을 고르시오.

(A) _____ (B) _____ (C) _____

35 What is the problem with taking only several seconds to look at a painting? Answer in English with a full sentence.

➡ _____

36 다음 중 밑줄 친 ⓐ와 쓰임이 같은 것은?

① It was cold yesterday morning.
② It is still bright outside.
③ It was difficult to tell you all of my secrets.
④ It hurt my feeling.
⑤ It is going up the tree.

[01~02] 다음 대화를 읽고 물음에 답하시오.

Sue: Have you (A)listened to Jane's new song, *Girl Friend*?

Tony: Yeah, it's really cool. The guitar part is great.

Sue: There is also a dance version (B)of the song (C)on the album.

Tony: I've listened to it, but I prefer the guitar version (D)than the dance version. It matches her voice (E)better.

📝 출제율 90%

01 위 대화의 (A)~(E) 중 어법상 어색한 것을 찾아 바르게 고치시오.

➡ _____

📝 출제율 95%

02 위 대화를 읽고 대답할 수 없는 것은?

① What are Sue and Tony talking about?

② What does Tony think about Jane's new song, *Girl Friend*?

③ How many versions of *Girl Friend* are there on the album?

④ Why does Tony like the guitar version more than the dance version?

⑤ What does Tony think about the dance version of *Girl Friend*?

[03~05] 다음 대화를 읽고 물음에 답하시오.

Jason: Hi, we are planning a school festival, so we want to find out students' favorite types of performances. May I ask you a few questions?

Emily: Sure.

Jason: _____(A)_____

Emily: I like music performances best.

Jason: Okay. Then, which do you prefer, rock or hip-hop?

Emily: I prefer rock to hip-hop.

Jason: (B)Who's your favorite musician? (which, like)

Emily: My favorite musician is TJ.

Jason: Great. Thank you for your answers.

📝 출제율 95%

03 위 대화의 빈칸 (A)에 들어갈 말을 〈보기〉에 주어진 단어를 모두 배열하여 완성하시오.

┌─ 보기 ─┐
of / you / what / best / like / do / kind / performance
└────────┘

➡ _____

📝 출제율 85%

04 위 대화의 밑줄 친 (B)를 주어진 단어를 사용하여 의미가 같도록 다시 쓰시오.

➡ _____

📝 출제율 100%

05 위 대화의 내용과 일치하지 않는 것을 고르시오.

① Jason은 학교 축제를 계획하고 있다.

② Jason은 학생들이 가장 선호하는 공연의 종류에 대해 알아보고 있다.

③ Emily는 음악 공연을 가장 좋아한다.

④ Emily는 힙합 공연을 록 공연보다 더 좋아한다.

⑤ Emily가 가장 좋아하는 음악가는 TJ이다.

[06~07] 다음 대화를 읽고 물음에 답하시오.

Anna: (*ringing*) Hello, Steve.

Steve: Hi, Anna. We're meeting at the arts festival tomorrow at 1:30, right?

Anna: Right. What kind of ____ⓐ____ do you want to watch first?

Steve: I want to watch the hip-hop dance performance first.

Anna: Sounds good. It's at 2 p.m. at the gym, right?

Steve: Yeah, and how about watching the play, *Romeo and Juliet*, at 4 p.m.?

Anna: Oh, the one at the Main Hall near the gym? Sure!

06 위 대화의 빈칸 ⓐ에 들어갈 적절한 말을 대화에서 찾아 쓰시오.

➡ _____

07 다음 대화의 내용과 일치하도록 빈칸을 완성하시오.

<Arts Festival Schedule>		
Performance	Time	Place
Dance: hip-hop	(A)	(B)
(C) : *Romeo and Juliet*	4:00 p.m	(D)

(A) _____ (B) _____

(C) _____ (D) _____

[08~09] 다음 대화를 읽고 물음에 답하시오.

Mina: I saw an interesting painting in an art book. Look at this. (A)

Jack: Wow, it looks like da Vinci's *Mona Lisa*. (B)

Mina: Actually, it's *Mona Lisa* by Fernando Botero. Which do you prefer? (C)

Jack: I prefer da Vinci's to Botero's. Da Vinci's *Mona Lisa* has an interesting smile. (D)

Mina: Well, I prefer Botero's to da Vinci's. His *Mona Lisa* is cute, and it looks modern. (E)

08 위 대화의 (A)~(E) 중 다음 주어진 문장이 들어가기에 적절한 곳은?

How about you?

① (A) ② (B) ③ (C) ④ (D) ⑤ (E)

09 위 대화를 읽고 대답할 수 없는 것은?

① What did Mina see in the art book?

② Which *Mona Lisa* does Jack prefer?

③ What does Jack think about da Vinci's *Mona Lisa*?

④ Why does Mina like Botero's *Mona Lisa*?

⑤ Why does Botero's *Mona Lisa* look modern?

10 다음 대화가 자연스럽게 이어지도록 순서대로 배열하시오.

(A) The scenes are very beautiful. And the tiger looks so real.

(B) The novel, *Life of Pi*. It's a story of a boy and a tiger.

(C) What are you reading, Jina?

(D) Why do you like it better?

(E) It's a great book. I've seen the movie of it, too. I prefer the movie to the novel.

➡ _____

11 다음 우리말을 영어로 바르게 옮긴 것은?

누가 너에게 그 비밀을 말해 줬는지 궁금해.

① I wonder who the secret you told.

② I wonder whom did you tell the secret.

③ I wonder who told you the secret.

④ I want to know who you told the secret.

⑤ Tell me who you want to tell the secret.

12 다음 빈칸에 들어갈 말이 바르게 짝지어진 것은?

> • They made us _____ by their house.
> • The teacher had students _____ softball.

① to drop – to play

② dropped – playing

③ dropped – played

④ drop – play

⑤ dropping – playing

13 다음 빈칸에 알맞은 말을 쓰시오.

> I don't know. What did you wear for the Halloween party?
> = I don't know _____
> for the Halloween party.

14 다음 빈칸에 들어갈 말로 적절하지 <u>않은</u> 것은?

> I _____ my sister set the table.

① had　　② made　　③ let

④ helped　　⑤ wanted

15 다음 중 어법상 바르지 <u>않은</u> 것은?

① Do you know what the teacher made us do?

② I wonder whether Jessy is sad or happy.

③ Please let her knows what he likes.

④ Can you tell me who let you go out at night?

⑤ Terry asks me if there was something to drink.

16 다음 빈칸에 들어갈 말이 바르게 짝지어진 것은?

> A: Can you tell me what kind of fruit _____?
> B: I like tomato most.

① you like least　　② you like most

③ you used to like　　④ do you like most

⑤ did you like

17 주어진 단어를 활용하여 다음 우리말을 영어로 쓰시오.

> 나의 부모님은 주말마다 내가 늦잠을 자도록 허락하신다. (let / late / on weekends)

➡ _____

[18~20] 다음 글을 읽고 물음에 답하시오.

　Now, let's move on to the next painting. Do you see the artist behind the large canvas? ① He is Diego Velázquez, and he actually painted this picture. ② Who do you think he is painting? Take a quick look. ③ The young princess seems to be the main person because she is in the center of the painting. ④ Then, is the artist drawing the two women beside the princess? Take a close look. ⑤ It will make you wonder about the painting more. Try to see which direction the artist is looking at. Can you see the king and the queen in the mirror in the background of the painting? Who do you think he is painting now?

18 ①~⑤ 중 다음 주어진 문장이 들어가기에 가장 적절한 곳은?

> But the title of the painting is *The Maids of Honour*.

①　　②　　③　　④　　⑤

19 다음 중 위 글을 읽고 답할 수 있는 것은?

① Why did Diego Velázquez paint the picture?

② When did Diego Velázquez paint the picture?

③ How many maids are there in the picture?

④ Where did Diego Velázquez paint the picture?

⑤ How often did Diego Velázquez meet the king to paint the picture?

20 다음 중 위 그림에서 찾을 수 없는 것은?

① an artist who painted the picture

② a young prince between two women

③ the young princess in the middle of the painting

④ the mirror in the background

⑤ the king and the queen

[21~22] 다음 글을 읽고 물음에 답하시오.

This is Icarus in the famous myth in Greece. In the myth, Icarus' father made wings for him with feathers and wax and told him to stay away from the sun. However, Icarus didn't listen. He flew too close to the sun.   (A) , the wax melted and he fell into the water. Now, look at the entire painting again. Despite the tragedy of Icarus, people are going on with their everyday activities. Does the painting still look peaceful? What do you think the artist is trying to tell us?

21 다음 중 빈칸 (A)에 들어갈 말로 알맞은 것은?

① So   ② But

③ Though   ④ Still

⑤ Instead

22 위 글에 대한 다음 질문을 완성하시오.

A: Can you tell me _____?
(이카루스에게 무슨 일이 생겼는지 말해 줄래?)

B: He flew too close to the sun and the wax of his wings melted.

[23~24] 다음 글을 읽고 물음에 답하시오.

Amazing Sand Art

Today, I went to the Amazing Art exhibition. At the exhibition, I saw many interesting pieces of art. Among them, I liked the piece called *Moon Tree*. It was made by French artist, David Myriam. Interestingly, sand was used in this painting. I like it because a tree in the moon makes me feel calm. Now I know that anything can be used to make art. Anything is possible!

23 위 글의 표현을 활용하여 다음 우리말을 영어로 쓰시오.

나는 네가 많은 흥미로운 예술 작품들을 보았는지 궁금해.

➡ _____

24 Which is NOT true about the passage?

① The writer went to an art exhibition.

② There were many interesting pieces of art at the Amazing Art exhibition.

③ *Moon Tree* was made by David Myriam.

④ David Myriam made *Moon Tree* by using paint.

⑤ The writer realized anything can be used to make art.

[01~03] 다음 대화를 읽고 물음에 답하시오.

Anna: (ringing) Hello, Steve.

Steve: Hi, Anna. We're meeting at the arts festival tomorrow at 1:30, right?

Anna: Right. What kind of performance do you want to watch first?

Steve: I want to watch the hip-hop dance performance first.

Anna: Sounds good. It's at 2 p.m. at the gym, right?

Steve: Yeah, and how about watching the play, *Romeo and Juliet*, at 4 p.m.?

Anna: Oh, the one at the Main Hall near the gym? Sure!

01 What festival will Anna and Steve go to?

➡ _____

02 중요 Where will Anna and Steve watch the hip-hop dance performance?

➡ _____

03 What time and where is *Romeo and Juliet*?

➡ _____

04 중요 간접의문문을 이용하여 다음 두 문장을 하나의 문장으로 쓰시오.

(1) Tell me. Where does Maria live?

➡ _____

(2) I wonder. Are you married?

➡ _____

(3) May I ask? Is he alone?

➡ _____

(4) Can you tell me? Who drove your car?

➡ _____

05 주어진 단어를 바르게 배열하여 다음 우리말을 영어로 쓰시오.

어떤 것도 내가 나의 마음을 바꾸도록 하지는 못할 거야.

(my mind / change / make / nothing / me / will)

➡ _____

06 다음 빈칸에 알맞은 말을 쓰시오.

누가 그 문을 열었는지 궁금해.

➡ I wonder _____.

07 중요 괄호 안의 말을 바르게 배열하여 대화를 완성하시오.

A: I want (how many / read / last year / know / to / books / you).

B: I read about 10 books.

➡ _____

Look at this painting first. The seaside landscape is so peaceful and beautiful, isn't it? The title of this painting is *Landscape with the Fall of Icarus*. So, can you see where Icarus is? Do you see two legs that are sticking out of the water near the ship? This is Icarus in the famous myth in Greece. In the myth, Icarus' father made wings for him with feathers and wax and told him to stay away from the sun. However, Icarus didn't listen. He flew too close to the sun. So, the wax ___(A)___ and he ___(B)___ the water. Now, look at the entire painting again. Despite the tragedy of Icarus, people are going on with their everyday activities. Does the painting still look peaceful? ⓐ화가가 우리에게 무엇을 말하려 한다고 생각하나요?(think, try)

08 위 글의 빈칸 (A)와 (B)에 알맞은 말을 쓰시오.

(A) _____ (B) _____

09 주어진 단어를 활용하여 밑줄 친 우리말 ⓐ를 영어로 쓰시오.

➡ _____

10 위 글의 내용에 맞게 빈칸에 알맞은 말을 쓰시오.

A: Where is Icarus?
B: He is _____ _____ _____. You can see his legs _____ _____ _____ _____ _____.

11 주어진 단어를 활용하여 다음 우리말을 영어로 쓰시오.

그는 그의 아들이 태양에서 멀리 떨어지게 하지 못했다. (make / stay)

➡ _____

12 위 글의 내용에 맞게 빈칸에 알맞은 말을 쓰시오.

Q: What happened to Icarus?
A: He _____ too _____ to the sun and the _____ of his wings _____.

[13~14] 다음 글을 읽고 물음에 답하시오.

Now, let's move ___ⓐ___ to the next painting. Do you see the artist behind the large canvas?

(A) The young princess seems to be the main person because she is in the center of the painting.

(B) It will make you wonder about the painting more. Try to see which direction the artist is looking at.

(C) But the title of the painting is *The Maids of Honour*. Then, is the artist drawing the two women beside the princess? Take a close look.

(D) He is Diego Velázquez, and he actually painted this picture. Who do you think he is painting? Take a quick look.

Can you see the king and the queen in the mirror ___ⓑ___ the background of the painting? Who do you think he is painting now?

13 자연스러운 글이 되도록 (A)~(D)를 바르게 나열하시오.

➡ _____

14 위 글의 빈칸 ⓐ와 ⓑ에 알맞은 말을 쓰시오.

ⓐ _____ ⓑ _____

01 다음 대화의 내용과 일치하도록 Mina의 일기를 완성하시오.

> **Mina:** I saw an interesting painting in an art book. Look at this.
> **Jack:** Wow, it looks like da Vinci's *Mona Lisa*.
> **Mina:** Actually, it's *Mona Lisa* by Fernando Botero. Which do you prefer?
> **Jack:** I prefer da Vinci's to Botero's. Da Vinci's *Mona Lisa* has an interesting smile. How about you?
> **Mina:** Well, I prefer Botero's to da Vinci's. His *Mona Lisa* is cute, and it looks modern.

> Mon, Oct 14th, 2019
> Today, I saw an interesting painting in an art book. It looked like da Vinci's *Mona Lisa*, but it was *Mona Lisa* by Fernando Botero. Between them, Jack preferred (A) _____ _____ to (B)_____, because of (C)_____ on da Vinci's *Mona Lisa*. However, I like (D)_____ much more because his *Mona Lisa* is cute and it looks modern.

02 다음 설문 조사표를 보고 대화를 완성하시오.

> Museum Survey   Name: Clark
> 01 What grade are you in?   □ 7th grade   ☑ 8th grade   □ 9th grade
> 02 How often do you go to a museum?
> □ once a month   ☑ twice a month   □ once a year   □ others: _____
> 03 What kind of museum do you like to go to?
> ☑ art museum   □ history museum   □ others: _____
> 04 How long do you usually spend time in the museum?
> □ about an hour   ☑ about two hours   □ about three hours   □ about four hours

> **Q:** I would like to know _____.
> **A:** I am in the 8th grade.
> **Q:** May I ask _____?
> **A:** I go to a museum twice a month.
> **Q:** I wonder _____.
> **A:** I like to go to the art museum.
> **Q:** Would you mind telling me _____?
> **A:** Certainly not. I usually spend about two hours in the museum.

단원별 모의고사

01 다음 문장에 공통으로 들어갈 말을 고르시오.

> • Tom, _____ your teeth clean.
> • I didn't need the _____ anymore.
> • This _____ was worn out.

① produce   ② stick
③ wax   ④ flat
⑤ brush

02 다음 문장의 빈칸에 들어갈 말을 〈보기〉에서 골라 쓰시오.

> ┌── 보기 ├──
> tourist / wonder / direction / melt / despite

(1) _____ the butter over low heat.
(2) _____ the bad weather, we went on a picnic at a beach.
(3) A foreign _____ asked me to take her picture.
(4) Everyone in the photo is looking in the same _____.
(5) I _____ why she did that.

[03~05] 다음 대화를 읽고 물음에 답하시오.

> M: (A)Can you help me? (hand) I want to buy a guitar.
> W: There are various kinds of guitars. (B)어떤 종류의 음악을 연주하고 싶으신가요?
> M: I want to play pop songs.
> W: Then you should get a classical guitar.
> M: Okay, I will take a classical guitar.

03 위 대화에서 밑줄 친 (A)와 의미가 같도록 주어진 단어를 사용하여 다시 쓰시오.

➡ _____

04 위 대화의 밑줄 친 우리말 (B)를 영작하시오.

➡ _____

05 위 대화에서 나타난 두 사람의 관계로 적절한 것은?

① student – teacher
② tourist – guide
③ customer – clerk
④ patient – doctor
⑤ interviewee – interviewer

[06~07] 다음 대화를 읽고 물음에 답하시오.

> Jason: Hi, we are planning a school festival, so we want to find out students' favorite types of performances. May I ask you (A)[a few / few] questions?
> Emily: Sure.
> Jason: What kind of performance do you like (B)[more / most]?
> Emily: I like music performances best.
> Jason: Okay. Then, which do you prefer, rock (C)[and / or] hip-hop?
> Emily: I prefer rock to hip-hop.
> Jason: Who's your favorite musician?
> Emily: My favorite musician is TJ.
> Jason: Great. Thank you for your answers.

06 위 대화의 (A)~(C)에 들어갈 말로 바르게 짝지어진 것은?

① a few – more – and
② a few – most – or
③ a few – most – and
④ few – most – or
⑤ few – more – and

07 위 대화를 읽고 대답할 수 없는 것은?

① What does Jason want Emily to do?
② What kind of performance does Emily like best?
③ What kind of music does Emily like?
④ Who is Emily's favorite musician?
⑤ Why does Emily like TJ most?

[08~09] 다음 대화를 읽고 물음에 답하시오.

Mina: I saw an (A)interesting painting in an art book. Look (B)at this.
Jack: Wow, it looks like da Vinci's *Mona Lisa*.
Mina: Actually, it's *Mona Lisa* by Fernando Botero. (C)How do you prefer?
Jack: I prefer da Vinci's (D)to Botero's. Da Vinci's *Mona Lisa* has an interesting smile. How (E)about you?
Mina: Well, I prefer Botero's to da Vinci's. His *Mona Lisa* is cute, and it looks modern.

08 위 대화의 밑줄 친 (A)~(E) 중 어색한 것을 찾아 바르게 고치시오.

➡ _____

09 위 대화의 내용과 일치하지 않는 것은?

① Mina는 미술책에서 페르난도 보테로의 '모나리자'를 보았다.
② Jack은 보테로의 '모나리자'보다 다빈치의 '모나리자'를 더 좋아한다.
③ Jack은 다빈치의 '모나리자'에 흥미로운 미소가 있다고 생각한다.
④ Mina는 다빈치의 '모나리자'보다는 보테로의 '모나리자'를 더 좋아한다.
⑤ Mina는 다빈치의 '모나리자'가 귀엽고 현대적이라고 생각한다.

[10~12] 다음 대화를 읽고 물음에 답하시오.

Susan: Brian, is your band going to play at the Teen Music Festival?
Brian: Yes, we're practicing (A)almost every day.
Susan: (B)너희는 올해 어떤 종류의 음악을 연주하려고 하니?
Brian: Rock music. We'll play songs from the (C)ninety.

10 위 대화의 밑줄 친 (A)와 같은 뜻의 단어를 쓰시오.

➡ _____

11 위 대화의 밑줄 친 (A)의 우리말을 영작하시오.

➡ _____

12 위 대화의 밑줄 친 (C)를 알맞은 형으로 고치시오.

➡ _____

13 다음 빈칸에 들어갈 말로 가장 적절한 것은?

Rapunzel's mom _____ in the tower.

① makes Rapunzel staying
② made herself to stay
③ made Rapunzel stayed
④ made herself staying
⑤ made Rapunzel stay

14 주어진 단어를 활용하여 다음 우리말을 7 단어로 이루어진 한 문장으로 쓰시오.

좋은 음악은 네가 기분이 더 좋아지도록 만들 것이다. (make / feel)

➡ _____

15 다음 빈칸에 들어갈 말로 적절하지 <u>않은</u> 것은?

> Do you know _____ ?

① who called you last night
② when the Morisons will arrive
③ where they are going to meet
④ how the word is spelled
⑤ what Tom made upset

16 간접의문문을 이용하여 다음 두 문장을 하나의 문장으로 쓰시오.

(1) Do you remember? Where did you find this bag?

➡ _____

(2) Can you tell me? Why does Kelly want to become a dancer?

➡ _____

17 다음 중 어법상 바르지 <u>않은</u> 것은?

① She made their dreams come true.
② Would you mind telling me who pushed you?
③ I want you to tell me when you will start the project.
④ Do you know who the lights turned off?
⑤ I had the man fix my chair.

[18~21] 다음 글을 읽고 물음에 답하시오.

Look at this painting first. The seaside landscape is so peaceful and beautiful, isn't it? The title of this painting is *Landscape with the Fall of Icarus*. So, can you see where Icarus is? Do you see two legs that are sticking out of the water near the ship? This is Icarus in the famous myth in Greece. In the myth, Icarus' father made wings for him with feathers and wax and told him to stay away __(A)__ the sun. However, Icarus didn't listen. He flew too close to the sun. So, the wax melted and he fell into the water. Now, look at the entire painting again. Despite the tragedy of Icarus, people are going on with their everyday activities. Does the painting still look peaceful? What do you think the artist is trying to tell us?

18 다음 중 빈칸 (A)에 들어갈 말과 같은 말이 들어가는 것은?

① I want you to listen _____ my words.
② Do you take good care _____ your plants?
③ Many people suffer _____ headache.
④ Turn _____ the lights when you go out.
⑤ She will be satisfied _____ your presents.

19 When Icarus fell into the water, what were the other people in the painting doing? Answer in English with a full sentence.

➡ _____

20 다음 중 위 글의 내용과 일치하지 <u>않는</u> 것은?

① Icarus flew too close to the sun.
② Icarus' legs are sticking out of the ship.
③ Icarus' father wanted his son not to fly close to the sun.
④ Icarus' wings were made by his father.
⑤ People in the painting didn't care about the tragedy of Icarus.

21 위 글의 내용에 맞게 다음 대화의 빈칸을 채우시오.

> A: I would like to know _____.
> B: Oh, that's because he flew too close to the sun.

➡ _____

[22~25] 다음 글을 읽고 물음에 답하시오.

Now, let's move on to the next painting. Do you see the artist behind the large canvas? He is Diego Velázquez, and he actually painted this picture. _____(A)_____ Take a quick look. The young princess seems to be the main person ①because she is in the center of the painting. But the title of the painting is *The Maids of Honour*. Then, is the artist ②drawing the two women ③beside the princess? Take a close look. It will make you ④wonder about the painting more. Try to see which direction ⑤is the artist looking at. Can you see the king and the queen in the mirror in the background of the painting? _____(B)_____

22 (A)와 (B)에 공통으로 들어갈 말로 가장 적절한 것은?

① When do you think he drew this painting?
② Who do you imagine he is painting?
③ How do you guess he is painting?
④ Do you know where he is painting?
⑤ What made him paint?

23 위 글의 ①~⑤ 중 어법상 바르지 않은 것은?

①   ②   ③   ④   ⑤

24 다음과 같이 풀이되는 단어를 위 글에서 찾아 쓰시오.

> a piece of thick cloth used by artists for painting on

➡ _____

25 Which is NOT true about the artist who painted *The Maids of Honour*?

① His name is Diego Velázquez.
② He drew the young princess in the painting.
③ The king and the queen appear in the painting.
④ He drew himself behind the large canvas.
⑤ He drew the king and the queen in front of the princess.

Lesson 8

Changes Ahead

 의사소통 기능

- 상대방의 의견 묻기
  A: What do you think about the present?
  B: I think it's really touching.

- 상대방의 의견과 같거나 다름을 표현하기
  A: I think it's great that many people see my posts.
  B: I'm (not) with you on that.

 언어 형식

- so ~ that ... can't
  We were **so** tired **that** we **could not** go out.

- 현재[과거]분사
  The seafood **fried** rice was amazing.

Words & Expressions

Key Words

- **agree** [əgríː] 동 동의하다
- **bakery** [béikəri] 명 빵집, 제과점
- **balance** [bǽləns] 동 균형을 잡다
- **counter** [káuntər] 명 계산대, 판매대
- **creative** [kriéitiv] 형 창의적인
- **debate** [dibéit] 명 토론, 논의
- **deliver** [dilívər] 동 전달하다, 배달하다
- **dependence** [dipéndəns] 명 의존, 의지
- **donate** [dóuneit] 동 기부하다
- **downtown** [dauntaun] 형 시내의
- **effect** [ifékt] 명 효과
- **elderly** [éldərli] 형 나이가 지긋한
- **experience** [ikspíəriəns] 명 경험
- **fry** [frai] 동 튀기다
- **guesthouse** [gesthaus] 명 (여행자 등의) 숙소, 여관
- **guidebook** [gaidbuk] 명 (여행) 안내서
- **handwritten** [hǽndrìtn] 형 손으로 쓴
- **hundred** [hʌ́ndrəd] 명 백, 100
- **importance** [impɔ́ːrtəns] 명 중요함
- **local** [lóukəl] 형 지역의, 현지의 명 주민, 현지인
- **machine** [məʃíːn] 명 기계
- **memory stick** 소형 메모리 카드
- **mixture** [míkstʃər] 명 혼합물, 혼합
- **moment** [móumənt] 명 순간
- **nearby** [nìərbái] 부 근처에
- **opinion** [əpínjən] 명 의견
- **post** [poust] 동 (웹 사이트에 정보, 사진을) 올리다
- **presence** [prézns] 명 존재
- **price** [prais] 명 가격
- **remain** [riméin] 동 남아 있다, 남다
- **scared** [skɛərd] 형 무서워하는, 겁먹은
- **side** [said] 명 면, 측면
- **smartphone** 명 스마트폰
- **sugar-free** [ʃúgərfrìː] 형 무가당의
- **suggest** [səgdʒést] 동 제안하다
- **surprise** [sərpráiz] 동 놀라게 하다
- **technology** [teknálədʒi] 명 (과학) 기술
- **thought** [θɔːt] 명 생각
- **trendy** [tréhdi] 형 최신 유행의
- **wisely** [wáizli] 부 현명하게

Key Expressions

- **be busy -ing** ~하느라 바쁘다
- **can't wait to** ~하기를 기대하다
- **even though** 비록 ~할지라도
- **fall asleep** 잠들다
- **get attention** 주목을 받다
- **get lost** 길을 잃다
- **keep -ing** 계속해서 ~하다
- **pay for** 대금을 지불하다
- **throw away** ~을 버리다
- **rely on** ~에 의존하다

Word Power

※ 서로 반대되는 뜻을 가진 어휘

- □ **agree** 동의하다 ↔ **disagree** 반대하다
- □ **heavy** 무거운 ↔ **right** 가벼운
- □ **balanced** 균형 잡힌 ↔ **imbalanced** 불균형의
- □ **near** 가까운 ↔ **far** 먼, 멀리 떨어진
- □ **important** 중요한 ↔ **unimportant** 중요하지 않은

- □ **dependence** 의존, 의지 ↔ **independence** 독립
- □ **wisely** 현명하게 ↔ **stupidly** 어리석게도
- □ **useful** 유용한 ↔ **useless** 쓸모없는
- □ **present** 있는, 출석한 ↔ **absent** 부재의, 결석한
- □ **succeed** 성공 ↔ **fail** 실패하다

English Dictionary

- □ **bakery** 빵집, 제과점
  → a place where bread and cakes are made or sold
  빵과 케이크를 만들거나 파는 곳

- □ **balance** 균형을 잡다
  → to be in a steady position without falling to one side
  한쪽으로 치우치지 않고 한결같은 자세를 취하다

- □ **downtown** 시내의, 도심지의
  → relating to or located in the center of a town or city
  마을이나 도시의 중심에 위치하거나 연관된

- □ **experience** 경험
  → knowledge or skill that you gain from doing a job or activity
  당신이 어떤 일이나 활동을 하며 얻은 지식 또는 기술

- □ **fry** 튀기다
  → to cook something in hot oil
  뜨거운 기름으로 무언가를 요리하다

- □ **guesthouse** (여행자 등의) 숙소, 여관
  → a private house where people can pay to stay and have meals
  사람들이 머무르고 식사하기 위해 돈을 지불할 수 있는 사적인 집

- □ **guidebook** (여행) 안내서
  → a book of directions and information for travelers
  여행자들을 위한 지침 또는 정보에 대한 책

- □ **local** 지역의, 현지의
  → relating to the particular area you live in
  당신이 살고 있는 특정 지역과 관련된

- □ **moment** 순간
  → a particular point in time
  시간상의 특정 시점

- □ **post** (웹사이트에 정보, 사진을) 올리다
  → to put a message or computer document on the Internet
  인터넷에 메시지 또는 컴퓨터 서류를 올리다

- □ **remain** 남아 있다, 남다
  → to continue to exist or be left after others have gone
  다른 사람들이 가버린 후 계속 존재하거나 남겨져 있다

- □ **suggest** 제안하다
  → to tell someone your ideas about what they should do, where they should go, etc.
  누군가에게 그들이 해야 하는 것, 그들이 가야 하는 곳 등에 대해 당신의 생각을 말하다

- □ **technology** (과학) 기술
  → new machines, equipment, and ways of doing things that are based on modern scientific knowledge
  현대의 과학적 지식을 바탕으로 한 무언가를 하는 새로운 기계, 장비 방법

- □ **wisely** 현명하게
  → in a way that show experience, knowledge, and good judgment
  경험, 지식, 그리고 좋은 판단을 보여주는 방식으로

서답형

01 다음 짝지어진 단어의 관계가 같도록 빈칸에 알맞은 말을 쓰시오.

> appear : disappear = agree : _____

02 다음 영영풀이가 가리키는 것을 고르시오.

> to tell someone your ideas about what they should do, where they should go, etc.

① remain   ② suggest

③ donate   ④ deliver

⑤ agree

중요

03 다음 중 밑줄 친 부분의 뜻풀이가 바르지 않은 것은?

① My sister is standing at the <u>counter</u>. 계산대

② James opened his new office near the <u>downtown</u>. 시내

③ I <u>agree</u>, but I'd like to listen to your reasons. 동의하다

④ How about offering your seat to an <u>elderly</u> person? 나이가 지긋한

⑤ Pour the <u>mixture</u> into the frying pan. 원료

서답형

04 다음 우리말에 맞게 빈칸에 알맞은 말을 쓰시오.

(1) 우리 부모님은 매년 돈을 기부하신다.
  ➡ My parents _____ money every year.

(2) 우리는 지역 신문에 우리의 차를 광고했다.
  ➡ We advertised our car in the _____ newspaper.

(3) 이 손을 쓸 필요가 없는 기기는 음성 명령으로 전화가 걸린다.
  ➡ This _____ device lets me make calls by voice commands.

서답형

05 다음 우리말에 맞게 주어진 단어를 사용하여 영작하시오.

(1) 우리는 환경의 중요성을 알아야만 한다. (should, environment)
  ➡ _____

(2) 나는 일과 놀이 사이에 균형을 잡으려고 노력한다. (try, work)
  ➡ _____

(3) 내 남동생은 시애틀 시내에서 일한다. (Seattle, in)
  ➡ _____

06 다음 주어진 문장의 밑줄 친 <u>post</u>와 같은 의미로 쓰인 것은?

> Would you <u>post</u> these advertisements on Sam's website?

① He has held the <u>post</u> for three years.

② You can <u>post</u> your suggestions on the board.

③ Tom will send the documents to you by <u>post</u>.

④ Was there any <u>post</u> to me?

⑤ I'm sorry that I forgot to <u>post</u> the letter.

01 다음 짝지어진 단어의 관계가 같도록 빈칸에 알맞은 말을 쓰시오.

> balanced : imbalanced =
> important : _____

02 다음 문장의 빈칸에 들어갈 말을 〈보기〉에서 골라 쓰시오.

> ┌ 보기 ┐
> get attention / throw away / rely on /
> fall asleep / even though

(1) Don't _____ _____ trash on the street.

(2) I used to _____ _____ my own judgement.

(3) Why do you want to _____ _____ from people?

(4) _____ _____ Emma is young, she is wise enough to handle the problems.

(5) I can't _____ _____ because of noise from the upper floor.

03 다음 우리말에 맞게 주어진 단어를 사용하여 영작하시오.

(1) 네 시간을 현명하게 써라. (spend)

➡ _____

(2) 우리는 이 사진들을 인터넷에 게시할 것이다. (will, these)

➡ _____

(3) 그 직업은 약간의 창의적인 상상력을 필요로 한다. (some, job)

➡ _____

04 다음 영영풀이가 가리키는 것을 쓰시오.

> a place where bread and cakes are made or sold

➡ _____

05 다음 주어진 우리말과 일치하도록 주어진 단어를 모두 배열하여 영작하시오.

(1) 몇몇 과학자들은 무가당 음료가 치아에 나쁘다고 말한다. (sugar-free / some / are / bad / your / for / teeth / say / scientists / drinks)

➡ _____
_____

(2) 그 어린 소녀는 소년의 존재에 수줍어했다. (little / presence / felt / boy's / the / shy / the / girl / in)

➡ _____

(3) 나의 반 친구들이 나를 위한 깜짝 파티를 열었다. (me / my / for / a / threw / party / classmates / surprise)

➡ _____

(4) 내 새 드레스에 대해 어떻게 생각하니? (about / my / new / do / dress / what / you / think)

➡ _____

(5) 그 여행은 내 인생에서 가장 흥미진진한 순간 중의 하나였다. (one / moments / the trip / my life / exciting / was / the most / in / of)

➡ _____
_____

1 상대방의 의견 묻기

> **A** What do you think about the present? 그 선물에 대해 어떻게 생각하니?
>
> **B** I think it's really touching. 나는 그것이 정말 감동적이라고 생각해.

■ "What do you think about ~?"은 어떤 일이나 사건, 사물, 사람들에 대하여 상대방의 의견을 물을 때 사용한다. 예를 들어, 상대방에게 자신의 새로운 머리 스타일에 대한 의견을 물을 때는 "What do you think about my new hair style?"과 같이 말할 수 있다.

상대방의 의견 묻기

- How do you feel about my study plan? 내 공부 계획에 대해 어떻게 생각하세요?
- What would you like to say about smartphones? 스마트폰에 대해 무슨 말을 하고 싶으세요?
- What is your opinion on extreme sports? 극한 스포츠에 대해 어떻게 생각하세요?

핵심 Check

1. 다음 주어진 우리말과 일치하도록 빈칸을 완성하시오.

(1) **A:** _____ _____ _____ _____ the School Rooftop Farm?
(학교 옥상 농장에 대해 어떻게 생각하니?)

B: I think it's cool. It can give us _____ _____ and make our school _____.
(나는 좋다고 생각해. 이것은 우리에게 신선한 야채들을 제공해 줄 수 있고 우리 학교를 더 푸르게 만들어 줄 수 있어.)

(2) **A:** How _____ _____ _____ _____ the Sharing Library?
(공유 도서관에 대해 어떻게 생각하니?)

B: _____ _____ _____ _____. It can be a great way to read various kinds of books _____ _____. (나는 좋다고 생각해. 이것은 무료로 다양한 종류의 책들을 읽을 수 있는 훌륭한 방식일 수 있어.)

(3) **A:** _____ your opinion on the Donation Walk? (기부 걷기에 대해 어떻게 생각하니?)

B: I think it's great. It can help people _____ _____ and make us _____, too. (나는 매우 좋다고 생각해. 어려움에 처한 사람들을 도울 수 있고 또한 우리를 건강하게 만들어 줄 수 있어.)

2 상대방의 의견과 같거나 다름을 표현하기

A I think it's great that many people see my posts.

나는 많은 사람들이 내 게시물들을 보는 것이 정말 좋다고 생각해.

B I'm (not) with you on that. 나도 그렇게 생각해. / 나는 그 점에 있어서 너랑 생각이 달라.

■ "I'm (not) with you on that."은 어떤 특정 이슈나 사안에 대하여 상대방의 의견에 동의하거나 이의를 나타낼 때 사용한다.

상대방의 의견에 동의를 나타낼 때

- I think so, too. 나도 그렇게 생각해.
- I believe so, too. 나도 그렇게 믿어.
- I agree with you. 당신의 의견에 동의해요.
- I see it that way, too. 나도 그렇게 생각해.

상대방의 의견에 이의를 나타낼 때

- I don't think so. 나는 그렇게 생각하지 않아.
- I don't believe so. 난 그렇게 믿지 않아.
- I don't agree with you. 저는 당신에게 동의하지 않아요.
- I disagree with you. 난 당신의 의견에 동의하지 않아요.

핵심 Check

2. 다음 주어진 우리말과 일치하도록 빈칸을 완성하시오.

(1) **A:** I think taking _____ classes is better than taking _____ classes.

(나는 온라인 수업들을 듣는 것이 오프라인 수업들을 듣는 것보다 더 낫다고 생각해.)

B: I'm _____ you _____ that. I can watch the lessons any time.

(나도 그렇게 생각해. 나는 언제든지 수업들을 볼 수가 있어.)

C: _____ _____ _____ _____. I can't focus well outside of the classroom. (나는 그렇게 생각하지 않아. 나는 교실 밖에서는 잘 집중할 수 없어.)

(2) **A:** I think watching movies at home is better than watching them at a _____.

(나는 집에서 영화를 보는 것이 극장에서 보는 것보다 더 낫다고 생각해.)

B: I'm _____ _____ _____ on that. I can't enjoy the large screen and the sound _____. (나는 그렇게 생각하지 않아. 나는 큰 화면과 음향 효과를 즐길 수 없어.)

Listen and Talk 1-B

Tony: Hey, Julie! ❶Have you heard about the *Quiz & Rice* game?

Julie: Yeah, isn't it the one that ❷donates rice when you get a right answer?

Tony: Yeah, ❸what do you think about the game?

Julie: I think ❹it's a creative game. ❺You can have fun and help out hungry people. Have you played ❹it yet?

Tony: No, but I'm going to ❻try ❹it out this weekend.

Tony: 저기, Julie! 너 '퀴즈와 쌀'이라는 게임에 대해 들어 봤니?

Julie: 응. 정답을 맞히면 쌀을 기부하는 게임 아니야?

Tony: 맞아. 넌 그 게임에 대해 어떻게 생각하니?

Julie: 난 그것이 창의적인 게임이라고 생각해. 재미있게 놀면서 배고픈 사람들을 도울 수 있잖아. 너 그거 이미 해 봤니?

Tony: 아니, 하지만 이번 주말에 해 보려고 해.

❶ 현재완료 시제를 사용하여 경험을 묻고 있다.
❷ donate: 기부하다
❸ 상대방의 의견을 묻는 표현으로 What's your opinion on that game?으로 바꾸어 쓸 수 있다.
❹ it은 모두 '퀴즈와 쌀'이라는 게임을 가리킨다.
❺ help out: ~을 돕다
❻ 이어동사의 목적어가 인칭대명사일 때는 목적어는 동사와 부사 사이에 위치한다.

Check(√) True or False

(1) People who play the *Quiz & Rice* game can donate money when they get the right answer.　T ☐ F ☐

(2) Tony is going to try out the *Quiz & Rice* game this weekend.　T ☐ F ☐

Listen and Talk 2-B

Emma: Excuse me. ❶Can you help me ❷order with this machine?

Tom: Sure. First, ❸press the Hot Dog button and choose your hot dog and drink.

Emma: Okay. How do I ❹pay for my order?

Tom: Touch the Done button at the bottom and ❹pay for them.

Emma: Wow, it's so simple. This machine is much faster than ordering at the counter.

Tom: ❺I'm with you on that. It really saves a lot of time when there's a long line.

Emma: 실례합니다. 제가 이 기계로 주문하는 것을 좀 도와주실 수 있나요?

Tom: 물론이죠. 먼저 '핫도그' 버튼을 누르시고, 드시고 싶은 핫도그와 음료를 고르세요.

Emma: 알겠습니다. 주문한 것에 대한 지불은 어떻게 하나요?

Tom: 맨 아래에 있는 '완료' 버튼을 누르시고 그것들에 대해 지불하세요.

Emma: 와, 정말 간단하네요. 이 기계가 계산대에서 주문하는 것보다 훨씬 더 빨라요.

Tom: 저도 그렇게 생각해요. 줄이 길 때, 그것은 정말 많은 시간을 절약해 줘요.

❶ 도움을 요청하는 구문으로 'Can you tell me how to order with this machine?'으로 바꾸어 쓸 수 있다.
❷ order: 주문하다
❸ 동사로 시작하는 명령문으로 이어지는 동사 choose와 병렬 구조이다.
❹ pay for: 지불하다
❺ 상대방의 의견에 동의하는 표현으로 'I agree with you.'로 바꾸어 쓸 수 있다.

Check(√) True or False

(3) Emma used to order hot dog with this machine.　T ☐ F ☐

(4) Tom disagrees with Emma's opinion about saving lots of time with the machine.　T ☐ F ☐

Listen and Talk 1 A-1

Jane: Look, Dad. This is Mom's birthday gift.

Dad: Oh, you're giving her a memory stick?

Jane: Yeah, I've made a family video clip for Mom and saved ❶it on this stick. ❷What do you think about the present?

Dad: I think ❸it's really ❹touching. She'll love ❸it.

❶ it은 a family video clip을 가리킨다.
❷ 상대방의 의견을 묻는 표현으로 'How do you feel about the present?'로 바꾸어 쓸 수 있다.
❸ it은 the present를 가리킨다.
❹ touching: 감동적인

Listen and Talk 1 A-2

Mike: Jenny, ❶what do you think about the new online comic *Scary Night*?

Jenny: I didn't like ❷it. I thought ❷it had too many sound ❸effects.

Mike: Really? I thought ❹they made the story more interesting.

Jenny: Not me. I couldn't focus because I was too ❺scared.

❶ 상대방의 의견을 묻는 표현으로 'What's your opinion on the new online comic *Scary Night*?'으로 바꾸어 물어볼 수 있다.
❷ it은 모두 the new online comic *Scary Night*을 가리킨다.
❸ effect: 효과
❹ they는 sound effects를 가리킨다.
❺ scared: 겁먹은

Listen and Talk 2 A-1

Jack: Sally, did you watch *Super Voice's* Top 10 finalists yesterday?

Sally: Yeah. They all sang much better than before.

Jack: Yeah, they did. I think this singing contest helps them ❶get closer to their dreams.

Sally: ❷I'm with you on that. I ❸can't wait to watch their next performances.

❶ help의 목적보어로 원형부정사가 이어졌다.
❷ 상대방의 의견에 동의하는 표현으로 'I think so, too.'라고 바꾸어 말할 수 있다.
❸ can't wait to: ~하기를 기대하다

Listen & Talk 2 A-2

Steve: Hey, Lisa. I've got ❶over a hundred comments on my SNS ❷posts.

Lisa: Oh, I wouldn't feel ❸comfortable to ❹ share my posts with so many people.

Steve: Really? I think it's great that a lot of people see my posts.

Lisa: ❺I'm not with you on that. I only want to share my posts with my close friends.

❶ over a hundred comments: 100개 이상의 댓글
❷ post: (명) 게시물, (동) 게시하다
❸ comfortable: 편안한
❹ share: 공유하다
❺ 상대방의 의견에 이의를 나타내는 표현으로 'I disagree with you.' 또는 'I don't think so, too.'로 바꾸어 말할 수 있다.

Communication

Sujin: Now, we will start the three-minute ❶ debate. Today's first topic is fast fashion. What do you think about ❷it? Please, begin, James.

James: I think fast fashion is good. We can wear ❸trendy clothes at a cheaper price.

Wendy: I'm not with you on that. ❷It makes us spend too much money and ❹throw away clothes too often.

Sujin: It looks like the two of you have different opinions on the first topic. Now, let's ❺ move on to the second topic.

❶ debate: 토론
❷ it은 fast fashion을 가리킨다.
❸ trendy: 최신의
❹ throw away: 버리다
❺ move on to: ~로 넘어가다

● 다음 우리말과 일치하도록 빈칸에 알맞은 말을 쓰시오.

Listen & Talk 1 A-1

Jane: Look, Dad. This is Mom's birthday gift.

Dad: Oh, you're giving her a _____ _____?

Jane: Yeah, I've made a family video clip for Mom and _____ it on this stick. What do you _____ about the _____?

Dad: I think it's really _____. She'll love it.

Jane: 보세요, 아빠. 이거 엄마의 생신 선물이에요.

Dad: 오, 너는 엄마에게 막대 기억 장치 (메모리 스틱)를 준다는 거지?

Jane: 네, 엄마를 위한 가족 동영상을 만들어서, 그것을 이 막대 기억 장치에 저장했어요. 이 선물에 대해 어떻게 생각하세요?

Dad: 정말 감동적인 것 같구나. 엄마가 그걸 정말 좋아할 거 같아.

Listen & Talk 1 A-2

Mike: Jenny, _____ _____ _____ _____ _____ the new online comic *Scary Night*?

Jenny: I didn't like it. I thought it had too many _____ _____.

Mike: Really? I thought they made the story more _____.

Jenny: Not me. I couldn't focus because I was too _____.

Mike: Jenny, 너는 새로운 온라인 만화 '무서운 밤'에 대해 어떻게 생각하니?

Jenny: 난 그거 별로였어. 거기에 음향 효과가 너무 많다고 생각했어.

Mike: 정말? 나는 그것이 이야기를 더욱 흥미진진하게 만들어 준다고 생각했는데.

Jenny: 난 아니야. 난 너무 무서워서 집중할 수가 없었거든.

Listen & Talk 1 B

Tony: Hey, Julie! Have you _____ about the *Quiz & Rice* game?

Julie: Yeah, isn't it the one that _____ rice when you get a right answer?

Tony: Yeah, _____ do you think about the game?

Julie: I think it's a _____ game. You can _____ _____ and _____ _____ hungry people. Have you played it yet?

Tony: No, but I'm going to _____ it _____ this weekend.

Tony: 저기, Julie! 너 '퀴즈와 쌀'이라는 게임에 대해 들어봤니?

Julie: 응, 정답을 맞히면 쌀을 기부하는 게임 아니야?

Tony: 맞아, 넌 그 게임에 대해 어떻게 생각하니?

Julie: 난 그것이 창의적인 게임이라고 생각해. 재미있게 놀면서 배고픈 사람들을 도울 수 있잖아. 너 그거 이미 해 봤니?

Tony: 아니, 하지만 이번 주말에 해 보려고 해.

Listen & Talk 2 A-1

Jack: Sally, did you watch *Super Voice's* Top 10 finalists yesterday?

Sally: Yeah. They all sang much _____ _____ _____.

Jack: Yeah, they did. I think this singing contest helps them _____ _____ to their dreams.

Sally: I'm _____ _____ _____ _____. I can't _____ _____ _____ their next performances.

Jack: Sally, 너 어제 '슈퍼 보이스'의 상위 10위 결정전을 봤니?

Sally: 응. 그들은 모두 전보다 훨씬 더 노래를 잘 불렀어.

Jack: 맞아, 그랬어. 나는 이 노래 경연 대회가 그들이 자신의 꿈에 더 가까워지도록 도와준다고 생각해.

Sally: 나도 그 말에 동의해. 그들의 다음 공연을 보는 것이 너무 기다려진다.

Listen & Talk 2 A-2

Steve: Hey, Lisa. I've got over a hundred _____ on my SNS posts.

Lisa: Oh, I wouldn't feel _____ to share my posts with so many people.

Steve: Really? I think it's great _____ a lot of people see my _____.

Lisa: I'm _____ _____ _____ _____ _____. I only want to _____ my posts with my close friends.

Listen & Talk 2 B

Emma: Excuse me. Can you _____ me _____ with this machine?

Tom: Sure. First, _____ the Hot Dog button and choose your hot dog and drink.

Emma: Okay. _____ do I _____ _____ _____ _____?

Tom: Touch the Done button at the _____ and _____ for them.

Emma: Wow, it's so _____. This machine is much faster than ordering at the _____.

Tom: I'm _____ _____ on that. It really _____ a lot of _____ when there's a long _____.

Communication

Sujin: Now, we will start the three-minute _____. Today's first topic is fast fashion. _____ do you _____ about it? Please, begin, James.

James: I think fast fashion is good. We can wear _____ clothes at a cheaper _____.

Wendy: I'm not with you _____ _____. It makes us spend too much money and _____ _____ clothes too often.

Sujin: It looks like the two of you have different _____ on the first topic. Now, let's _____ _____ to the second topic.

Wrap Up 1

Alex: I've just finished _____ _____ _____ for Leon, Mom. _____ _____ _____ _____ _____ _____ _____?

Mom: Oh, the title "LOST CAT" in big letters at the top is easy to see.

Alex: Yeah, I did it to _____ _____. How about these photos _____ the title?

Mom: Hmm... the _____ on the _____ doesn't show Leon's face well.

Alex: Okay, I'll _____ the photo.

Mom: Oh, I _____ we can _____ Leon.

해석

Steve: 저기, Lisa. 나 내 SNS 게시물들에 100개가 넘는 댓글을 받았어.

Lisa: 아, 나는 내 게시물들을 너무 많은 사람들과 공유하는 게 편하지 않을 거야.

Steve: 정말? 나는 많은 사람들이 내 게시물들을 보는 게 정말 좋다고 생각해.

Lisa: 나는 그 점에 있어서 너랑 생각이 달라. 나는 그냥 가까운 친구들하고만 내 게시물들을 공유하고 싶어.

Emma: 실례합니다. 제가 이 기계로 주문하는 것을 좀 도와주실 수 있나요?

Tom: 물론이죠. 먼저 '핫도그' 버튼을 누르시고, 드시고 싶은 핫도그와 음료를 고르세요.

Emma: 알겠습니다. 주문한 것에 대한 지불을 어떻게 하나요?

Tom: 맨 아래에 있는 '완료' 버튼을 누르시고 그것들에 대해 지불하세요.

Emma: 와, 정말 간단하네요. 이 기계가 계산대에서 주문하는 것보다 훨씬 더 빨라요.

Tom: 저도 그렇게 생각해요. 줄이 길 때, 그것은 정말 많은 시간을 절약해 줘요.

Sujin: 자, 3분 토론을 시작하겠습니다. 오늘의 첫 번째 주제는 '패스트 패션'입니다. 여러분들은 그것에 대해 어떻게 생각하십니까? 시작해 주세요, James.

James: 저는 '패스트 패션'이 좋다고 생각합니다. 우리는 보다 저렴한 가격으로 최신 유행의 옷들을 입을 수 있습니다.

Wendy: 저는 그 의견에 동의하지 않습니다. 그것은 우리가 너무 많은 돈을 쓰고 너무 자주 옷을 버리게 합니다.

Sujin: 첫 번째 주제에 대해서는 두 사람이 다른 의견을 갖고 있는 것 같습니다. 이제 두 번째 주제로 넘어가 보도록 하겠습니다.

Alex: 엄마, Leon을 위한 인터넷 게시물 만드는 걸 막 끝냈어요. 이것에 대해 어떻게 생각하세요?

Mom: 오, 맨 위에 큰 글자로 된 제목 "LOST CAT"이 잘 보이는구나.

Alex: 네, 주목을 끌기 위해 그렇게 했어요. 제목 밑에 있는 이 사진들은 어때요?

Mom: 흠… 오른쪽에 있는 사진에서 Leon의 얼굴이 잘 보이지 않아.

Alex: 알겠어요. 그 사진을 바꿀게요.

Mom: 오, 우리가 Leon을 찾을 수 있으면 좋겠구나.

[01~02] 다음 대화를 읽고 물음에 답하시오.

Tony: Hey, Julie! Have you ⓐheard about the *Quiz & Rice* game?

Julie: Yeah, isn't it the one that ⓑdonates rice when you get a right answer?

Tony: Yeah, what do you think about the game?

Julie: I think it's a ⓒcreative game. You can have fun and ⓓhelp out hungry people. Have you played it yet?

Tony: No, but I'm going to ⓔtry out it this weekend.

01 위 대화의 밑줄 친 ⓐ~ⓔ 중 어법상 어색한 것을 찾아 바르게 고치시오.

➡ _____

02 위 대화의 내용과 일치하지 않는 것은?

① '퀴즈와 쌀' 게임은 정답을 맞히면 쌀을 기부하는 게임이다.
② Julie는 '퀴즈와 쌀' 게임이 창의적인 게임이라고 생각한다.
③ '퀴즈와 쌀' 게임은 재미있게 놀면서 배고픈 사람들을 도울 수 있다.
④ Tony는 이번 주말에 '퀴즈와 쌀' 게임을 해보려고 한다.
⑤ Julie는 '퀴즈와 쌀' 게임을 하며 많은 쌀을 기부하였다.

[03~04] 다음 대화를 읽고 물음에 답하시오.

Jack: Sally, did you watch *Super Voice's* Top 10 finalists yesterday?

Sally: Yeah. They all sang much better than before.

Jack: Yeah, they did. I think this singing contest helps them get closer to their dreams.

Sally: I'm with you on that. (A)I can't wait to watch their next performances.

03 위 대화의 밑줄 친 (A)에서 나타난 Sally의 의도로 알맞은 것은?

① 일정 설명하기
② 기대감 표현하기
③ 긴장감 묘사하기
④ 불만 표현하기
⑤ 만족 표현하기

04 What does Jack think about this singing contest?

➡ _____

[01~03] 다음 대화를 읽고 물음에 답하시오.

Jane: Look, Dad. This is Mom's birthday gift.

Dad: Oh, you're giving her a memory stick?

Jane: Yeah, I've made a family video clip for Mom and saved (A)it on this stick.

ⓐ _____

Dad: I think (B)it's really touching. She'll love it.

 서답형

01 위 대화의 빈칸 ⓐ에 들어갈 말을 <보기>에 주어진 단어를 모두 배열하여 영작하시오.

┌─ 보기 ┐
about / do / the / think /
present / you / what
└───────────┘

➡ _____

서답형

02 위 대화의 (A)와 (B)의 it이 가리키는 것을 각각 쓰시오.

(A) _____ (B) _____

중요

03 위 대화의 내용과 일치하지 않는 것은?

① Jane은 엄마의 생일 선물로 가족 동영상을 만들었다.

② Jane은 가족 동영상을 메모리 칩에 담았다.

③ 아빠는 Jane의 선물이 매우 감동적이라고 생각한다.

④ 아빠는 엄마가 Jane의 선물을 매우 좋아할 것이라고 생각한다.

⑤ 아빠는 Jane의 가족 동영상을 본 후 감동 받았다.

[04~05] 다음 대화를 읽고 물음에 답하시오.

Tony: (A) Hey, Julie! Have you heard about the *Quiz & Rice* game?

Julie: (B) Yeah, isn't it the one that donates rice when you get a right answer?

Tony: (C) Yeah, what do you think about the game?

Julie: (D) You can have fun and help out hungry people. Have you played it yet?

Tony: (E) No, but I'm going to try it out this weekend.

04 위 대화의 (A)~(E) 중 주어진 문장이 들어가기에 알맞은 곳은?

┌─────────────────────────┐
│ I think it's a creative game. │
└─────────────────────────┘

① (A) ② (B) ③ (C) ④ (D) ⑤ (E)

 중요

05 위 대화를 읽고 대답할 수 없는 것은?

① What is the *Quiz & Rice* game?

② When can you donate the rice, playing the *Quiz & Rice* game?

③ What is Julie's opinion about the *Quiz & Rice* game?

④ When will Tony try out the *Quiz & Rice* game?

⑤ How much rice is Tony going to donate to hungry people?

서답형

06 다음 대화가 자연스럽게 이어지도록 순서대로 배열하시오.

┌──────────────────────────────────┐
│ (A) Really? I thought they made the story more interesting. │
│ (B) I didn't like it. I thought it had too many sound effects. │
│ (C) What do you think about the new online comic *Scary Night*? │
│ (D) Not me. I couldn't focus because I was too scared. │
└──────────────────────────────────┘

➡ _____

[07~09] 다음 대화를 읽고 물음에 답하시오.

Emma: Excuse me. ⓐCan you help me order with this machine?

Tom: Sure. First, press the Hot Dog button and choose your hot dog and drink.

Emma: Okay. How do I pay for my order?

Tom: Touch the Done button at the bottom and pay for them.

Emma: Wow, it's so simple. This machine is ___(A)___ faster than ordering at the counter.

Tom: I'm with you on that. It really saves a lot of time when there's a long line.

07 위 대화의 빈칸 (A)에 들어가기에 어색한 것은?

① much ② far ③ even
④ a lot ⑤ very

08 위 대화의 밑줄 친 ⓐ와 같은 의미를 나타내는 것을 모두 고르시오.

① Do you need any help to order with this machine?

② Can you give me your hand to order with this machine?

③ Can I order with this machine?

④ How can I help you?

⑤ Would you mind helping me order with this machine?

서답형

09 다음 도표를 보고 빈칸을 완성하시오.

<How to order your food here>

Step	What to do
1	Press the Hot Dog button.
2	(A)
3	Touch the Done button.
4	(B)

(A) _____

(B) _____

[10~11] 다음 대화를 읽고 물음에 답하시오.

Alex: I've just finished (A)[to make / making] the posting for Leon, Mom. What do you think about it?

Mom: Oh, the title "LOST CAT" in big letters at the top (B)[is / are] easy to see.

Alex: Yeah, I did it to get (C)[attentive / attention]. How about these photos below the title?

Mom: Hmm... the one on the right doesn't show Leon's face well.

Alex: Okay, I'll change the photo.

Mom: Oh, I hope we can find Leon.

10 위 대화의 괄호 (A)~(C)에 들어갈 말로 알맞게 짝지어진 것은?

① to make – is – attentive

② to make – are – attention

③ making – is – attention

④ making – are – attentive

⑤ making – is – attentive

11 위 대화의 내용과 일치하지 <u>않는</u> 것은?

① Alex는 잃어버린 Leon을 찾기 위해 게시물을 만들었다.

② 게시물 맨 위에 큰 글자로 된 "LOST CAT"이 잘 보인다.

③ 게시물 오른쪽에 있는 사진에서 Leon의 얼굴이 잘 보이지 않는다.

④ Alex는 제목 밑에 있는 사진들을 모두 바꿀 것이다.

⑤ 엄마는 Leon을 찾기를 희망한다.

[01~03] 다음 대화를 읽고 물음에 답하시오.

Jane: Look, Dad. This is Mom's birthday gift.

Dad: Oh, you're giving her a memory stick?

Jane: Yeah, I've made a family video clip for Mom and saved it on this stick. What do you think about the present?

Dad: I think it's really touching. She'll love it.

01 What is Jane talking about with her dad?

➡ _____

_____

02 What will Jane give her mom as a birthday gift?

➡ _____

_____

03 What did Jane save on the memory stick?

➡ _____

04 다음 대화의 내용과 일치하도록 Jenny의 일기를 완성하시오.

Mike: Jenny, what do you think about the new online comic *Scary Night*?

Jenny: I didn't like it. I thought it had too many sound effects.

Mike: Really? I thought they made the story more interesting.

Jenny: Not me. I couldn't focus because I was too scared.

⬇

Mon, Dec 2nd, 2019
Today, I talked about the new online comic *Scary Night* with Mike. Actually, I didn't like it because of (A)_____ _____ _____ _____. I was so (B)_____ that I couldn't focus on the story. On the other hand, Mike told me that (C)_____ _____ _____ made the story more interesting.

[05~06] 다음 대화를 읽고 물음에 답하시오.

Tony: Hey, Julie! Have you heard about the *Quiz & Rice* game?

Julie: Yeah, isn't it the one that donates rice when you get a right answer?

Tony: Yeah, (A)넌 그 게임에 대해 어떻게 생각하니?

Julie: I think it's a creative game. You can have fun and help out hungry people. Have you played it yet?

Tony: No, but I'm going to try it out this weekend.

05 위 대화의 밑줄 친 (A)의 우리말을 영작하시오.

➡ _____

06 위 대화의 내용과 일치하도록 빈칸을 완성하시오.

<Try the *Quiz & Rice* game!>
Get the (A)_____ answer and (B)_____ rice. Not only you can have fun but also (C)_____ _____ _____ _____.

Grammar

1 so ~ that ... can't

- He is **so** tired **that** he **can't** finish his homework. 그는 너무 피곤해서 숙제를 끝낼 수 없다.
- I am **so** sad **that** I **can't** stay here. 나는 너무 슬퍼서 이곳에 머물 수 없어.

■ 'so+형용사/부사+that+주어+can't+동사원형'은 '너무 ~해서 …할 수 없다'는 의미로, 형용사나 부사가 that절의 원인이 되고, that절은 그 결과를 이끈다. 'too+형용사/부사+to V'로 바꾸어 쓸 수 있다.

- Jimmy is **so** weak **that** he **can't** lift it.
  = Jimmy is **too** weak **to** lift it. Jimmy는 너무 약해서 그것을 들 수 없다.

- She was **so** busy **that** she **couldn't** talk with us.
  = She was **too** busy **to** talk with us. 그녀는 너무 바빠서 우리와 이야기할 수 없었다.

- Patrick was **so** upset **that** he **couldn't** go to the party.
  = Patrick was **too** upset **to** go to the party. Patrick은 너무 화가 나서 파티에 갈 수 없었다.

■ '아주 ~해서 …할 수 있다'는 의미를 나타낼 때에는 'so+형용사/부사+that+주어+can+동사원형'을 쓰고, 이는 '형용사/부사+enough+to부정사'와 같다.

- The man is **so** kind **that** he can help you. 그 남자는 아주 친절해서 너를 도울 수 있어.
  = The man is kind **enough to** help you.

- Julie was **so** happy **that** she could invite anyone. Julie는 아주 행복해서 누구든 초대할 수 있었다.
  = Julie was happy **enough to** invite anyone.

- Amelia is **so** wise **that** she can give us advice. Amelia는 아주 현명해서 우리에게 조언을 해 줄 수 있다.
  = Amelia is wise **enough to** give us advice.

핵심 Check

1. 다음 우리말과 같도록 빈칸에 알맞은 말을 쓰시오.

(1) 너는 너무 어려서 일을 할 수 없어.
➡ You are _____ _____ _____ you _____ _____.
➡ You are _____ _____ _____ _____.

(2) 그는 너무 피곤해서 저녁을 먹을 수 없었다.
➡ He was _____ _____ _____ he _____ have dinner.
➡ He was _____ _____ _____ have dinner.

② 명사를 수식하는 현재분사와 과거분사

- Look at the **sleeping** baby. 잠자고 있는 아이를 보아라.
- Is this a **baked** potato? 이것은 구워진 감자인가요?

■ 분사는 Ving 형태를 취하는 현재분사와, p.p. 형태를 취하는 과거분사로 나뉘며, 모두 명사를 수식하거나 설명하는 형용사 역할을 한다. 현재분사는 '~하는'이라는 의미로 주로 해석되어 능동이나 진행의 의미를 나타내고, 과거분사는 '~된'이라는 의미로 해석되어 수동이나 완료의 의미를 나타낸다.

- I saw a **crying** baby. 나는 우는 아기를 봤어.
- The **disappointing** result made me sad. 그 실망스러운 결과는 나를 슬프게 했다.

■ 분사가 단독으로 명사를 수식할 때에는 일반적으로 명사 앞에서 수식하지만, 분사가 다른 어구와 함께 명사를 수식할 때에는 명사 뒤에서 수식한다.

- Do you see the children **playing** together? 함께 놀고 있는 아이들이 보이세요?
- Kevin found a letter **written** on his note. Kevin은 자신의 노트 위에 쓰여진 편지를 발견했다.
- People **living** in the town felt happy. 그 마을에 사는 사람들은 행복했다.

■ '사역동사(have, make)+목적어+과거분사', '지각동사+목적어+과거분사', 'help(또는 get)+목적어+과거분사'는 목적어와 목적보어의 관계가 수동인 경우 쓰인다.

- Jason **has** the man **repair** his car. Jason은 그 남자가 자신의 차를 수리하게 한다.
  = Jason **has** his car **repaired** by the man. Jason은 그의 차가 그 남자에 의해 수리되게 한다.

■ 'Ving'로 형태가 같은 현재분사와 동명사의 차이를 구별하자. 현재분사는 '~하는', '~하는 중인'이라고 해석되고, 동명사는 '~하는 것'이라고 해석되거나 'V를 용도로 하는 명사'로 해석된다.

- There is a **sleeping** baby. 잠자는 아기가 있다.
- Did you find your **sleeping bag**? 너의 침낭을 찾았니? (잠자는 데 쓰이는 가방 – 침낭)

핵심 Check

2. 다음 주어진 동사를 어법에 맞게 빈칸에 쓰시오.

(1) 노래 부르는 그 소녀를 보았니?
  ➡ Did you see the _____ girl?

(2) 나는 John에 의해 쓰여진 책을 읽었어.
  ➡ I read the book _____ by John. (write)

(3) 무언가를 쓰고 있는 저 소녀를 아니?
  ➡ Do you know the girl _____ something? (write)

01 다음 문장에서 어법상 <u>어색한</u> 부분을 바르게 고치시오.

(1) The shirt is so big to wear.

_____ ➡ _____

(2) She was so old that she can't drive safely.

_____ ➡ _____

(3) I watched the excited bowling game on TV.

_____ ➡ _____

(4) Who is the boy thrown a ball?

_____ ➡ _____

02 주어진 단어를 어법에 맞게 빈칸에 쓰시오.

(1) He came too late _____ _____ part in the race. (take)

(2) I smelled something _____ in the kitchen. (burn)

(3) The rose is beautiful enough _____ _____ many people.
(attract)

(4) A girl _____ Jiho called you an hour ago. (name)

(5) The _____ robot is really expensive. (talk)

03 주어진 어구를 바르게 배열하여 다음 우리말을 영어로 쓰시오. 필요하다면 단어를 추가하시오.

(1) Olivia는 너무 추워서 잠들 수 없었다.

(asleep / Olivia / cold / felt / fall / that / she / couldn't)

➡ _____

(2) 그 집은 살기에 충분히 따뜻해.

(in / the house / warm / is / live / enough)

➡ _____

(3) 나는 떨어지는 낙엽을 보았어. (the / falling / I / leaves / looked at)

➡ _____

(4) 관객은 게임이나 연극을 지켜보는 사람이다.

(a game or a play / a spectator / watching / someone / is)

➡ _____

01 다음 중 빈칸에 들어갈 말로 가장 적절한 것은?

> Blair was too tired _____ the movie.

① watching
② to watching
③ watched
④ to watch
⑤ watch

02 다음 빈칸에 들어갈 말이 바르게 짝지어진 것은?

> • The girl _____ a book is my sister.
> • There was a _____ window.

① read – breaking
② read – broken
③ reading – broken
④ read – break
⑤ reading – break

03 다음 중 주어진 문장과 같은 의미의 문장으로 가장 적절한 것은?

> She is too young to get married.

① She is too young that she can't get married.
② She is so young that she can't get married.
③ She is so young that she can get married.
④ She is young enough to get married.
⑤ She is too young that she can get married.

서답형
04 다음 빈칸에 알맞은 말을 일곱 단어로 쓰시오.

> I can't drink the milk. It is too hot.
> = The milk _____.

05 다음 중 어법상 바르지 <u>않은</u> 것은?

> ①The injured man was ②taken to a hospital. But he ③arrived too ④late ⑤to getting proper treatment.

①   ②   ③   ④   ⑤

중요
06 다음 중 주어진 문장의 밑줄 친 부분과 쓰임이 <u>다른</u> 하나는?

> <u>Playing</u> the violin is very fun.

① Are you interested in <u>baking</u> bread?
② <u>Making</u> a film was not that easy.
③ It was a very <u>embarrassing</u> moment.
④ Julie really enjoyed <u>playing</u> soccer.
⑤ His hobby is <u>flying</u> a drone.

07 다음 빈칸에 들어갈 말을 바르게 짝지은 것은?

> The wall was _____ high _____ over.

① too – to climbing
② too – that we can't climb
③ so – that we can't climb
④ so – to climb
⑤ so – that we couldn't climb

서답형
08 주어진 단어를 활용하여 다음 우리말을 지시에 맞게 영어로 쓰시오.

> 이 지갑은 너무 커서 내 주머니에 넣을 수 없었어. (wallet / pocket / big)

(1) to부정사를 사용하여 10단어로
➡ _____

(2) that절을 사용하여 13단어로
➡ _____
_____

09 다음 우리말을 영어로 바르게 표현한 것은?

> 그 목걸이는 너무 비싸서 살 수 없어.

① The necklace is expensive enough to buy.

② It is an expensive necklace to buy.

③ The necklace is too expensive to buying.

④ The necklace is so expensive that we can't buy it.

⑤ It is expensive to buy the necklace.

10 다음 중 문장의 전환이 바르지 <u>않은</u> 것은?

① 나는 그 상자를 들 만큼 충분히 힘이 세.

→ I am strong enough to lift the box.

② 그는 너무 뚱뚱해서 오랫동안 걸을 수 없었다.

→ He was too fat to walk for a long time.

③ 그녀는 어제 머리카락을 잘랐다.

→ She had her hair cut yesterday.

④ 우리는 우리의 사진이 찍히도록 했다.

→ We had our picture taking.

⑤ Jamie는 너무 아파서 학교에 갈 수 없었다.

→ Jamie was so sick that he couldn't go to school.

11 다음 중 어법상 <u>틀린</u> 문장은?

① I wonder who the man talking with her is.

② The weather was too hot to go out.

③ She is talented enough to be a singer.

④ They were so scared that they couldn't say a word.

⑤ The movie was so moved that we wanted to watch it again.

서답형

12 주어진 단어를 활용하여 다음 우리말을 일곱 단어로 이루어진 한 문장의 영어로 쓰시오.

> 우리는 낙엽 위를 걷는 것을 좋아합니다.
> (like / on / fall / leaves)

➡ _____

13 다음 빈칸에 들어갈 말로 알맞은 것을 고르시오.

> A: Did you hear what Karen was saying?
> B: No, I was _____ what she was saying.

① close enough to hear

② too far away hear

③ so far away to hear

④ too far away to hear

⑤ too close to hear

14 다음 중 빈칸에 들어갈 말로 적절하지 <u>않은</u> 것은? (2개)

> We _____ the house painted.

① saw   ② wanted   ③ got

④ had   ⑤ appeared

서답형

15 다음 문장을 영어로 옮길 때 표시된 곳에 들어가는 단어를 차례대로 쓰시오.

> 그는 너무 게을러서 그 일을 할 수 없어.
> ➡ _____ _____ ★ _____
> _____ _____ ★
> _____ _____

➡ _____

서답형

16 다음 빈칸에 알맞은 말을 쓰시오.

> 저 춤추는 소년은 누구니?
> ➡ Who is that _____ _____?

17 다음 중 서로 의미가 같지 <u>않은</u> 문장은?

① Charlie was too sick to go on a picnic.
  = Charlie was so sick that he couldn't go on a picnic.
② I had my room cleaned by my brother.
  = I had my brother clean my room.
③ Dick is tall enough to play basketball well.
  = Dick is so tall that he can play basketball well.
④ I can't play with you because I am very busy.
  = I am too busy to play with you.
⑤ Jimmy was too nervous to say hello.
  = Jimmy was so nervous that he could say hello.

18 다음 중 빈칸에 들어갈 말이 바르게 짝지어진 것은?

> • I am _____ to attend the meeting. So I have to wait outside.
> • Tom was _____ buy the car. But he didn't buy it.

① late enough – so rich that he can
② late enough – too rich to
③ too late – so rich that he could
④ too late – enough rich to
⑤ too late – so rich that he couldn't

19 주어진 단어를 활용하여 다음 문장을 영어로 쓰시오.

> 그는 그 날아오는 공을 쳤다.
> (hit / fly)

➡ _____

20 다음 빈칸에 알맞은 말을 쓰시오.

> 그 잠자는 고양이는 너무 귀여워서 나는 그것에서 눈을 뗄 수 없다.
> ➡ The _____ cat is _____ _____ _____ _____ _____ take my eyes off it.

21 다음 빈칸에 들어갈 말로 가장 적절한 것은?

> 나는 구운 생선을 좋아해.
> ➡ I like _____ fish.

① baking   ② bake   ③ bakes
④ baked   ⑤ being baked

22 다음 중 어법상 바르지 <u>않은</u> 것은?

① I was too tired to go out.
② She looked at their smiling faces.
③ I was boring with the movie.
④ Mindy was so happy that she hugged everyone.
⑤ The scaring film was interesting.

23 주어진 단어를 바르게 배열하여 다음 우리말을 영어로 쓰시오. 세 개의 단어를 적절히 변형하시오.

> 그 놀라운 소식은 나를 흥분되게 만들었다.
> (excite / surprise / make / news / me)

➡ The _____.

24 다음 빈칸에 들어갈 알맞은 말을 쓰시오.

> The train was so fast that we couldn't catch it.
> = The train was _____ _____ for us _____ _____.

01 다음 문장과 같은 의미의 문장을 조건에 맞게 쓰시오.

> Nobody could move the table. It was too heavy.

(1) to부정사를 사용하여 한 문장으로

➡ _____

(2) that절을 사용하여 한 문장으로

➡ _____

_____

02 주어진 단어를 어법에 맞게 활용하여 다음 우리말을 다섯 단어로 이루어진 한 문장의 영어로 쓰시오.

> 그 부서진 의자를 내게 보여줘. (break)

➡ _____

03 주어진 단어를 활용하여 다음 우리말을 영어로 쓰시오.

> 그녀의 가족은 너무 가난해서 그 집을 살 수 없었다.
> (so / they / buy)

➡ _____

_____

04 다음 빈칸에 알맞은 말을 다섯 단어로 쓰시오.

> My brother can't stay home alone because he is so young.
> = My brother is _____
>   home alone.
> = My brother is _____
>   home alone.

05 다음 주어진 단어를 어법에 맞게 빈칸에 쓰시오.

> hit / excite / play / amaze / repair

(1) The girl _____ badminton is my sister.

(2) I have an _____ story to tell you.

(3) We had the car _____ by Potter and Parker.

(4) Jina is an _____ basketball player.

(5) Did you see the building _____ by a dump truck?

06 다음 두 문장의 해석을 쓰고 밑줄 친 부분의 어법상 차이를 설명하시오.

> (1) Jane likes sliced cheese.
> (2) Jane likes slicing cheese.

(1) 해석: _____

(2) 해석: _____

(3) 어법상 차이: _____

_____

07 접속사 that을 활용하여 다음 두 문장을 하나의 문장으로 표현하시오.

> The room is very small. You can't invite all the friends to your party.

➡ _____

_____

08 다음 빈칸에 알맞은 말을 쓰시오.

> 나는 숨겨진 보물을 찾으려는 중이야.
> ➡ I am trying to find _____ treasure.

09 접속사 that을 이용하여 다음 주어진 문장과 같은 의미의 문장을 쓰시오.

> The news is too good to be true.

➡ _____

10 주어진 단어를 바르게 배열하여 다음 우리말을 영어로 쓰시오.

> 산타클로스는 너무 자주 전화기를 확인해서 일에 집중할 수가 없다.
> (focus / Santa Claus / often / can't / on / his work / he / his phone / that / checks / so)

➡ _____
_____

11 다음 대화의 빈칸에 주어진 단어를 어법에 맞게 쓰시오.

> A: Maria makes me so _____(annoy) that I don't want her to be around me.
> B: But she is our guest. You should be nice to her during the _____(remain) days.

12 다음 우리말을 조건에 맞게 영어로 쓰시오.

> 나는 너무 피곤해서 눈을 뜰 수 없었다.

(1) to부정사를 사용하여 한 문장으로
➡ _____

(2) that절을 사용하여 한 문장으로
➡ _____

13 다음 문장과 같은 의미의 문장을 쓰시오.

(1) Daisy was too nervous to speak in front of many people.
➡ _____
_____

(2) Christopher is so tall that he can be a model.
➡ _____

(3) Jamie is too scared to be alone at home.
➡ _____

(4) Amelia was rich enough to throw a big party for her friend.
➡ _____

14 주어진 단어를 활용하여 다음 우리말을 영어로 쓰시오.

> 그것은 신나는 게임처럼 들리는구나.
> (it / like / excite)

➡ _____

15 다음 문장과 같은 의미의 문장을 조건에 맞게 쓰시오.

> He can't sleep because he has much work.

(1) to부정사를 사용하여 한 문장으로
➡ _____

(2) that절을 사용하여 한 문장으로
➡ _____

Reading

My Tech-Free Trip Story

Last summer, my father suggested a surprising event: a family trip
without smartphones! He said, "I hate to see you sitting together and
only looking at your smartphones." My sister and I explained the need
for smartphones, but he kept saying that we could not fully enjoy
the trip with them. So we started a technology-free trip to a new city,
Barcelona, Spain.

Our first day was terrible. On the way to our guesthouse around Plaza
Reial, we got lost in downtown Barcelona. Dad was busy looking at
the map and asking for directions with a few Spanish words he got
from a tour guidebook. Even though our guesthouse was right next to
the Plaza, it took us about two hours to get there. We were so tired that
we could not go out for dinner. I went to bed but couldn't fall asleep
because I was worried about what would happen the next day.

After looking around Gaudi's Park Guell, we decided to have seafood
fried rice for lunch. However, we didn't know which restaurant to go
to.

suggest 제안하다
surprise 놀라게 하다
technology (과학) 기술
keep -ing 계속해서 ~하다
guesthouse (여행자 등의) 숙소, 여관
get lost 길을 잃다
downtown 시내의, 도심지의
be busy -ing ~하느라 바쁘다
guidebook (여행) 안내서
even though 비록 ~할지라도
fall asleep 잠들다

 확인문제

● 다음 문장이 본문의 내용과 일치하면 T, 일치하지 <u>않으면</u> F를 쓰시오.

1 The writer's father proposed a trip without smartphones. ☐

2 Not only the writer but also his sister explained the need for smartphones. ☐

3 They got lost in Plaza Reial. ☐

4 Dad didn't know Spanish words at all. ☐

We needed help, so Mom went up to an elderly lady and tried to ask for directions to a popular seafood restaurant.

Luckily, she seemed to understand Mom's few Spanish words. She took us to a small local restaurant nearby. The seafood fried rice was amazing. I really wanted to take pictures of the food and post them on my blog. But without my phone, I just decided to enjoy the moment.

During the remaining days, we relied more and more on the locals. We were able to meet and talk with various people on the streets, in the bakeries, and in the parks. They were always kind enough to show us different sides of Barcelona with a smile. Also, our family talked a lot with each other. We spent much of our time together on the Spanish train, on the bus, and at the restaurants.

Our technology-free trip was a new and different experience. Before the trip, I was so dependent on my smartphone that I couldn't do anything without it. But now I see that I can enjoy the moment without it. From the experience, I have learned the importance of a balanced use of the smartphone. So, next time, would I travel without a smartphone? Probably not. But I will try to use it more wisely.

fry 튀기다
elderly 나이가 지긋한
nearby 근처에
local 현지의, 지역의; 주민
post (웹사이트에 정보나 사진을) 올리다
moment 순간
remain 남아 있다, 남다
rely on ~에 의존하다
various 다양한
bakery 빵집, 제과점
experience 경험
dependent 의존적인
importance 중요함
balance 균형을 잡다

확인문제

다음 문장이 본문의 내용과 일치하면 T, 일치하지 않으면 F를 쓰시오.

1 They found a local seafood restaurant with a help from an elderly woman.

2 The writer posted the pictures of the food on his blog.

3 As the writer didn't have his smartphone, he didn't know how to enjoy the moment.

4 As time goes by, they became independent from the locals.

5 The writer learned how to use his smartphone wisely after the trip.

• 우리말을 참고하여 빈칸에 알맞은 말을 쓰시오.

1 Last summer, my father _____ a _____ event: a family trip _____ smartphones!

2 He said, "I hate _____ _____ you _____ together and only _____ _____ your smartphones."

3 My sister and I _____ the need for smartphones, but he _____ _____ _____ we could not fully enjoy the trip with them.

4 So we _____ a technology-free trip _____ a new city, Barcelona, Spain.

5 Our first day was _____.

6 _____ _____ _____ _____ our guesthouse around Plaza Reial, we _____ _____ in downtown Barcelona.

7 Dad _____ _____ _____ at the map and _____ for directions _____ a few Spanish words he got _____ a tour guidebook.

8 _____ _____ our guesthouse was _____ _____ _____ the Plaza, _____ took us about two hours _____ _____ there.

9 We _____ _____ _____ _____ we could not go out for dinner.

10 I went to bed but couldn't _____ _____ because I was _____ about _____ _____ _____ the next day.

11 _____ looking around Gaudi's Park Guell, we decided _____ _____ seafood _____ rice for lunch.

12 However, we didn't know _____ _____ _____ _____ _____.

13 We needed help, so Mom _____ _____ _____ an elderly lady and _____ _____ _____ for directions to a popular seafood restaurant.

1 지난여름, 아빠가 깜짝 놀랄 만한 이벤트로 스마트폰 없는 가족 여행을 제안하셨다!

2 아빠는 "나는 우리 가족이 함께 앉아서 각자의 스마트폰만 보고 있는 걸 보는 게 참 싫구나."라고 말씀하셨다.

3 여동생과 내가 스마트폰이 필요하다고 설명했지만, 아빠는 스마트폰이 있으면 여행을 충분히 즐길 수 없을 거라고 계속해서 말씀하셨다.

4 그래서 우리는 새로운 도시인 스페인의 바르셀로나로 '첨단 과학 기술 없는 여행'을 시작했다.

5 우리의 첫째 날은 엉망이었다.

6 레이알 광장 주변에 있는 여행자 숙소로 가는 길에 우리는 바르셀로나 시내에서 길을 잃었다.

7 아빠는 지도를 보며 여행안내 책자에서 배운 스페인어 몇 마디로 길을 묻느라 분주하셨다.

8 우리의 숙소가 광장 바로 옆에 있었음에도 불구하고, 우리가 그곳에 도착하는 데는 거의 두 시간이 걸렸다.

9 우리는 너무 피곤해서 저녁을 먹으러 나갈 수가 없었다.

10 나는 잠자리에 들었지만 내일 무슨 일이 일어날지 걱정이 되어서 잠들 수가 없었다.

11 가우디가 지은 구엘 공원을 둘러본 후, 우리는 점심으로 해산물 볶음밥을 먹기로 했다.

12 그러나 우리는 어떤 식당으로 가야 할지 몰랐다.

13 우리는 도움이 필요해서, 엄마가 한 노부인에게 가서 인기 있는 해산물 식당으로 가는 길을 물어보려고 애쓰셨다.

14 Luckily, she seemed _____ _____ Mom's few Spanish _____.

15 She _____ _____ to a small local restaurant _____.

16 The seafood _____ _____ was _____.

17 I really wanted to _____ _____ _____ the food and post _____ on my blog.

18 But _____ my phone, I just decided _____ _____ the moment.

19 During the _____ days, we _____ more and more _____ the locals.

20 We _____ _____ _____ _____ and talk with various people on the streets, in the bakeries, and in the parks.

21 They were always _____ _____ _____ _____ us different sides of Barcelona with a smile.

22 Also, our family _____ a lot _____ each other.

23 We spent _____ _____ _____ _____ _____ on the Spanish train, on the bus, and at the restaurants.

24 Our technology-free trip was a _____ _____ _____ experience.

25 Before the trip, I was _____ _____ _____ my smartphone _____ I couldn't do anything without it.

26 But now I see _____ I can enjoy the moment _____ _____.

27 _____ the experience, I _____ _____ the importance of a _____ of the smartphone.

28 So, next time, _____ _____ without a smartphone?

29 Probably not. But I will _____ _____ _____ more wisely.

---

14 운이 좋게도 그녀는 몇 마디 안 되는 엄마의 스페인어를 이해하는 듯했다.

15 그녀는 우리를 근처에 있는 작은 현지 식당으로 데려다 주었다.

16 그 해산물 볶음밥은 놀랍도록 맛있었다.

17 나는 음식 사진을 찍어 그것을 내 블로그에 올리고 싶은 마음이 정말 간절했다.

18 그러나 스마트폰이 없었기 때문에 나는 그냥 그 순간을 즐기기로 했다.

19 (여행의) 남아 있는 날들 동안, 우리는 점점 더 현지 사람들에게 의존하게 되었다.

20 우리는 거리에서, 빵집에서, 공원에서 다양한 사람들을 만나 이야기할 수 있었다.

21 그들은 항상 웃으면서 너무나 친절히도 바르셀로나의 다양한 면을 우리에게 보여 주었다.

22 또한 우리 가족은 서로 많은 대화를 나누었다.

23 우리는 스페인의 기차에서, 버스에서, 그리고 식당에서 많은 시간을 함께 보냈다.

24 우리의 '첨단 과학 기술 없는' 여행은 새롭고 색다른 경험이었다.

25 여행 전에 나는 내 스마트폰에 너무 의존해서 그것 없이는 아무것도 할 수 없었다.

26 하지만 지금은 내가 스마트폰 없이도 그 순간을 즐길 수 있음을 알고 있다.

27 그 경험을 통해, 나는 스마트폰을 균형 있게 사용하는 것이 중요함을 배우게 되었다.

28 그러면, 다음번에 나는 스마트폰 없이 여행을 하게 될까?

29 아마도 그렇지는 않을 것이다. 하지만 나는 그것을 좀 더 현명하게 사용하기 위해 노력할 것이다.

● 우리말을 참고하여 본문을 영작하시오.

1 지난여름, 아빠가 깜짝 놀랄 만한 이벤트로 스마트폰 없는 가족 여행을 제안하셨다!

➡ _____

2 아빠는 "나는 우리 가족이 함께 앉아서 각자의 스마트폰만 보고 있는 걸 보는 게 참 싫구나."라고 말씀하셨다.

➡ _____

3 여동생과 내가 스마트폰이 필요하다고 설명했지만, 아빠는 스마트폰이 있으면 여행을 충분히 즐길 수 없을 거라고 계속해서 말씀하셨다.

➡ _____

_____

4 그래서 우리는 새로운 도시인 스페인의 바르셀로나로 '첨단 과학 기술 없는 여행'을 시작했다.

➡ _____

5 우리의 첫째 날은 엉망이었다.

➡ _____

6 레이알 광장 주변에 있는 여행자 숙소로 가는 길에 우리는 바르셀로나 시내에서 길을 잃었다.

➡ _____

7 아빠는 지도를 보며 여행안내 책자에서 배운 스페인어 몇 마디로 길을 묻느라 분주하셨다.

➡ _____

_____

8 우리의 숙소가 광장 바로 옆에 있었음에도 불구하고, 우리가 그곳에 도착하는 데는 거의 두 시간이 걸렸다.

➡ _____

9 우리는 너무 피곤해서 저녁을 먹으러 나갈 수가 없었다.

➡ _____

10 나는 잠자리에 들었지만 내일 무슨 일이 일어날지 걱정이 되어서 잠들 수가 없었다.

➡ _____

_____

11 가우디가 지은 구엘 공원을 둘러본 후, 우리는 점심으로 해산물 볶음밥을 먹기로 했다.

➡ _____

12 그러나 우리는 어떤 식당으로 가야 할지 몰랐다.

➡ _____

13 우리는 도움이 필요해서, 엄마가 한 노부인에게 가서 인기 있는 해산물 식당으로 가는 길을 물어보려고 애쓰셨다.

➡ _____

_____

14 운이 좋게도 그녀는 몇 마디 안 되는 엄마의 스페인어를 이해하는 듯했다.

➡ _____

15 그녀는 우리를 근처에 있는 작은 현지 식당으로 데려다 주었다.

➡ _____

16 그 해산물 볶음밥은 놀랍도록 맛있었다.

➡ _____

17 나는 음식 사진을 찍어 그것을 내 블로그에 올리고 싶은 마음이 정말 간절했다.

➡ _____

18 그러나 스마트폰이 없었기 때문에 나는 그냥 그 순간을 즐기기로 했다.

➡ _____

19 (여행의) 남아 있는 날들 동안, 우리는 점점 더 현지 사람들에게 의존하게 되었다.

➡ _____

20 우리는 거리에서, 빵집에서, 공원에서 다양한 사람들을 만나 이야기할 수 있었다.

➡ _____

21 그들은 항상 웃으면서 너무나 친절히도 바르셀로나의 다양한 면을 우리에게 보여 주었다.

➡ _____

22 또한 우리 가족은 서로 많은 대화를 나누었다.

➡ _____

23 우리는 스페인의 기차에서, 버스에서, 그리고 식당에서 많은 시간을 함께 보냈다.

➡ _____

24 우리의 '첨단 과학 기술 없는' 여행은 새롭고 색다른 경험이었다.

➡ _____

25 여행 전에 나는 내 스마트폰에 너무 의존해서 그것 없이는 아무것도 할 수 없었다.

➡ _____

26 하지만 지금은 내가 스마트폰 없이도 그 순간을 즐길 수 있음을 알고 있다.

➡ _____

27 그 경험을 통해, 나는 스마트폰을 균형 있게 사용하는 것이 중요함을 배우게 되었다.

➡ _____

28 그러면, 다음번에 나는 스마트폰 없이 여행을 하게 될까?

➡ _____

29 아마도 그렇지는 않을 것이다. 하지만 나는 그것을 좀 더 현명하게 사용하기 위해 노력할 것이다.

➡ _____

[01~04] 다음 글을 읽고 물음에 답하시오.

Last summer, my father suggested a surprising event: a family trip without smartphones! He said, "I hate to see you sitting together and only looking at your smartphones." My sister and I explained the need for smartphones, ___(A)___ he kept ___(B)___ that we could not fully enjoy the trip with them. So we started a technology-free trip to a new city, Barcelona, Spain.

01 다음 중 빈칸 (A)에 들어갈 말로 가장 적절한 것은?

① for   ② but   ③ while
④ if   ⑤ unless

02 동사 say를 어법에 맞게 빈칸 (B)에 쓰시오.

➡ _____

03 Where did they go for a family trip? Answer in English with five words.

➡ _____

 04 다음 중 글의 내용과 일치하지 <u>않는</u> 것은?

① The writer's father suggested an event which was surprising.
② The writer's father wanted to have a family trip.
③ The writer explained the need for smartphones with his sister.
④ The writer's father wanted to enjoy the trip without smartphones.
⑤ The writer's father didn't want to see the writer and his sister sitting together.

[05~07] 다음 글을 읽고 물음에 답하시오.

Our first day was terrible. ①On the way to our guesthouse around Plaza Reial, we ②got lost in downtown Barcelona. Dad ③was busy looking at the map and asking for directions with a few Spanish words he got from a tour guidebook. Even though our guesthouse was ④right next to the Plaza, it took us about two hours to get there. We were so tired that we could not go out for dinner. I went to bed but ⑤couldn't fall asleep because I was worried about what would happen the next day.

05 다음 중 밑줄 친 ①~⑤의 의미로 알맞지 <u>않은</u> 것은?

① ~로 가는 길에
② 길을 잃었다
③ 지도를 보느라 바빴다
④ 광장 오른쪽에
⑤ 잠들 수 없었다

 06 다음 중 위 글을 읽고 답할 수 <u>없는</u> 것은?

① Where was the writer's guesthouse?
② Where did the writer's dad get a few Spanish words?
③ How long did it take to get to the guesthouse?
④ Why couldn't they go out for dinner?
⑤ How big was the Plaza Reial?

07 According to the writer, how was their first day of the trip? Answer in English with three words.

➡ _____

[08~10] 다음 글을 읽고 물음에 답하시오.

After looking around Gaudi's Park Guell, we decided to have seafood fried rice for lunch. ① ___(A)___ , we didn't know which restaurant to go to. ② We needed help, so Mom went up to an elderly lady and tried to ask for directions to a popular seafood restaurant. ③ She took us to a small local restaurant nearby. ④ The seafood fried rice was amazing. ⑤ I really wanted to take pictures of the food and post them on my blog. But without my phone, I just decided to enjoy the moment.

08 다음 중 빈칸 (A)에 들어갈 말로 적절한 것은?

① Therefore
② Moreover
③ However
④ Instead
⑤ For example

09 위 글의 ①~⑤ 중 주어진 문장이 들어가기에 가장 적절한 곳은?

> Luckily, she seemed to understand Mom's few Spanish words.

①   ②   ③   ④   ⑤

10 다음 중 글의 내용을 <u>잘못</u> 이해한 사람은?

① Jason: They looked around the Gaudi's Park Guell before having lunch.
② Claire: They had to decide which restaurant to go to.
③ Brady: Thanks to the elderly lady, they could eat what they wanted to.
④ Amy: The writer made up his mind to enjoy the moment.
⑤ Frank: I am looking forward to seeing the writer's blog to see pictures of the food.

[11~13] 다음 글을 읽고 물음에 답하시오.

During the remaining days, we relied more and more on the locals. We were able to meet and talk with various people on the streets, in the bakeries, and in the parks. They were always kind enough to show us different sides of Barcelona with a smile. Also, our family talked a lot with each other. We spent much of our time together on the Spanish train, on the bus, and at the restaurants.

Our technology-free trip was a new and different experience. Before the trip, I was so dependent on my smartphone that I couldn't do anything without it. But now I see that I can enjoy the moment without it. From the experience, I have learned the importance of a balanced use of the smartphone. So, next time, would I travel without a smartphone? Probably not. But I will try to use it more wisely.

서답형

11 다음과 같이 풀이되는 말을 위 글에서 찾아 쓰시오.

> to be in a steady position without falling to one side

서답형 ➡ _____

12 What did the writer learn from the trip?

➡ _____

13 다음 중 위 글의 내용과 일치하는 것은?

① They didn't depend on the locals.
② They were too busy to talk with various people.
③ They had a technology-free trip.
④ The writer wasn't interested in the smartphone before the trip.
⑤ The writer doesn't want to use his smartphone any more.

[14~18] 다음 글을 읽고 물음에 답하시오.

Last summer, my father suggested a surprising event: a family trip without smartphones! He said, "I hate to see you sitting together and only (A)[look / looking] at your smartphones." My sister and I explained the need for smartphones, but he kept saying that we could not fully enjoy the trip with them. So we started a technology-free trip to a new city, Barcelona, Spain.

Our first day was terrible. On the way to our guesthouse around Plaza Reial, we (B)[lost / got lost] in downtown Barcelona. Dad was busy looking at the map and asking for directions with a few Spanish words he got from a tour guidebook. Even though our guesthouse was right next to the Plaza, it took us about two hours (C)[getting / to get] (D)there. We were so tired that we could not go out for dinner. I went to bed but couldn't fall asleep because I was worried about what would happen the next day.

14 다음 괄호 (A)~(C)에서 어법상 옳은 것을 바르게 짝지은 것은?

① look – lost – getting
② look – got lost – to get
③ look – lost – to get
④ looking – got lost – to get
⑤ looking – lost – getting

15 밑줄 친 (D)가 가리키는 것을 위 글에서 찾아 쓰시오.

➡ _____

서답형

16 What surprising event did the writer's dad suggest last summer? Answer in English.

➡ _____

17 다음 중 글쓴이가 여행 중 느낀 감정으로 가장 적절한 것은?

① excited and lively
② worried and lonely
③ anxious and tired
④ tired but pleased
⑤ embarrassed and upset

18 다음 중 위 글을 읽고 답할 수 <u>없는</u> 것은?

① When did the writer's father suggest the event?
② What did the writer's father hate to see?
③ Where did they have their dinner?
④ Why couldn't the writer fall asleep?
⑤ Where is Barcelona?

[19~21] 다음 글을 읽고 물음에 답하시오.

After looking around Gaudi's Park Guell, we decided to have seafood fried rice for lunch.
(A) The seafood fried rice was amazing. I really wanted to take pictures of the food and post them on my blog. But without my phone, I just decided to enjoy the moment.
(B) Luckily, she seemed to understand Mom's few Spanish words. She took us to a small local restaurant nearby.
(C) However, we didn't know which restaurant to go to. We needed help, so Mom went up to an elderly lady and tried to ask for directions to a popular seafood restaurant.

19 자연스러운 글이 되도록 (A)~(C)를 바르게 배열한 것은?

① (A) - (B) - (C)   ② (B) - (A) - (C)
③ (B) - (C) - (A)   ④ (C) - (A) - (B)
⑤ (C) - (B) - (A)

20 What did the writer want to do with a smartphone at the restaurant? Answer in English with a full sentence.

➡ _____

_____

21 다음 중 위 글의 내용과 일치하는 것은?

① The writer's family wanted to have seafood fried rice for dinner.
② The writer thought Gaudi's Park Guell was amazing.
③ The writer took many pictures of the food.
④ The writer went up to an elderly lady and asked for directions.
⑤ The elderly lady took the family to a seafood restaurant.

[22~26] 다음 글을 읽고 물음에 답하시오.

During the remaining days, we relied more and more on the locals. We were able to meet and talk with various people on the streets, in the bakeries, and in the parks. They were always kind enough to show us different sides of Barcelona with a smile. Also, our family talked a lot with each other. We spent much of our time together on the Spanish train, on the bus, and at the restaurants.

Our technology-free trip was a new and different experience. Before the trip, I was so dependent on my smartphone that I couldn't do anything without it. But now I see that I can enjoy the moment without it. From (A) the experience, I have learned the importance of a balanced use of the smartphone. So, next time, would I travel without a smartphone? Probably not. But I will try to use it more wisely.

22 밑줄 친 (A)가 의미하는 것을 위 글에서 찾아 쓰시오.

➡ _____

23 다음 중 글쓴이가 여행 중 한 일이 아닌 것은?

① depending on the locals
② meeting a number of people
③ talking with many people in the parks
④ showing people different sides of Barcelona
⑤ spending much time with his family

24 다음 중 위 글에서 반의어를 찾을 수 없는 것은?

① independent ② same
③ sensibly ④ old
⑤ less

25 Choose the one which is NOT true.

① The writer's family depended upon the local people.
② Thanks to the locals, the writer's family could see different sides of the city.
③ The writer used to be dependent on his smartphone.
④ The trip was an unfamiliar experience to the writer.
⑤ The writer hopes to travel without a smartphone someday.

26 What will the writer try to do when he goes on a trip next time? Answer in English with nine words.

➡ _____

[01~06] 다음 글을 읽고 물음에 답하시오.

Last summer, my father suggested a surprising event: a family trip without smartphones! He said, "I hate to see you sitting together and only looking at your smartphones." My sister and I explained the need for smartphones, but he kept saying that we could not fully enjoy the trip with them. So we started a technology-free trip to a new city, Barcelona, Spain.

Our first day was terrible. On the way to our guesthouse around Plaza Reial, we got lost in downtown Barcelona. Dad was busy looking at the map and asking for directions with a few Spanish words he got from a tour guidebook. Even though our guesthouse was right next to the Plaza, it took us about two hours to get there. (A)We were so tired that we could not go out for dinner. I went to bed but couldn't fall asleep because I was worried about what would happen the next day.

01 According to the passage, what is a technology-free trip? Answer in English.

➡ _____

02 What did the writer do when he heard his father's suggestion? Answer in English and use the word 'with.'

➡ _____

_____

03 to부정사를 활용하여 밑줄 친 (A)와 같은 의미의 문장을 쓰시오.

➡ _____

04 According to the passage, where did the writer's dad get a few Spanish words from? Answer in English, using 'them.'

➡ _____

05 다음은 가족 여행을 제안한 아버지의 말이다. 글의 내용에 맞게 빈칸에 알맞은 말을 쓰시오.

Dad: In order to fully _____ _____
_____ , we should travel _____
_____ .

06 Where was the family's guesthouse?

➡ _____

[07~10] 다음 글을 읽고 물음에 답하시오.

After looking around Gaudi's Park Guell, we decided to have seafood fried rice for lunch. However, we didn't know which restaurant to go to. We ①needed help, so Mom went up to an elderly lady and tried ②to ask for directions to a popular seafood restaurant. Luckily, she seemed ③to understand Mom's few Spanish words. She took us to a small local restaurant nearby. The seafood fried rice was ④amazing. I really wanted to take pictures of the food and post (A)them on my blog. But ⑤with my phone, I just decided to enjoy the moment.

07 Write the reason why the family needed help. Use the phrase 'It's because.'

➡ _____

_____

08 다음은 여행을 다녀온 글쓴이가 친구에게 한 말이다. 글의 내용에 맞게 빈칸에 알맞은 말을 쓰시오.

> We didn't know where we should go to have lunch, but an elderly lady was kind _____ _____ _____ us to a small local restaurant nearby.

09 밑줄 친 (A)가 가리키는 것을 위 글에서 찾아 쓰시오.

➡ _____

10 🅰️ 위 글의 ①~⑤ 중 글의 흐름에 맞지 <u>않는</u> 것을 골라 바르게 고치시오.

➡ _____

[11~15] 다음 글을 읽고 물음에 답하시오.

　During the remaining days, we relied more and more on the locals. We were able to meet and talk with various people on the streets, in the bakeries, and in the parks. They were always kind enough to show us different sides of Barcelona with a smile. Also, our family talked a lot with each other. We spent much of our time together on the Spanish train, on the bus, and at the restaurants.

　Our technology-free trip was a new and different experience. Before the trip, I was so dependent on my smartphone that I couldn't do anything without it. But now I see that I can enjoy the moment without it. From the experience, I have learned the importance of a ___(A)___ use of the smartphone. So, next time, would I travel without a smartphone? (B)<u>Probably not. But I will try to use it more wisely.</u>

11 주어진 단어를 어법에 맞게 빈칸 (A)에 쓰시오.

> balance

➡ _____

12 위 글의 내용에 맞게 빈칸에 알맞은 말을 쓰시오.

> The family not only _____ _____ _____ with various people in Barcelona but also _____ _____ _____ with each other.

13 🅰️ 다음 대화의 빈칸에 알맞은 말을 쓰시오.

> A: Was the technology-free trip a familiar experience to the writer?
> B: _____, _____ _____. It _____ _____ _____ _____ _____ to the writer.

14 🅰️ 다음은 밑줄 친 (B)의 의미이다. 빈칸에 알맞은 말을 쓰시오.

> Probably I wouldn't _____ _____ _____ _____ next time, but I will try to use it more wisely.

15 According to the passage, who did the writer's family depend on during the remaining days? Answer in English with five words.

➡ _____

Read and Think

Technology-Free Trip to Barcelona
~이 없는

Last summer, I had a new and different experience: a family trip without smartphones.

Troubles

- On the first day, we got lost on our way to the guesthouse.
특정한 날 앞에 전치사 on   ~로 가는 길에
- I couldn't take pictures of the food and post them on my blog.
pictures of the food

Joys

- I enjoyed the places and the people around me.
~의 주위에 있는
- I talked a lot with my family all the time and everywhere.
언제든, 항상

Changes after the Trip

- My thoughts on using a smartphone
동명사
Before: I couldn't do anything without it.

Now: I understand the importance of a balanced use of it.

구문해설 • technology-free: 첨단 과학 기술이 없는 • get lost: 길을 잃다 • thought: 생각

• importance: 중요성 • balanced: 균형 잡힌

해석

바르셀로나로의 첨단 과학 기술 없는 여행
지난여름, 나는 새롭고 색다른 경험으로 '스마트폰 없는 가족 여행'을 갔다.

• 힘들었던 점
– 첫째 날, 우리는 숙소로 가는 도중에 길을 잃었다.
– 나는 음식 사진을 찍어 블로그에 올릴 수 없었다.

• 좋았던 점
– 나는 내 주위에 있는 장소들과 사람들을 즐겼다.
– 나는 가족들과 언제 어디서든 많은 대화를 나누었다.

• 여행 후 달라진 점
– 스마트폰 사용에 대한 나의 생각
이전: 나는 그것 없이는 아무것도 할 수 없었다.
지금: 나는 그것을 균형 있게 사용하는 것이 중요함을 이해한다.

Grammar in Real Life B

1. Wash one apple under running water and cut it into small pieces.
현재분사(흐르는)
2. Cook the cut apple pieces with brown sugar on low heat.
과거분사(잘린 사과 조각)
3. Add salt, milk, and a beaten egg to make the egg mixture.
to부정사의 부사적 용법(~하기 위해서)
4. Roll the bread out and put the cooked apple filling on it.
과거분사(조리된) (음식의) 소, 속
5. Put the rolled bread in the egg mixture and take it out quickly. Then bake it
take out it (X)
   for 3 minutes.

6. Decorate a dish with the bread rolls and the remaining apple filling.

구문해설 • piece: 조각 • low: 낮은 • mixture: 혼합물 • roll out: 밀어 펴다 • decorate: 장식하다

1. 사과 한 개를 흐르는 물에 씻어 작은 조각으로 자르세요.
2. 잘라진 사과 조각들을 갈색 설탕과 함께 약한 불에서 조리세요.
3. 계란 혼합물을 만들기 위해 소금, 우유, 그리고 휘저은 계란을 더하세요.
4. 식빵을 얇게 밀어서 펴고 그 위에 조리된 사과 소를 올리세요.
5. 돌돌 말은 빵을 계란 혼합물에 넣었다가 빠르게 꺼내세요. 그러고 나서 그것을 3분간 구우세요.
6. 돌돌 말은 빵과 남아 있는 사과 소로 접시를 장식하세요.

01 다음 짝지어진 단어의 관계가 같도록 빈칸에 알맞은 말을 쓰시오.

> live : die = _____ : absent

02 다음 영영풀이가 가리키는 것을 쓰시오.

> to cook something in hot oil

➡ _____

03 다음 중 밑줄 친 부분의 뜻풀이가 바르지 <u>않은</u> 것은?

① Have you tried <u>sugar-free</u> juice? 무가당의

② I was <u>scared</u> after watching the horror movie. 겁먹은

③ I <u>suggest</u> to him that he should take a walk every day. 설득하다

④ The <u>debate</u> was highly emotional at times. 토론

⑤ I studied the beneficial <u>effects</u> of exercise. 효과

04 다음 우리말에 맞게 빈칸에 알맞은 말을 쓰시오.

(1) 나는 캐나다를 방문하는 것이 너무 기다려져!

➡ I can't _____ _____ visit Canada.

(2) 너는 너 자신을 믿고 계속 나아가야 한다.

➡ You should believe in yourself and _____ _____.

(3) 신용카드로 그것을 지불할 수 있을까요?

➡ Can I _____ _____ it with a credit card?

05 다음 문장에 공통으로 들어갈 말을 고르시오.

> • It is important for you to _____ various things and learn from failure.
> • We _____ these problems at some time in our lives.
> • To get the position as the manager, you should have skills and _____.

① deliver ② donate ③ post
④ experience ⑤ surprise

06 다음 문장의 빈칸에 들어갈 말을 〈보기〉에서 골라 쓰시오.

> ┤ 보기 ├
> importance / thought / side / effect / scared

(1) I want you to realize the _____ of working hard.

(2) I was surprised when I saw the serious _____ of the situation.

(3) I don't like acting without _____.

(4) My younger sister was _____ and began to cry.

(5) Weather has an _____ on our moods.

07 다음 주어진 문장의 밑줄 친 counter와 다른 의미로 쓰인 것은?

> Pay for this at the <u>counter</u>, please.

① Many people are lined up at the ticket <u>counter</u>.

② My father is standing behind the <u>counter</u>.

③ Would you put things up on the <u>counter</u>?

④ You can keep your valuables at the <u>counter</u>.

⑤ We read the <u>counter</u> proposal written from different point of view.

Conversation

[08~10] 다음 대화를 읽고 물음에 답하시오.

> Mike: Jenny, what do you think about the new online comic *Scary Night*?
>
> Jenny: I didn't like it. I thought it had too many sound effects.
>
> Mike: Really? I thought they made the story more interesting.
>
> Jenny: Not me. I couldn't focus because I was too (A)scared.

08 위 대화의 밑줄 친 (A)와 바꾸어 쓸 수 있는 것은?

① terrified ② terrific
③ brilliant ④ pleased
⑤ satisfied

09 What did Mike think about the sound effects in *Scary Night*?

➡ _____

10 How did Jenny feel when she was watching *Scary Night*?

➡ _____

[11~12] 다음 대화를 읽고 물음에 답하시오.

> Steve: Hey, Lisa. I've got over a hundred comments on my SNS posts.
>
> Lisa: Oh, I wouldn't feel comfortable to share my posts with so many people.
>
> Steve: Really? I think it's great that a lot of people see my posts.
>
> Lisa: (A)I'm not with you on that. I only want to share my posts with my close friends.

11 위 대화의 밑줄 친 (A)의 의도와 다른 것은?

① I don't think so.
② I don't believe so.
③ I don't agree with you.
④ I disagree with you.
⑤ I see it that way, too.

12 위 대화의 내용과 일치하지 않는 것은?

① Steve는 그의 SNS 게시물들에 100개가 넘는 댓글을 받았다.
② Lisa는 게시물 공유에 관해 Steve와 같은 의견을 갖고 있다.
③ Steve는 많은 사람들이 그의 게시물들을 보는 것을 좋아한다.
④ Lisa는 가까운 친구들하고만 그녀의 게시물을 공유하고 싶어 한다.
⑤ Lisa는 너무 많은 사람들과 게시물들을 공유하는 것이 편하지 않다.

[13~14] 다음 대화를 읽고 물음에 답하시오.

> Sujin: Now, we will start the three-minute debate. Today's first topic is fast fashion. (A) What do you think about it? Please, begin, James.
>
> James: (B) I think fast fashion is good. We can wear trendy clothes at a cheaper price.
>
> Wendy: (C) It makes us spend too much money and throw away clothes too often.
>
> Sujin: (D) It looks like the two of you have different opinions on the first topic. (E) Now, let's move on to the second topic.

13 위 대화의 (A)~(E) 중 주어진 문장이 들어가기에 알맞은 곳은?

I'm not with you on that.

① (A) ② (B) ③ (C) ④ (D) ⑤ (E)

14 위 대화를 읽고 대답할 수 <u>없는</u> 것은?

① What are students doing now?

② What is the first topic of the debate?

③ What does James think about the fast fashion?

④ Why doesn't Wendy like the fast fashion?

⑤ What did Wendy throw away too often?

Grammar

15 다음 중 빈칸에 들어갈 말로 가장 적절한 것은?

> My dad had his shoes _____.

① to shine   ② shining

③ shined   ④ to shining

⑤ shine

16 다음 중 빈칸에 들어갈 말로 적절하지 <u>않은</u> 것은?

> You look so _____ that I can't help looking at you.

① lovely   ② nice   ③ pretty

④ beautifully ⑤ cool

17 다음 빈칸에 들어갈 말이 바르게 짝지어진 것은?

> • I am too _____ to find any mistakes in your essay.
> • The shop offers _____ prices.

① careful – discounting

② careless – discounting

③ careless – discounted

④ carelessly – discount

⑤ carelessly – discounted

18 주어진 단어를 활용하여 다음 우리말을 11 단어로 이루어진 한 문장의 영어로 쓰시오.

> 나의 방은 너무 더러워서 내 친구들을 초대할 수 없어. (so / invite)

➡ _____

19 다음 중 어법상 바르지 <u>않은</u> 것은?

① He had his wallet stolen.

② Jane was so mad that he couldn't say a word.

③ The computer game looked boring.

④ You are not kind enough taking care of my plants.

⑤ Tom is too talkative to listen to his friends.

20 다음 중 우리말을 영어로 바르게 옮기지 <u>않은</u> 것은?

① 나는 너무 바빠서 지금 당장 너와 이야기할 수 없어.

= I am too busy to talk with you right now.

② Katherine은 너무 배불러서 음식을 더 먹을 수 없었다.

= Katherine was so full that she couldn't eat more food.

③ 땅 위에 떨어진 오렌지들을 봐!

= Look at the oranges fallen on the ground!

④ 나는 혼자 여행을 할 만큼 충분히 건강해.

= I am healthy enough to take a trip alone.

⑤ 그녀는 그 결과에 만족하는 것처럼 보였어.

= She looked satisfying with the result.

21 다음 중 주어진 문장의 밑줄 친 부분과 쓰임이 다른 하나는?

> Did you see the underline{swimming} pool?

① Kevin was not interested in playing soccer.
② My hobby is taking pictures.
③ The boys are riding bikes together.
④ They enjoyed cooking with her.
⑤ Dana focused on studying English.

22 다음 빈칸에 들어갈 말로 가장 적절한 것은?

> I am ＿＿＿＿＿＿ make a decision by myself.

① too old that
② so old to
③ enough old to
④ old enough
⑤ so old that I can

23 다음 중 빈칸에 들어갈 단어 use의 형태가 다른 하나는?

① I found her ＿＿＿＿ my pen.
② The boy ＿＿＿＿ your computer is my son.
③ David is ＿＿＿＿ the copy machine.
④ They bought a ＿＿＿＿ car.
⑤ She isn't good at ＿＿＿＿ the tool.

24 주어진 단어를 활용하여 다음 우리말을 영어로 쓰시오.

> 나는 너무 화가 나서 그 소식을 들을 수 없었어.
> (too / upset)

➡ ＿＿＿＿＿＿＿＿＿＿＿＿＿＿＿＿＿

Reading

[25~29] 다음 글을 읽고 물음에 답하시오.

Last summer, my father suggested ① a surprising event: a family trip without smartphones! He said, "I hate to see you sitting together and ②only looking at your smartphones." My sister and I explained the need for smartphones, but he kept saying that we could not fully enjoy the trip ③without them. So we started a technology-free trip to a new city, Barcelona, Spain.

Our first day was terrible. On the way to our guesthouse around Plaza Reial, we ④got lost in downtown Barcelona. Dad was busy looking at the map and asking for directions with a few Spanish words he got from a tour guidebook. ＿＿(A)＿＿ our guesthouse was right next to the Plaza, it (B)took us about two hours to get there. We were so tired that we ⑤could not go out for dinner. I went to bed but couldn't fall asleep because I was worried about what would happen the next day.

25 다음 중 빈칸 (A)에 들어갈 말로 가장 적절한 것은?

① Unless
② Because
③ Although
④ When
⑤ If

26 위 글의 밑줄 친 ①~⑤ 중 글의 흐름상 적절하지 않은 것은?

①　　②　　③　　④　　⑤

27 다음 중 밑줄 친 (B)와 같은 의미로 쓰인 것은?

① A girl <u>took</u> us to our room.
② <u>Take</u> this to the hotel for me.
③ Grace <u>took</u> the grey jacket.
④ The journey <u>took</u> half an hour.
⑤ He <u>took</u> a bus to get there.

28 위 글의 내용에 맞게 다음 질문의 답변을 완성하시오.

> Q: Why did the writer's dad suggest a family trip without smartphones?

➡ Because _____

_____.

29 다음 중 위 글의 내용과 일치하지 <u>않는</u> 것은?

① Barcelona was a new city to the family.
② The guesthouse was next to Plaza Reial.
③ The writer's father spoke a few Spanish words to ask for directions.
④ The writer was busy looking at the map.
⑤ The writer was too worried to fall asleep.

[30~32] 다음 글을 읽고 물음에 답하시오.

After looking around Gaudi's Park Guell, we decided to have seafood ①<u>fried</u> rice for lunch. However, we didn't know ②<u>which restaurant</u> to go to. We needed help, so Mom went up to an elderly lady and tried to ask for directions to a popular seafood restaurant. Luckily, she seemed ③<u>to understand</u> Mom's few Spanish words. She took us to a small local restaurant nearby. The seafood fried rice was ④<u>amazing</u>. I really wanted to take pictures of the food and ⑤<u>posted</u> them on my blog. But without my phone, I just decided to enjoy the moment.

30 위 글의 ①~⑤ 중 어법상 바르지 <u>않은</u> 것을 골라 바르게 고쳐 쓰시오.

➡ _____

31 다음 중 위 글의 내용과 일치하지 <u>않는</u> 것은?

> After we looked around Gaudi's Park Guell, we ①wanted to eat seafood fried rice. Because ②Mom could speak a few Spanish words, she asked ③an elderly lady where we should go. She took us ④ to a local restaurant far from the park. Even though the food was amazing, I ⑤ couldn't take pictures of it.

①   ②   ③   ④   ⑤

32 다음 중 위 글을 읽고 답할 수 <u>없는</u> 것은?

① What did they decide to do after looking around Gaudi's Park Guell?
② How did they get to the restaurant?
③ Why did the writer's mom go up to the elderly lady?
④ How was the seafood fried rice at the restaurant?
⑤ How popular was the seafood restaurant?

[01~02] 다음 대화를 읽고 물음에 답하시오.

Mike: Jenny, what do you think about the new online comic *Scary Night*?

Jenny: I didn't like (A)it. I thought it had too many sound effects.

Mike: Really? I thought (B)they made the story more interesting.

Jenny: Not me. I couldn't focus because I was too scared.

출제율 90%

01 위 대화의 (A)it과 (B)they가 가리키는 것을 각각 찾아 쓰시오.

(A) _____

(B) _____

출제율 95%

02 위 대화의 내용과 일치하지 <u>않는</u> 것은?

① *Scary Night* is a new online comic.

② Jenny didn't like *Scary Night* because of lots of sound effects.

③ Mike was with Jenny on *Scary Night*.

④ Mike liked *Scary Night* because many sound effects made the story more interesting.

⑤ Jenny was so scared that she couldn't focus on *Scary Night*.

[03~05] 다음 대화를 읽고 물음에 답하시오.

Tony: Hey, Julie! Have you heard about the *Quiz & Rice* game?

Julie: Yeah, isn't it the one that donates rice when you get a right answer?

Tony: Yeah, what do you think about the game?

Julie: I think it's a creative game. You can have fun and help out hungry people. Have you played it yet?

Tony: No, but I'm going to try it out this weekend.

출제율 90%

03 What can you donate when you get the right answer in the *Quiz & Rice* game?

➡ _____

출제율 85%

04 What does Julie think about the *Quiz & Rice* game?

➡ _____

출제율 95%

05 When will Tony try out the *Quiz & Rice* game?

➡ _____

[06~07] 다음 대화를 읽고 물음에 답하시오.

Jack: Sally, did you watch *Super Voice's* Top 10 finalists yesterday?

Sally: Yeah. They all sang much better than before.

Jack: Yeah, they did. I think this singing contest helps them get closer to their dreams.

Sally: _____(A)_____ (B)I can't wait to watch their next performances.

출제율 100%

06 위 대화의 빈칸 (A)에 들어갈 말로 나머지와 의도가 <u>다른</u> 것은?

① I'm with you on that.

② I think so, too.

③ I see it that way, too.

④ I agree with you.

⑤ I disagree with you.

07 위 대화의 밑줄 친 (B)와 의미가 같도록 forward를 사용하여 다시 쓰시오.

➡ _____

_____

[08~10] 다음 대화를 읽고 물음에 답하시오.

Sujin: Now, we will start the three-minute debate. Today's first topic is fast fashion. What do you think about it? Please, begin, James.

James: I think fast fashion is good. We can wear trendy clothes at a cheaper price.

Wendy: I'm not with you on that. It makes us spend too much money and throw away clothes too often.

Sujin: It looks like the two of you have different opinions on the first topic. Now, let's move on to the second topic.

08 What are students debating now?

➡ _____

09 Why does James think that fast fashion is good?

➡ _____

_____

10 What does Wendy think about fast fashion?

➡ _____

_____

11 다음 중 빈칸에 들어갈 말이 바르게 짝지어진 것은?

> • Claire was _____ worried to do her homework.
> • The stick is light _____ to float on water.
> • Thank you for your _____ gift.

① so – that – amazed
② so – that – amaze
③ so – enough – amazing
④ too – enough – amazing
⑤ too – enough – amazed

12 다음 중 어법상 바르지 <u>않은</u> 것은?

> David runs ①too ②fast ③that no one ④can catch ⑤him.

①   ②   ③   ④   ⑤

13 주어진 단어를 바르게 배열하여 다음 우리말을 영어로 쓰시오. 필요하다면 단어의 형태를 변형하시오.

> 그 걷고 있는 로봇은 내가 가장 좋아하는 장난감이야.
> (toy / walk / favorite / robot / the / my / is)

➡ _____

14 다음 중 밑줄 친 부분의 쓰임이 같은 것끼리 바르게 묶은 것은?

> ⓐ Can you see the girl <u>wearing</u> a cap?
> ⓑ We are curious about <u>making</u> the cookies.
> ⓒ Are you still doing the <u>boring</u> game?
> ⓓ George's hobby is <u>playing</u> chess.

① ⓐ-ⓓ, ⓑ-ⓒ   ② ⓐ-ⓒ, ⓑ-ⓓ
③ ⓐ-ⓑ-ⓒ, ⓓ   ④ ⓑ-ⓒ-ⓓ, ⓐ
⑤ ⓐ-ⓑ-ⓒ, ⓓ

15 다음 중 어법상 바르지 <u>않은</u> 것은?

① The news made him disappointed.
② I am too angry to forgive you right now.
③ Mike was so full that he couldn't eat the dessert.
④ Chris kept the door closed.
⑤ We had the tree plant in the garden.

16 다음 빈칸에 알맞은 말을 다섯 단어로 쓰시오.

> Molly was too busy to take care of her children.
> = Molly was _____ take care of her children.

17 동사 write를 어법에 맞게 빈칸에 쓰시오.

> • My cousin is the boy _____ something on his note.
> • Did you see a letter _____ in Korean?

[18~21] 다음 글을 읽고 물음에 답하시오.

> During the remaining days, we relied more and more on the locals.
> (A) Also, our family talked a lot with each other.
> (B) They were always kind enough to show us different sides of Barcelona with a smile.
> (C) We were able to meet and talk with various people on the streets, in the bakeries, and in the parks.
> We spent much of our time together on the Spanish train, on the bus, and at the restaurants.
>
> Our technology-free trip was a new and different experience. Before the trip, I was so dependent on my smartphone that I couldn't do anything without it. But now I see that I can enjoy the moment without it. From the experience, I have learned the importance of a balanced use of the smartphone. So, next time, would I travel without a smartphone? Probably not. But I will try to use it more wisely.

18 자연스러운 글이 되도록 (A)~(C)를 바르게 배열하시오.

➡ _____

19 다음 중 위 글의 내용과 일치하는 것은?

① The family took the trip without relying on the locals.
② The writer was independent enough to do something without his smartphone before the trip.
③ The writer understands that he can enjoy moments without a smartphone.
④ The writer looks forward to going on another trip without his smartphone.
⑤ There's nothing that the writer learned from the trip.

✎ 출제율 90%

20 According to the passage, where did the family meet and talk with the locals? Answer in English with a full sentence.

➡ _____

_____

✎ 출제율 100%

21 다음 중 위 글을 읽고 찾아볼 수 없는 것은?

① the writer's family talking with each other
② the writer's family getting on the bus
③ the writer's family talking with the locals at the restaurant
④ the writer's family meeting people in the parks
⑤ the locals showing the family different sides of Barcelona

[22~25] 다음 글을 읽고 물음에 답하시오.

　Wash one apple under ①running water and cut it into small pieces. Cook the ②cutting apple pieces with brown sugar on low heat. Add salt, milk, and a beaten egg to make the egg mixture. Roll the bread out and put the ③cooked apple filling on it. Put the ④ rolled bread in the egg mixture and take it out quickly. Then bake it ___(A)___ 3 minutes. Decorate a dish with the bread rolls and the ⑤ remaining apple filling.

✎ 출제율 90%

22 다음 중 빈칸 (A)에 들어갈 말로 가장 적절한 것은?

① at　　　　② in　　　　③ for
④ about　　⑤ to

✎ 출제율 95%

23 위 글의 밑줄 친 ①~⑤ 중 어법상 바르지 않은 것은?

①　　　　②　　　　③　　　　④　　　　⑤

✎ 출제율 100%

24 다음 중 위 글의 내용을 잘못 이해한 사람은?

① 은주: 가장 먼저 사과를 씻어야 해.
② 준휘: 계란 혼합물을 만들려면 소금, 우유, 그리고 계란이 필요하네.
③ 재영: 식빵을 얇게 밀어서 펴야 해.
④ 혜준: 식빵 위에 올린 사과 소는 조리할 필요가 없어.
⑤ 서현: 남아 있는 사과 소로 접시를 장식해야 해.

✎ 출제율 95%

25 다음 중 위 글을 읽고 답할 수 없는 것은?

① What did we have to do with the apple after washing it?
② What sugar do we have to use?
③ What do we have to prepare to make the dish?
④ What do we decorate the dish with?
⑤ How long do we have to cook the cut apple pieces?

[01~03] 다음 대화를 읽고 물음에 답하시오.

Steve: Hey, Lisa. I've got over a hundred comments on my SNS posts.

Lisa: Oh, I wouldn't feel comfortable to share my posts with so many people.

Steve: Really? I think it's great that a lot of people see my posts.

Lisa: _____ (A) _____ I only want to share my posts with my close friends.

01 위 대화의 빈칸 (A)에 들어갈 말을 <보기>에 주어진 단어들을 모두 배열하여 영작하시오.

┌─ 보기 ─┐
with / that / I'm / you / not / on
└────────┘

➡ _____

02 What does Steve think about sharing his posts with many people?

➡ _____

03 With whom does Lisa want to share her posts?

➡ _____

04 다음 대화가 자연스럽게 이어지도록 순서대로 배열하시오.

(A) I think it's really touching. She'll love it.
(B) Oh, you're giving her a memory stick?
(C) Look, Dad. This is Mom's birthday gift.
(D) Yeah, I've made a family video clip for Mom and saved it on this stick. What do you think about the present?

➡ _____

05 다음 주어진 단어를 어법에 맞게 빈칸에 쓰시오.

Angela said _____ words to me. So I was _____. (encourage)

06 다음 우리말 의미에 맞게 빈칸에 알맞은 말을 쓰시오.

(1) 그 젊은 주자들은 응원하는 군중 옆을 지나갔다.
➡ The young runners passed by the _____ crowd.

(2) 그 요리사는 얇게 잘린 양파를 차가운 물에 넣었다.
➡ The chef put the _____ onions in cold water.

07 주어진 어구를 활용하여 다음 우리말을 조건에 맞게 영어로 쓰시오.

그녀는 선반 꼭대기에 닿을 만큼 키가 커.
(reach, the top shelf)

(1) to부정사를 활용하여 한 문장으로
➡ _____

(2) that절을 활용하여 한 문장으로
➡ _____

08 주어진 단어를 활용하여 다음 대화의 빈칸에 알맞은 말을 쓰시오.

A: Do you know why the dog didn't bark at a stranger?
B: I think _____.
(hungry / that)

➡ _____
_____

Our first day was terrible. On the way to our guesthouse around Plaza Reial, we got lost in downtown Barcelona. Dad was busy looking at the map and asking for directions with a few Spanish words he got from a tour guidebook. Even though our guesthouse was right next to the Plaza, it took us about two hours to get there. We were so tired that we could not go out for dinner. I went to bed but couldn't fall asleep because I was worried about what would happen the next day.

09 How did the writer's dad ask for directions? Answer in English with a full sentence.

➡ _____

_____

10 Why couldn't the writer fall asleep? Use the word 'because.'

➡ _____

_____

11 Where did they get lost? Answer in English with a full sentence.

➡ _____

It is my 15th birthday today. Last night, I was so excited that I couldn't sleep well. However, my birthday started badly. I woke up too late to have my birthday breakfast. All day, I felt so sleepy that I couldn't focus during class. I was sad because nothing was going right. But something unexpected happened. My classmates threw a surprise party for me. (A)I was too moved to say anything. It was a wonderful day. ※ I=Jesse

12 to부정사를 활용하여 다음 물음에 답하시오.

Q: Why couldn't Jesse focus during class?

➡ _____

13 How did Jesse feel when his classmates threw a surprise party for him? Answer in English with three words.

➡ _____

14 that절을 활용하여 밑줄 친 (A)와 같은 의미의 문장을 쓰시오.

➡ _____

창의사고력 서술형 문제

01 다음 대화의 내용과 일치하도록 Mina의 일기를 완성하시오.

If you have seen him, please CALL! 880-335-7975

Alex: I've just finished making the posting for Leon, Mom. What do you think about it?

Mom: Oh, the title "LOST CAT" in big letters at the top is easy to see.

Alex: Yeah, I did it to get attention. How about these photos below the title?

Mom: Hmm··· the one on the right doesn't show Leon's face well.

Alex: Okay, I'll change the photo.

Mom: Oh, I hope we can find Leon.

Alex made the posting to (A)_____ his lost cat, Leon. He wrote the title "LOST CAT" in (B)_____ at the top to get attention. He added (C)_____ below the title on the posting. His mom wanted to change the one on the right because (D)_____. His mom wished to find Leon soon.

02 다음 주어진 문장과 같은 의미의 문장을 쓰시오.

(1) The man was so shocked that he couldn't say anything.

➡ _____

(2) The book was so difficult that it couldn't be read easily.

➡ _____

(3) The dog was so hungry that he couldn't bark at a stranger.

➡ _____

(4) She was so frightened that she couldn't phone us.

➡ _____

단원별 모의고사

01 다음 문장에 공통으로 들어갈 말을 고르시오.

> • I would like to listen to your _____s on this issue.
> • Have you ever _____ about becoming a lawyer?
> • I _____ that you were afraid of trying something new.

① suggest ② remain ③ presence
④ post ⑤ thought

02 다음 우리말에 맞게 빈칸에 알맞은 말을 쓰시오.

(1) 나의 아버지는 멀리 떨어져 계시지만, 나의 마음은 항상 그와 함께 있다.
➡ _____ _____ my father is far away, my heart is always with him.

(2) 그는 그녀의 관심을 얻기 위해 노력했다.
➡ He tried to _____ her _____.

03 다음 문장의 빈칸에 들어갈 말을 〈보기〉에서 골라 쓰시오.

> ┌ 보기 ┐
> elderly / handwritten / guidebook /
> local / guesthouse

(1) I brought this _____ to get some information about China.

(2) Jessica felt touched when she got the _____ letters from her daughter.

(3) I decided to stay at the _____ for three days.

(4) How about offering your seat to the _____ lady?

(5) Have you ever visited that restaurant serving organic and _____ food?

04 다음 우리말을 주어진 단어를 이용하여 영작하시오.

(1) 나는 내 방을 청소하느라 바빴다.
(cleaning, was)
➡ _____

(2) 나는 커피 한 잔을 마신 후 잠이 들 수 없었다.
(asleep, drinking)
➡ _____

(3) 젊은 사람들은 기술에 너무 많이 의존한다.
(rely, much, young)
➡ _____

[05~06] 다음 대화를 읽고 물음에 답하시오.

Emma: Excuse me. Can you help me order with this machine?

Tom: Sure. First, press the Hot Dog button and choose your hot dog and drink.

Emma: Okay. How do I pay for my order?

Tom: Touch the Done button at the bottom and pay for them.

Emma: Wow, it's so simple. This machine is much faster than ordering at the counter.

Tom: I'm with you on that. It really saves a lot of time when there's a long line.

05 Which button should Emma touch before paying for the order?

➡ _____

06 What does Tom think about the machine?

➡ _____
_____

[07~09] 다음 대화를 읽고 물음에 답하시오.

> Sujin: Now, we will start the three-minute debate. Today's first topic is fast fashion. What do you think about it? Please, begin, James.
>
> James: I think fast fashion is good. We can wear trendy clothes at a ⓐcheaper price.
>
> Wendy: I'm not ⓑwith you on that. It makes us spend too much money and ⓒthrows away clothes too often.
>
> Sujin: It ⓓlooks like the two of you have different opinions on the first topic. Now, let's ⓔmove on to the second topic.

07 위 대화에서 다음 주어진 영영풀이가 나타내는 말을 찾아 쓰시오.

> an argument or a discussion expressing different opinions

➡ _____

08 위 대화의 밑줄 친 ⓐ~ⓔ 중 어법상 어색한 것을 찾아 바르게 고치시오.

➡ _____

09 위 대화의 내용과 일치하지 <u>않는</u> 것은?

① Students are debating the pros and cons of fast fashion.
② James thinks that fast fashion is good because trendy clothes are available at a cheaper price.
③ Wendy has the same opinion as James about the fast fashion.
④ Wendy thinks that trendy clothes make us waste much money.
⑤ Wendy insists that fast fashion is bad because it makes us throw away clothes too often.

[10~11] 다음 대화를 읽고 물음에 답하시오.

> Emma: Excuse me. Can you help me order with this machine?
>
> Tom: (A) Sure. First, press the Hot Dog button and choose your hot dog and drink.
>
> Emma: (B) Okay. How do I pay for my order?
>
> Tom: (C) Touch the Done button at the bottom and pay for them.
>
> Emma: (D) Wow, it's so simple. This machine is much faster than ordering at the counter.
>
> Tom: (E) It really saves a lot of time when there's a long line.

10 위 대화의 (A)~(E) 중 주어진 문장이 들어가기에 알맞은 곳은?

> I'm with you on that.

① (A) ② (B) ③ (C) ④ (D) ⑤ (E)

11 위 대화의 내용과 일치하지 <u>않는</u> 것은?

① Emma는 기계로 주문을 하려고 한다.
② Emma는 먼저 '핫도그' 버튼을 누르고 먹고 싶은 핫도그와 음료를 골라야 한다.
③ Emma는 맨 아래의 '완료' 버튼을 누르고 결제할 수 있다.
④ 기계에서 주문하는 것이 계산대에서 주문하는 것보다 훨씬 더 빠르다.
⑤ 줄이 길 때, 계산대에서 주문하면 많은 시간을 절약할 수 있다.

12 다음 우리말과 일치하도록 주어진 단어를 모두 배열하여 영작하시오.

> 나는 온라인 쇼핑이 상점에서 쇼핑하는 것보다 낫다고 생각해.
>
> (shopping / think / is / better / shopping / at / the stores / I / online / than)

➡ _____

_____

13 주어진 단어를 활용하여 다음 우리말을 영어로 쓰시오.

> 그녀는 그 충격적인 소식에 실망할 거야.
> (will / shock / disappoint / with)

➡ _____

14 다음 문장과 같은 의미의 문장을 <u>모두</u> 고르시오.

> You can't eat the soup because it is very hot.

① The soup is too hot for you to eat.
② The soup is hot enough to eat.
③ The soup is so hot that you can eat it.
④ The soup is too hot that you can't eat it.
⑤ The soup is so hot that you can't eat it.

15 다음 중 어법상 바르지 <u>않은</u> 것은?

① There are many excited people in the hall.
② Did you find your broken camera?
③ The movie is interesting enough to watch several times.
④ They were so busy that they can't have lunch.
⑤ The book is too difficult to understand.

[16~19] 다음 글을 읽고 물음에 답하시오.

After looking around Gaudi's Park Guell, we decided to have seafood fried rice for lunch. However, we didn't know which restaurant to go to. We needed help, so Mom went up to an (a)elderly lady and tried to ask for directions to a popular seafood restaurant. Luckily, she seemed to understand Mom's few Spanish words. She took us to a small local restaurant nearby. The seafood fried rice was amazing. I really wanted to take pictures of the food and (b)post them on my blog. But without my phone, I just decided to enjoy the (c)moment.

During the remaining days, we relied more and more on the locals. We were able to meet and talk with various people on the streets, in the (d)bakeries, and in the parks. They were always kind enough to show us different sides of Barcelona with a smile. Also, our family talked a lot with each other. We spent much of our time together on the Spanish train, on the bus, and at the restaurants.

16 다음 중 (a)~(d)를 풀이한 말에 해당하지 <u>않는</u> 것은?

① a particular point in time
② to put a message or computer document on the Internet
③ old or aging
④ a book of directions and information for travelers
⑤ a building where bread is baked or sold

17 다음 중 위 글을 읽고 답할 수 <u>없는</u> 것은?

① What did they do before they decided to have lunch?
② Why did they need help?
③ Who took them to a small restaurant?
④ How was the seafood fried rice?
⑤ How far was it from Park Guell to the restaurant?

18 Where did the family spend their time together during the trip? Answer in English with a full sentence.

➡ _____

_____

19 How did the locals act toward the family? Answer in English with a full sentence.

➡ _____

_____

[20~22] 다음 글을 읽고 물음에 답하시오.

It is my 15th birthday today. Last night, I was so excited that I couldn't sleep well. ___(A)___ , my birthday started badly. I woke up too late to have my birthday breakfast. All day, I felt so sleepy that I couldn't focus during class. I was sad because nothing was going right. But something unexpected happened. My classmates threw a surprise party for me. I was so moved that I couldn't say anything. It was a wonderful day.

20 다음 중 빈칸 (A)에 들어갈 말로 가장 적절한 것은?

① Therefore
② Besides
③ However
④ Luckily
⑤ On the other hand

21 위 글의 내용에 맞게 빈칸에 알맞은 말을 쓰시오.

A: Jesse, did you have your birthday breakfast?

B: No. I woke up _____ _____ _____ _____ _____ have my birthday breakfast.

22 다음 중 위 글의 내용과 일치하지 <u>않는</u> 것은?

① The writer wrote this story on his birthday.
② The writer was too excited to sleep well.
③ The writer felt sleepy all day long.
④ The surprise party made the writer feel moved.
⑤ The writer knew that there would be a surprise party for him.

23 자연스러운 글이 되도록 (A)~(C)를 바르게 나열한 것은?

Our technology-free trip was a new and different experience.

(A) But now I see that I can enjoy the moment without it. From the experience, I have learned the importance of a balanced use of the smartphone.

(B) Before the trip, I was so dependent on my smartphone that I couldn't do anything without it.

(C) So, next time, would I travel without a smartphone? Probably not. But I will try to use it more wisely.

① (A)–(C)–(B)
② (B)–(A)–(C)
③ (B)–(C)–(A)
④ (C)–(A)–(B)
⑤ (C)–(B)–(A)

Lesson

Special

The Stone

교과서
Words & Expressions

Key Words

- □ **arrive** [əráiv] 동 도착하다
- □ **bear** [bɛər] 동 (새끼를) 낳다
- □ **beard** [biərd] 명 수염
- □ **cart** [kɑːrt] 명 수레, 우마차
- □ **cow** [kau] 명 소, 암소
- □ **decide** [disáid] 동 결심하다, 결정하다
- □ **delight** [diláit] 명 기쁨
- □ **destroy** [distrɔ́i] 동 파괴하다, 없애다
- □ **dwarf** [dwɔːrf] 명 난쟁이
- □ **explain** [ikspéin] 동 설명하다
- □ **field** [fiːld] 명 들판, 밭
- □ **free** [friː] 동 빼내다, 풀어 주다 형 자유로운
- □ **glad** [glæd] 형 기쁜
- □ **grandchild** [grǽndtʃàild] 명 손주
- □ **ground** [graund] 명 땅, 지면
- □ **hand** [hænd] 동 건네주다
- □ **log** [lɔg] 명 통나무
- □ **magic** [mǽdʒik] 형 마술의
- □ **nothing** [nʌ́θiŋ] 대 아무것도 아닌 것
- □ **reward** [riwɔ́ːrd] 명 보상, 보답
- □ **season** [síːzn] 명 계절
- □ **stone** [stoun] 명 돌
- □ **tooth** [tuːθ] 명 이, 치아
- □ **trouble** [trʌbl] 명 문제
- □ **unless** [ənlés] 접 ~하지 않는 한
- □ **warn** [wɔːrn] 동 경고하다
- □ **wife** [waif] 명 아내, 부인

Key Expressions

- □ **be proud of** ~을 자랑스러워하다
- □ **change into** ~으로 바꾸다
- □ **far from** ~에서 멀리
- □ **get rid of** ~을 없애다
- □ **give birth** 출산하다, 새끼를 낳다
- □ **go away** 떠나가다
- □ **go by** 흐르다, 지나가다
- □ **keep ~ from -ing** ~가 …하지 못하게 하다
- □ **keep -ing** 계속 ~하다
- □ **look forward to** ~을 기대하다, ~을 고대하다
- □ **on one's way to** ~로 가는 길에
- □ **throw away** ~을 버리다
- □ **try to** ~하려고 노력하다
- □ **worry about** ~에 대해 걱정하다

Word Power

※ 서로 반대되는 뜻을 가진 어휘

- [ ] **arrive** 도착하다 ↔ **depart** 출발하다, 떠나다
- [ ] **delight** 기쁨 ↔ **grief** 슬픔
- [ ] **destroy** 파괴하다 ↔ **construct** 건설하다
- [ ] **wife** 아내 ↔ **husband** 남편
- [ ] **sick** 아픈 ↔ **healthy** 건강한
- [ ] **old** 늙은 ↔ **young** 젊은

- [ ] **dwarf** 난쟁이 ↔ **giant** 거인
- [ ] **slow** 느린 ↔ **fast** 빠른
- [ ] **if** ~한다면 ↔ **unless** ~하지 않으면
- [ ] **proud** 자랑스러운 ↔ **shameful** 부끄러운
- [ ] **nothing** 아무것도 아닌 것 ↔ **everything** 모든 것
- [ ] **far from** ~에서 멀리 ↔ **close to** ~에 가까이

English Dictionary

- [ ] **arrive** 도착하다
  → to get to a place, especially at the end of a journey
  어떤 장소, 특히 여행의 끝에 다다르다

- [ ] **bear** (아이나 새끼를) 낳다
  → to give birth to a child
  아이를 낳다

- [ ] **beard** 수염
  → hair that grows on the chin and cheeks of a man's face
  남자 얼굴의 턱과 뺨에 자라는 털

- [ ] **cart** 수레, 우마차
  → a vehicle with two or four wheels that is pulled by a horse and used for carrying loads
  말이 끌고 짐을 나르기 위해 사용되는 두 개 또는 네 개의 바퀴가 있는 수송 수단

- [ ] **destroy** 파괴하다
  → to damage something so badly that it no longer exists, works, etc.
  무언가를 매우 심하게 손상시켜 더 이상 존재하거나 작동하지 않게 하다

- [ ] **free** 빼내다, 풀어 주다
  → to remove something that is unpleasant or not wanted from somebody/something
  누군가나 무언가로부터 불쾌하거나 원하지 않는 무언가를 제거하다

- [ ] **grandchild** 손주
  → a child of your son or daughter
  당신의 아들이나 딸의 아이

- [ ] **hand** 건네주다
  → to pass or give something to somebody
  누군가에게 무언가를 전달하거나 주다

- [ ] **log** 통나무
  → a thick piece of wood that is cut from or has fallen from a tree
  나무에서 떨어졌거나 베어진 두꺼운 나무 조각

- [ ] **reward** 보상
  → a thing that you are given because you have done something good, worked hard, etc.
  당신이 무언가 잘했거나 열심히 일을 했기 때문에 당신에게 주어진 것

- [ ] **warn** 경고하다
  → to tell somebody about something, especially something dangerous or unpleasant that is likely to happen, so that they can avoid it
  누군가에게 특히 일어나기 쉬운 위험하거나 불쾌한 무언가에 대해 그들이 그것을 피할 수 있도록 이야기하다

- [ ] **wife** 아내, 부인
  → the woman that somebody is married to
  누군가와 결혼한 여성

The Stone

One day, Maibon was driving down the road on his horse and cart when he saw an old man. The old man looked very sick. Maibon began to worry about growing old. Later that day, he saw a dwarf, Doli, in the field. He was trying to get his leg out from under a log. Maibon pulled the log away and freed the dwarf. "You'll have your reward. What do you want?" "I've heard that you have magic stones that can keep a man young. I want one." "Oh, you humans have it all wrong. Those stones don't make you young again. They only keep you from getting older." "Just as good!" Doli tried to explain the problem with the stones, but Maibon didn't listen. So Doli handed him a magic stone and went away.

After a few days, Maibon saw that his beard didn't grow at all. He became happy, but his wife, Modrona, got upset. "The eggs don't change into chickens!" "Oh, the season's slow, that's all." But she was not happy. "The cow doesn't give birth!" Maibon, then, told her about the stone, and she got very angry and told him to throw it away. He didn't want to, but he listened to his wife and threw the stone out the window.

cart 수레, 우마차
worry about ~에 대해 걱정하다
dwarf 난쟁이
field 들판
log 통나무
free 빼내다, 풀어 주다
reward 보상, 보답
keep ~ from Ving ~가 V하지 못하게 하다
go away 떠나가다
not ~ at all 전혀 ~ 않다
change into ~으로 바뀌다
give birth 새끼를 낳다
throw away 버리다

📎 확인문제

● 다음 문장이 본문의 내용과 일치하면 T, 일치하지 않으면 F를 쓰시오.

1 Maibon helped the old man who looked sick. ☐

2 Maibon wanted a magic stone from the dwarf as a reward. ☐

3 Maibon understood that the magic stone could keep him from getting older. ☐

4 Maibon's wife didn't like the stone. ☐

However, the next morning, he found the stone sitting by the window!
현재분사(목적보어)
Maibon was worried about the animals, but he was glad that he was
that 이하가 기뻤다
still young. Now Maibon's baby was having trouble. No tooth was seen
in his mouth. His wife told him to throw away the stone and this time,
tell+목적어+to부정사: 목적어가 V하도록 말하다
Maibon put the stone under the ground. But, the next day, the stone
came back! Time went by and nothing grew or changed. Maibon began
to worry. "There's nothing to look forward to, nothing to show for
to부정사의 형용사적 용법(nothing 수식)   *to부정사의 형용사적 용법(nothing 수식)*
my work." Maibon tried to destroy the stone, but it kept coming back.
keep Ving: 계속해서 V하다
Maibon decided to throw away the stone far from his house. On his
to부정사를 목적어로 취하는 동사
way to the field, he saw the dwarf. Maibon got angry with him. "Why
didn't you warn me about the stone?" "I tried to, but you wouldn't
= to warn you about the stone
listen." Doli explained that Maibon couldn't get rid of the stone unless
명사절 접속사(+완전한 문장)
he really wanted to. "I want no more of it. Whatever may happen, let
= if he really didn't want to   *복잡관계대명사*   *사역동사+목적어+동사원형*
it happen!" Doli told him to throw the stone onto the ground and go
back home. Maibon did as Doli said. When he arrived home, Modrona
접속사(~하는 대로)
told him the good news — the eggs changed into chickens and the cow
bore her baby. And Maibon laughed with delight when he saw the first
bear-bore-born   *기뻐서*
tooth in his baby's mouth. Maibon, Modrona and their children and
grandchildren lived for many years. Maibon was proud of his white
~을 자랑스러워했다
hair and long beard.

nothing 아무것도 아닌 것
destroy 파괴하다, 없애다
go by 흐르다, 지나가다
warn 경고하다
unless ~하지 않는 한
bear 새끼를 낳다
grandchild 손주
get rid of ~을 없애다

 확인문제

⊛ 다음 문장이 본문의 내용과 일치하면 T, 일치하지 않으면 F를 쓰시오.

1   Doli forgot to warn about the stone. ☐

2   Doli told Maibon to throw the stone onto the ground and went home. ☐

3   As soon as Maibon arrived home, he got the good news. ☐

● 우리말을 참고하여 빈칸에 알맞은 말을 쓰시오.

1 One day, Maibon was _____ the road on his horse and cart _____ he saw an old man.

2 The old man _____ very _____. Maibon began _____ _____ _____ growing old.

3 _____ _____ _____, he saw a dwarf, Doli, in the field.

4 He was trying _____ _____ his leg _____ _____ under a log.

5 Maibon _____ the log _____ and _____ the dwarf.

6 "You'll have your _____. What do you want?"

7 "I've heard that you have magic stones _____ can keep a man _____. I want one."

8 "Oh, you humans have _____ _____ _____. Those stones don't make you _____ _____. They only _____ you _____ getting older."

9 "Just as good!" Doli tried _____ _____ the problem with the stones, but Maibon didn't _____.

10 So Doli _____ _____ a magic stone and went away.

11 After _____ _____ days, Maibon saw that his beard didn't _____ _____ _____.

12 He _____ happy, but his wife, Modrona, _____ _____.

13 The eggs don't _____ _____ chickens!" "Oh, the season's _____, that's all."

14 But she was not happy. "The cow doesn't _____ _____!" Maibon, then, told her about the stone, and she _____ very _____ and told him _____ _____ _____ _____.

15 He didn't want to, but he _____ _____ his wife and _____ the stone _____ the window.

16 However, the next morning, he _____ the stone _____ by the window!

---

1 어느 날, Maibon이 한 노인을 보았을 때, 그는 마차를 타고 길을 내려가고 있던 중이었다.

2 그 노인은 매우 아파 보였다. Maibon은 늙어 가는 것이 걱정되기 시작했다.

3 그날 오후, 그는 들판에서 Doli라는 난쟁이를 보았다.

4 그는 통나무 아래에 깔린 그의 다리를 빼내려고 하고 있었다.

5 Maibon은 통나무를 잡아당겨서 난쟁이를 풀어주었다.

6 "너는 보상을 받게 될 거야. 원하는게 뭐니?"

7 "나는 네가 사람의 젊음을 유지해 주는 마법의 돌들을 가지고 있다고 들었어. 나는 그것을 원해."

8 "오, 너희 인간들은 잘못 알고 있어. 그 돌들은 너희들이 다시 젊어지게 해 주지 않아. 단지 더 늙지 않게 막아 줄 뿐이라고."

9 "그것대로 좋아!" Doli는 그 돌에 관한 문제를 설명하려고 했지만, Maibon은 듣지 않았다.

10 그래서 Doli는 그에게 마법의 돌을 건네고는 가버렸다.

11 며칠이 지나서, Maibon은 그의 수염이 전혀 자라지 않았음을 알았다.

12 그는 행복해졌지만, 그의 아내 Modrona는 화가 났다.

13 "달걀이 닭이 되지 않아요!" "아, 시기가 더딘 거예요. 그 뿐이에요."

14 하지만 그녀는 탐탁해하지 않았다. "소가 새끼를 낳지 않아요!" 그때 Maibon은 그 돌에 대해 그녀에게 이야기를 했고 그녀는 매우 화를 내며 그에게 그것을 버리라고 말했다.

15 그는 원하지 않았지만, 아내의 말을 듣고 창밖으로 돌을 던졌다.

16 그러나 다음날 아침 그는 창가에 그 돌이 있는 것을 발견했다!

17 Maibon was _____ _____ the animals, but he was _____ _____ he was still young.

18 Now Maibon's baby was _____ _____ . No tooth was _____ in his mouth.

19 His wife told him _____ _____ _____ the stone and this time, Maibon _____ the stone _____ the ground.

20 But, the next day, the stone _____ _____ ! Time _____ _____ and nothing _____ or _____ .

21 Maibon began _____ _____ . "There's _____ _____ _____ _____ _____ , nothing to show for my work."

22 Maibon tried _____ _____ the stone, but it kept _____ _____ .

23 Maibon decided _____ _____ _____ _____ the stone _____ _____ his house.

24 _____ his way _____ the field, he saw the dwarf. Maibon _____ _____ with him.

25 "Why _____ _____ _____ me about the stone?"

26 "I tried to, but you wouldn't _____ ."

27 Doli _____ that Maibon couldn't _____ _____ the stone _____ he really wanted to.

28 "I want _____ _____ _____ it. _____ may happen, _____ it _____ !"

29 Doli told him _____ _____ the stone _____ the ground and go back home.

30 Maibon _____ as Doli _____ . When he _____ home, Modrona told him the good news — the eggs _____ _____ chickens and the cow _____ her baby.

31 And Maibon _____ _____ _____ _____ when he saw the first tooth in his baby's mouth.

32 Maibon, Modrona and their children and grandchildren _____ _____ many years.

33 Maibon _____ _____ his white hair and long beard.

17 Maibon은 동물들이 걱정되긴 했지만, 자신이 여전히 젊어서 기뻤다.

18 이제 Maibon의 아기에게 문제가 생겼다. 아기의 입에서 이가 보이지 않았다.

19 그의 아내는 그에게 그 돌을 버리라고 말했고 Maibon은 이번엔 그 돌을 땅속에 묻었다.

20 그런데 그 다음날 그 돌은 다시 돌아왔다! 시간이 흘렀고 어떤 것도 자라거나 변하지 않았다.

21 Maibon은 걱정이 되기 시작했다. "기대할 것도 내 일의 결과를 보여 줄 것도 아무것도 없어."

22 Maibon은 그 돌을 없애려고 노력했지만 돌은 계속 되돌아왔다.

23 Maibon은 그 돌을 그의 집에서 멀리 떨어진 곳에 버리기로 결심했다.

24 그는 들판으로 가는 길에 난쟁이를 보았다. Maibon은 그에게 화를 냈다.

25 "너는 왜 내게 그 돌에 대해 경고하지 않았어?"

26 "나는 하려고 했지만, 너는 들으려 하지 않았어."

27 Doli는 Maibon이 진심으로 원하지 않는 한 그 돌을 없앨 수 없다고 설명했다.

28 "나는 그것을 더 이상 원하지 않아. 무슨 일이 있어도 일어나게 해!"

29 Doli는 그에게 그 돌을 땅에 던지고 집으로 돌아가라고 말했다.

30 Maibon은 Doli가 말한 대로 했다. 그가 집에 도착했을 때, Modrona는 그에게 달걀이 닭이 되고 소가 새끼를 낳았다는 좋은 소식을 말해 주었다.

31 그리고 Maibon은 아기의 입에 첫 이가 난 것을 보고 기뻐서 웃었다.

32 Maibon과 Modrona, 그리고 그들의 자녀들과 손주들은 오랫동안 살았다.

33 Maibon은 그의 흰 머리와 긴 수염을 자랑스러워했다.

• 우리말을 참고하여 본문을 영작하시오.

1 어느 날, Maibon이 한 노인을 보았을 때, 그는 마차를 타고 길을 내려가고 있던 중이었다.

➡ _____

2 그 노인은 매우 아파 보였다. Maibon은 늙어 가는 것이 걱정되기 시작했다.

➡ _____

3 그날 오후, 그는 들판에서 Doli라는 난쟁이를 보았다.

➡ _____

4 그는 통나무 아래에 깔린 그의 다리를 빼내려고 하고 있었다.

➡ _____

5 Maibon은 통나무를 잡아당겨서 난쟁이를 풀어 주었다.

➡ _____

6 "너는 보상을 받게 될 거야. 원하는 게 뭐니?"

➡ _____

7 "나는 네가 사람의 젊음을 유지해 주는 마법의 돌들을 가지고 있다고 들었어. 나는 그것을 원해."

➡ _____

8 오, 너희 인간들은 잘못 알고 있어. 그 돌들은 너희들이 다시 젊어지게 해 주지 않아. 단지 더 늙지 않게 막아 줄 뿐이라고."

➡ _____

➡ _____

9 "그것대로 좋아!" Doli는 그 돌에 관한 문제를 설명하려고 했지만, Maibon은 듣지 않았다.

➡ _____

10 그래서 Doli는 그에게 마법의 돌을 건네고는 가버렸다.

➡ _____

11 며칠이 지나서, Maibon은 그의 수염이 전혀 자라지 않았음을 알았다.

➡ _____

12 그는 행복해졌지만, 그의 아내 Modrona는 화가 났다.

➡ _____

13 "달걀이 닭이 되지 않아요!" "아, 시기가 더딘 거예요. 그 뿐이에요."

➡ _____

14 하지만 그녀는 탐탁해하지 않았다. "소가 새끼를 낳지 않아요!" 그때 Maibon은 그 돌에 대해 그녀에게 이야기를 했고 그녀는 매우 화를 내며 그에게 그것을 버리라고 말했다.

➡ _____

➡ _____

15 그는 원하지 않았지만, 아내의 말을 듣고 창밖으로 돌을 던졌다.

➡ _____

16 그러나 다음날 아침 그는 창가에 그 돌이 있는 것을 발견했다!

➡ _____

17 Maibon은 동물들이 걱정되긴 했지만, 자신이 여전히 젊어서 기뻤다.

➡ _____

18 이제 Maibon의 아기에게 문제가 생겼다. 아기의 입에서 이가 보이지 않았다.

➡ _____

19 그의 아내는 그에게 그 돌을 버리라고 말했고 Maibon은 이번엔 그 돌을 땅속에 묻었다.

➡ _____

20 그런데 그 다음날 그 돌은 다시 돌아왔다! 시간이 흘렀고 어떤 것도 자라거나 변하지 않았다.

➡ _____

21 Maibon은 걱정이 되기 시작했다. "기대할 것도 내 일의 결과를 보여 줄 것도 아무것도 없어."

➡ _____

22 Maibon은 그 돌을 없애려고 노력했지만 돌은 계속 되돌아왔다.

➡ _____

23 Maibon은 그 돌을 그의 집에서 멀리 떨어진 곳에 버리기로 결심했다.

➡ _____

24 그는 들판으로 가는 길에 난쟁이를 보았다. Maibon은 그에게 화를 냈다.

➡ _____

25 "너는 왜 내게 그 돌에 대해 경고하지 않았어?"

➡ _____

26 "나는 하려고 했지만, 너는 들으려 하지 않았어."

➡ _____

27 Doli는 Maibon이 진심으로 원하지 않는 한 그 돌을 없앨 수 없다고 설명했다.

➡ _____

28 "나는 그것을 더 이상 원하지 않아. 무슨 일이 있어도 일어나게 해!"

➡ _____

29 Doli는 그에게 그 돌을 땅에 던지고 집으로 돌아가라고 말했다.

➡ _____

30 Maibon은 Doli가 말한 대로 했다. 그가 집에 도착했을 때, Modrona는 그에게 달걀이 닭이 되고 소가 새끼를 낳았다는 좋은 소식을 말해 주었다.

➡ _____

➡ _____

31 그리고 Maibon은 아기의 입에 첫 이가 난 것을 보고 기뻐서 웃었다.

➡ _____

32 Maibon과 Modrona, 그리고 그들의 자녀들과 손주들은 오랫동안 살았다.

➡ _____

33 Maibon은 그의 흰 머리와 긴 수염을 자랑스러워했다.

➡ _____

01 다음 주어진 우리말과 의미가 같도록 빈칸을 완성하시오.

(1) 그녀는 아들을 낳았고 그를 Tony라고 불렀다.
➡ She _____ a son and called him Tony.

(2) 수염이 있는 그 남자는 내가 가장 좋아하는 배우이다.
➡ The man with a _____ is my favorite actor.

(3) 농부들은 들판에서 쌀을 재배한다.
➡ Farmers grow rice in the _____.

(4) 내 친구의 집은 통나무로 만들어졌다.
➡ My friend's house is made of _____.

02 다음 문장의 빈칸에 들어갈 말을 〈보기〉에서 골라 알맞은 형태로 쓰시오.

┌── 보기 ──┐
throw away / change into /
worry about / go by / go away
└──────────┘

(1) I hope this year _____ _____ quickly.

(2) She _____ _____ without saying goodbye yesterday.

(3) _____ _____ garbage in the trash can.

(4) Parents always _____ _____ their children's safety.

(5) It can _____ _____ different types of clothes.

03 다음 우리말을 주어진 단어를 사용하여 영작하시오.

(1) 나는 나의 나쁜 습관들을 없애기 위해 노력한다. (try, rid)
➡ _____

(2) 나의 선생님은 우리가 학교에서 휴대폰을 사용하지 못하게 하신다. (cell, keeps)
➡ _____
_____

(3) 나의 이모는 귀여운 아기를 낳았다. (cute, gave)
➡ _____

04 주어진 단어를 이용하여 우리말을 영어로 옮기시오.

(1) 그들은 우리에게 그 컴퓨터를 사용하지 말라고 말했다. (tell)
➡ _____

(2) 나는 이번 주말에 삼촌을 방문할 계획이야. (plan)
➡ _____

05 다음 문장을 능동태는 수동태로, 수동태는 능동태로 전환하시오.

(1) David repaired my car yesterday.
➡ _____

(2) The man on the street was hit by a car.
➡ _____

One day, Maibon was driving down the road on his horse and cart when he saw an old man. The old man looked very sick. Maibon began to worry about growing old.
(A) Maibon pulled the log away and freed the dwarf. "You'll have your reward. What do you want?"
(B) "Just as good!" Doli tried to explain the problem with the stones, but Maibon didn't listen.
(C) "I've heard that you have magic stones that can keep a man young. I want ⓐone."
(D) Later that day, he saw a dwarf, Doli, in the field. He was trying to get his leg out from under a log.
(E) "Oh, you humans have it all wrong. Those stones don't make you young again. They only keep you from getting older."
So Doli handed him a magic stone and went away.

06 자연스러운 글이 되도록 (A)~(E)를 바르게 배열하시오.

➡ _____

07 How did the old man look? Answer in English with a full sentence.

➡ _____

08 What did Maibon worry about? Answer in English with five words.

➡ _____

09 What is the name of the dwarf?

➡ _____

10 밑줄 친 ⓐ가 의미하는 것을 우리말로 쓰시오.

➡ _____

[11~13] 다음 글을 읽고, 물음에 답하시오.

After a few days, Maibon saw that his beard didn't grow at all. He became happy, but his wife, Modrona, got upset. "The eggs don't change into chickens!" "Oh, the season's slow, that's all." But she was not happy. "The cow doesn't give birth!" Maibon, then, told her about the stone, and she got very angry and told him to throw it away. (A)He didn't want to, but he listened to his wife and threw the stone out the window. However, the next morning, he found the stone sitting by the window! Maibon was worried about the animals, but he was glad that he was still young.

11 Who is Modrona?

➡ _____

12 밑줄 친 문장 (A)를 생략된 말을 보충하여 다시 쓰시오.

➡ _____

13 After throwing away the stone, what did Maibon find the next morning?

➡ _____

01 다음 밑줄 친 단어의 뜻이 바르지 <u>않은</u> 것은?

① The best student will receive a <u>reward</u>. 보상

② <u>Unless</u> you buy a ticket, you can't enter this museum. ~하지 않으면

③ We sometimes have <u>trouble</u> with our friends. 문제

④ Teachers <u>warned</u> us not to cheat on the test. 경고했다

⑤ The police decided to <u>free</u> the man. 자유로운

02 다음 문장의 빈칸에 공통으로 들어갈 말로 적절한 것은?

- Mike couldn't _____ the pain caused by the disease.
- Stephanie was not able to _____ children anymore.
- Mike was as strong as the _____ when he was young.

① bear ② free ③ hand
④ stand ⑤ reward

03 다음 문장의 빈칸에 들어갈 말을 〈보기〉에서 골라 적절한 형태로 쓰시오.

┌─ 보기 ─┐
reward / trouble / warn / glad / hand

(1) My aunt _____ed me not to leave my cousin alone.

(2) Would you _____ the salt to me?

(3) You won't get any _____s as long as you don't do chore.

(4) My heart is full of _____.

(5) I'm _____ that you have come here.

04 다음 영영풀이가 나타내는 말을 고르시오.

hair that grows on the chin and cheeks of a man's face

① beard ② delight
③ log ④ field
⑤ cart

05 다음 우리말을 주어진 단어를 사용하여 영작하시오.

(1) 나는 이 의자가 필요 없어. 그것을 버리자. (away, let)

➡ _____

(2) 내 고향은 서울로부터 멀지 않아요. (far, hometown)

➡ _____

(3) 나는 홍콩 방문을 기대하고 있다. (forward, visiting)

➡ _____

(4) 나는 학교 가는 길에, 외국인을 만났다. (way, on)

➡ _____

(5) 해가 갈수록, 일이 더 어려워진다. (go, as)

➡ _____

06 다음 중 어법상 바르지 <u>않은</u> 것은?

① Tell me how she is doing.

② The boy crying over there is my brother.

③ Did you know that they would come here?

④ They made her so angrily.

⑤ We made you do your best.

출제율 90%

07 다음 두 문장을 하나의 문장으로 쓰시오.

> • Paul met a woman.
> • She knew Ann's best friend.

➡ _____

출제율 95%

08 다음 빈칸에 들어갈 말로 알맞지 <u>않은</u> 것은?

> Brandy's parents _____ her go to the party.

① helped   ② made   ③ told
④ had   ⑤ let

출제율 90%

09 다음 중 밑줄 친 부분의 쓰임이 <u>다른</u> 하나는?

① They need <u>to do</u> something special.
② Did you decide <u>to go</u> to the field trip?
③ I would like <u>to throw</u> a party for you.
④ They have nothing <u>to tell</u> you.
⑤ Do you want <u>to give</u> her a present?

출제율 100%

10 다음 중 주어진 문장의 밑줄 친 부분과 쓰임이 <u>다른</u> 하나는?

> Did you hear <u>that</u> Michael made her cry?

① I thought <u>that</u> he needed to hear what others said.
② Is it true <u>that</u> Ms. James is our homeroom teacher?
③ The fact <u>that</u> she helped us doesn't change.
④ Don't say <u>that</u> you can't do it.
⑤ The letter <u>that</u> he sent to you is on the table.

출제율 90%

11 주어진 단어를 활용하여 다음 우리말을 여섯 단어로 이루어진 한 문장으로 쓰시오.

> 그녀는 그녀의 삶에 관하여 계속 말했다.
> (keep / talk)

➡ _____

출제율 90%

12 다음 주어진 동사를 어법에 맞게 빈칸에 쓰시오.

(1) 마실 무언가를 주세요. (drink)
➡ Please give me something _____
_____.

(2) 너에게 할 말이 있어. (say)
➡ I have something _____ _____
to you.

출제율 85%

13 다음 우리말에 맞게 빈칸에 알맞은 말을 쓰시오.

(1) 그녀는 나에게 두 송이의 꽃을 건넸다.
➡ She _____ _____ _____ _____.

(2) 한 선생님은 우리에게 피자를 사 주셨다.
➡ Mr. Han _____ _____ _____.

[14~20] 다음 글을 읽고, 물음에 답하시오.

One day, Maibon was driving down the road on his horse and cart when he saw an old man. ① The old man looked very sick. Maibon began to worry about growing old. ② Later that day, he saw a dwarf, Doli, in the field. ③ Maibon pulled the log away and freed the dwarf. ④ "You'll have your reward. What do you want?" "I've heard that you have magic stones that can keep a man young. I want one." ⑤ "Oh, you humans have it all wrong. Those stones don't make you young again. They only keep you from getting older." "Just as good!" Doli tried to explain the problem with the stones, but Maibon didn't listen. So Doli handed him a magic stone and went away.

14 출제율 95% 다음 중 주어진 문장이 들어가기에 가장 적절한 곳은?

He was trying to get his leg out from under a log.

①   ②   ③   ④   ⑤

15 출제율 100% 다음 중 위 글을 읽고 답할 수 없는 것은?

① Where did Maibon see Doli?
② What did Maibon do for Doli?
③ What did Maibon want from Doli?
④ How many stones did Doli give Maibon?
⑤ Why did Doli go to the field?

16 출제율 85% What did Doli do after he gave a stone to Maibon? Answer in English.

➡ _____

17 출제율 90% What was Maibon doing when he saw an old man? Answer in English.

➡ _____

18 출제율 95% 다음 중 위 글의 내용과 일치하지 <u>않는</u> 것은?

① Maibon met a dwarf on the same day that he saw an old man.
② Maibon came to worry about growing old because of an old man.
③ The name of a dwarf is Doli.
④ Maibon wanted to give reward to the dwarf.
⑤ There was a problem with the magic stone.

19 출제율 85% 다음 물음에 알맞은 답을 하시오.

Q: Does the stone make people young?
A: _____, _____
_____.

20 출제율 95% What did Doli try to explain? Answer in English with a full sentence.

➡ _____

[21~28] 다음 글을 읽고, 물음에 답하시오.

After a few days, Maibon saw that his beard didn't grow at all. He became happy, but his wife, Modrona, got upset. "The eggs don't change into chickens!" "Oh, the season's slow, that's all." But she was not happy. "The cow doesn't give birth!" Maibon, then, told her about the stone, and she got very angry and told him to throw it away. He didn't want to, but he listened to his wife and threw the stone out the window. ___(A)___, the next morning, he found the stone sitting ___(B)___ the window! Maibon was worried about the animals, but he was glad that he was still young.

Now Maibon's baby was having trouble. No tooth was seen in his mouth. His wife told him to throw away the stone and this time, Maibon put the stone under the ground. But, the next day, the stone came back! Time went ___(C)___ and nothing grew or changed. Maibon began to worry. "There's nothing to look forward to, nothing to show for my work." Maibon tried to destroy the stone, but it kept ___(D)___.

21 다음 중 빈칸 (A)에 들어갈 말로 가장 적절한 것은?

① Therefore ② However
③ Luckily ④ For example
⑤ In contrast

22 다음 빈칸 (B)와 (C)에 공통으로 들어갈 말로 적절한 것은?

① on ② to ③ by
④ in ⑤ for

23 위 글의 빈칸 (D)에 들어갈 말을 위 글에서 찾아 어법에 맞게 쓰시오.

➡ _____

24 Which are NOT true about the passage? Select all.

① The cow didn't give birth because of the stone.
② As his wife said, Maibon threw the stone away.
③ Although his baby had a trouble, Maibon didn't throw the stone away.
④ As nothing grew and changed, Maibon began to worry.
⑤ When Maibon tried to throw the stone away for the second time, he threw it out the window.

25 What trouble did Maibon's baby have?

➡ _____

26 What did Doli try to explain? Answer in English with a full sentence.

➡ _____

27 Write the reason why Maibon was glad even though he was worried about the animals. Use the phrase 'it's because.'

➡ _____

28 주어진 어구를 바르게 배열하여 위 글의 내용에 맞게 답변을 완성하시오.

> A: Did Maibon succeed in destroying the stone?
>
> B: _____
>
> (tried to / failed / it / he / he / no / but / to / destroy)

[29~35] 다음 글을 읽고 물음에 답하시오.

Maibon decided ___(A)___ away the stone far from his house. On ①his way to the field, he saw the dwarf. Maibon got angry with ②him. "Why didn't you warn me about the stone?" "I tried to, but you wouldn't listen." Doli explained that Maibon couldn't get rid of the stone unless ③he really wanted to. "I want no more of it. Whatever may happen, let it ___(B)___ !" Doli told ④him to throw the stone onto the ground and go back home. Maibon did as Doli said. When ⑤he arrived home, Modrona told him the good news — the eggs changed into chickens and the cow bore her baby. And Maibon laughed with delight when he saw the first tooth in his baby's mouth. Maibon, Modrona and their children and grandchildren lived for many years. Maibon was proud of his white hair and long beard.

29 다음 중 빈칸 (A)와 (B)에 들어갈 말이 바르게 짝지어진 것은?

① throwing – happen
② throwing – to happen
③ throw – happen
④ to throw – happened
⑤ to throw – happen

30 위 글의 ①~⑤ 중 지칭하는 것이 다른 하나는?

①   ②   ③   ④   ⑤

31 다음 중 Maibon의 감정 변화로 가장 적절한 것은?

① upset → sad
② angry → lonely
③ happy → scared
④ angry → delighted
⑤ pleased → relieved

32 What did Doli tell Maibon to do? Answer in English with a full sentence.

➡ _____

_____

33 Why couldn't Maibon get rid of the stone? Use the word 'because.' (6 words)

➡ _____

34 위 글의 내용에 맞게 다음 물음에 완전한 문장의 영어로 답하시오.

Q: Why did Maibon laugh with delight at home?

A: _____

35 What was Maibon proud of?

➡ _____

INSIGHT
on the textbook

교과서 파헤치기

Step1

※ 다음 영어를 우리말로 쓰시오.

01	prince	
02	classical	
03	melt	
04	produce	
05	direction	
06	exhibit	
07	feather	
08	artist	
09	promise	
10	brush	
11	landscape	
12	novel	
13	despite	
14	art work	
15	teen	
16	maze	
17	production	
18	notice	
19	wonder	
20	flat	
21	seaside	

22	detail	
23	tragedy	
24	prefer	
25	wing	
26	modern	
27	queen	
28	rock	
29	real	
30	novelist	
31	since	
32	myth	
33	tourist	
34	version	
35	wax	
36	canvas	
37	prefer A to B	
38	loot at	
39	glance at	
40	stay away from	
41	right away	
42	take a look	
43	move on	

※ 다음 우리말을 영어로 쓰시오.

01	녹다	
02	생산하다	
03	깃털	
04	날개	
05	방향	
06	왕비, 여왕	
07	예술가	
08	붓	
09	왕자	
10	전시하다	
11	개구리	
12	미로	
13	약속하다	
14	소설	
15	~에도 불구하고	
16	현대의	
17	납작한	
18	십 대	
19	~을 알아차리다	
20	풍경	
21	예술 작품	

22	(어떤 것의) 변형	
23	세부 사항	
24	신화	
25	생산	
26	비극	
27	더 좋아하다	
28	궁금해하다	
29	진짜의, 현실적인	
30	화폭, 캔버스	
31	관광객	
32	밀랍, 왁스	
33	록 음악	
34	소설가	
35	희극	
36	~ 때문에, ~이므로	
37	해변, 바닷가	
38	~로 이동하다, 넘어가다	
39	A를 B보다 더 좋아하다	
40	~을 힐끗 보다	
41	~을 보다	
42	~을 가까이하지 않다	
43	즉시, 바로	

※ 다음 영영풀이에 알맞은 단어를 <보기>에서 골라 쓴 후, 우리말 뜻을 쓰시오.

1 _____ : one of the light soft things that cover a bird's body: _____

2 _____ : an area that is close to the sea: _____

3 _____ : to change from a solid to a liquid by applying heat: _____

4 _____ : a very sad event, especially one involving death: _____

5 _____ : the way something or someone moves, faces, or is aimed: _____

6 _____ : to want to know more about something because it interests you:
_____

7 _____ : an area of countryside, especially in relation to its appearance:
_____

8 _____ : to see or become conscious of something or someone: _____

9 _____ : to put it in a position where other people can see a part of your body:
_____

10 _____ : someone who produces art: _____

11 _____ : one of the parts of a bird's or insect's body that it uses for flying:
_____

12 _____ : a single piece of some information of fact about something: _____

13 _____ : to show something in a public place for people to enjoy or to give them
information: _____

14 _____ : a kind of popular music with a strong beat that is played on instruments
that are made louder electronically: _____

15 _____ : a piece of thick cloth used by artists for painting on, usually with oil
paints, or the painting itself: _____

16 _____ : an ancient story, especially one invented in order to explain natural or
historical events: _____

보기			
canvas	melt	seaside	landscape
wonder	myth	notice	wing
direction	stick	artist	tragedy
feather	rock	detail	exhibit

※ 다음 우리말과 일치하도록 빈칸에 알맞은 말을 쓰시오.

Listen & Talk 1 A-1

W: Brian, is your band _____ _____ _____ at the Teen Music Festival?

M: Yes, we're _____ _____ _____ _____.

W: _____ _____ _____ _____ are you going to play this year?

M: Rock music. We'll _____ _____ from the _____.

W: Brian, 너희 밴드는 '십 대 음악 축제' 에서 연주할 거야?
M: 응, 우리는 거의 매일 연습하고 있어.
W: 너희는 올해 어떤 종류의 음악을 연주하려고 해?
M: 록 음악. 우리는 90년대 곡들을 연주할 거야.

Listen & Talk 1 A-2

W: Can you help me? I don't know _____ _____ _____ _____ _____.

M: _____ _____ _____ _____ were you _____?

W: This _____ _____.

M: _____ you _____ lines, a _____ brush is _____. _____ this one.

W: Okay, thank you.

W: 나 좀 도와줄래? 나는 선을 깔끔하게 그리는 방법을 모르겠어.
M: 어떤 종류의 붓을 사용하고 있었니?
W: 이 둥근 붓이야.
M: 선을 그릴 때는 납작한 붓이 더 나아. 이것을 써 봐.
W: 알았어, 고마워.

Listen & Talk 1 B

W: (ringing) Hello, Steve.

M: Hi, Anna. We're _____ at the arts festival tomorrow at 1:30, _____?

W: Right. What kind of _____ _____ _____ _____ _____ _____?

M: I _____ _____ watch the hip-hop dance _____ first.

W: _____ good. It's at 2 p.m. at the gym, _____?

M: Yeah, and how _____ _____ _____ _____, Romeo and Juliet, at 4 p.m.?

W: Oh, _____ _____ at the Main Hall _____ the gym? Sure!

W: (전화벨 소리) 안녕, Steve.
M: 안녕, Anna. 우리 내일 1시 30분에 예술 축제에서 만나는 거 맞지?
W: 맞아. 먼저 어떤 종류의 공연을 보고 싶어?
M: 난 힙합 댄스 공연을 먼저 보고 싶어.
W: 좋은 생각이야. 체육관에서 오후 2시에 하는 거 맞지?
M: 응, 그리고 오후 4시에 '로미오와 줄리엣' 연극을 보는 건 어때?
W: 아, 체육관 근처 대강당에서 하는 연극 말이지? 좋아!

Listen & Talk 2 A-1

M: What _____ you _____, Jina?

W: The novel, Life of Pi. It's _____ _____ of a boy and a tiger.

M: It's a great book. I've _____ the movie _____ _____, _____. I _____ the movie _____ the novel.

W: _____ do you _____ it _____?

M: The _____ are very beautiful. And the tiger _____ so _____.

M: 지나야, 너 무엇을 읽고 있니?
W: '파이 이야기'라는 소설이야. 한 소년과 호랑이에 대한 이야기이지.
M: 훌륭한 책이야. 나는 그것을 영화로도 봤어. 나는 소설보다는 영화가 더 좋아.
W: 왜 영화가 더 좋은데?
M: 장면이 매우 아름다워. 그리고 호랑이가 매우 진짜같이 보이거든.

Listen & Talk 2 A-2

W: _____ you _____ to Jane's new song, *Girl Friend*?

M: Yeah, it's really _____. The guitar _____ is _____.

W: There is also a _____ _____ of the song on the album.

M: I've _____ _____ it, but _____ _____ _____ _____ _____ to the dance version. It _____ her voice _____.

W: 너는 Jane의 새 노래인 '여자 친구'를 들어 봤니?

M: 응, 정말 멋져. 기타 부분이 굉장하지.

W: 앨범에는 그 노래의 댄스 버전도 있어.

M: 나는 그것을 들었는데 댄스 버전보다는 기타 버전이 더 좋아. 그 버전이 그녀의 목소리와 더 잘 어울리거든.

Listen & Talk 2 B

W: I saw an _____ _____ in an art book. _____ _____ this.

M: Wow, it _____ _____ da Vinci's *Mona Lisa*.

W: Actually, it's *Mona Lisa* by Fernando Botero. _____ _____ _____ _____?

M: I _____ da Vinci's _____ Botero's. Da Vinci's *Mona Lisa* has an interesting _____. _____ _____ _____?

W: Well, I _____ Botero's _____ da Vinci's. His *Mona Lisa* is cute, and it _____ _____.

W: 나 미술 책에서 흥미로운 그림을 봤어. 이것 봐.

M: 와, 그것은 다빈치의 '모나리자'처럼 보이는데.

W: 사실 이 그림은 페르난도 보테로의 '모나리자'야. 넌 어느 것이 더 마음에 드니?

M: 나는 보테로의 그림보다 다빈치의 모나리자가 더 좋아. 다빈치의 '모나리자'에는 흥미로운 미소가 있어. 너는 어때?

W: 음, 나는 다빈치의 모나리자보다는 보테로의 모나리자가 더 좋아. 그의 '모나리자'는 귀엽고 현대적으로 보여.

Communication

M: Hi, we _____ _____ a school festival, _____ we want to _____ _____ students' favorite types of performances. _____ I _____ you _____ _____ _____ _____?

W: Sure.

M: _____ _____ _____ _____ _____ _____ do you like best?

W: I like music _____ _____ _____.

M: Okay. Then, which _____ you _____, rock or hip-hop?

W: I _____ _____ _____ _____ _____.

M: Who's your _____ _____?

W: My _____ _____ is TJ.

M: Great. _____ you _____ your answers.

M: 안녕하세요, 저희는 학교 축제를 계획 중이고, 그래서 학생들이 어떤 종류의 공연을 좋아하는지 알고 싶습니다. 몇 가지 질문을 해도 될까요?

W: 물론이죠.

M: 어떤 종류의 공연을 가장 좋아하나요?

W: 저는 음악 공연을 가장 좋아해요.

M: 알겠습니다. 그러면 록과 힙합 중 어떤 것을 더 좋아하나요?

W: 저는 힙합보다 록을 더 좋아해요.

M: 가장 좋아하는 뮤지션은 누구인가요?

W: 제가 가장 좋아하는 뮤지션은 TJ입니다.

M: 좋습니다. 답변해 주셔서 감사합니다.

Wrap Up 1

M: _____ you _____ me? I want _____ _____ a guitar.

W: There are _____ _____ of guitars. _____ _____ _____ _____ do you want _____ _____?

M: I _____ _____ play pop songs.

W: Then you _____ _____ a classical guitar.

M: Okay, I will _____ a _____ _____.

M: 저 좀 도와주시겠어요? 저는 기타를 하나 사고 싶어요.

W: 다양한 종류의 기타가 있어요. 어떤 종류의 음악을 연주하고 싶으신가요?

M: 저는 팝송을 연주하려고 해요.

W: 그럼 클래식 기타를 사셔야 해요.

M: 알겠습니다, 클래식 기타로 살게요.

※ 다음 우리말에 맞도록 대화를 영어로 쓰시오.

Listen & Talk 1 A-1

W: _____

M: _____

W: _____

M: _____

W: Brian, 너희 밴드는 '십 대 음악 축제'에서 연주할 거야?
M: 응, 우리는 거의 매일 연습하고 있어.
W: 너희는 올해 어떤 종류의 음악을 연주하려고 해?
M: 록 음악. 우리는 90년대 곡들을 연주할 거야.

Listen & Talk 1 A-2

W: _____

M: _____

W: _____

M: _____

W: _____

W: 나 좀 도와줄래? 나는 선을 깔끔하게 그리는 방법을 모르겠어.
M: 어떤 종류의 붓을 사용하고 있었니?
W: 이 둥근 붓이야.
M: 선을 그릴 때는 납작한 붓이 더 나아. 이것을 써 봐.
W: 알았어, 고마워.

Listen & Talk 1 B

W: _____

M: _____

W: _____

M: _____

W: _____

M: _____

W: _____

W: (전화벨 소리) 안녕, Steve.
M: 안녕, Anna. 우리 내일 1시 30분에 예술 축제에서 만나는 거 맞지?
W: 맞아. 먼저 어떤 종류의 공연을 보고 싶어?
M: 난 힙합 댄스 공연을 먼저 보고 싶어.
W: 좋은 생각이야. 체육관에서 오후 2시에 하는 거 맞지?
M: 응, 그리고 오후 4시에 '로미오와 줄리엣' 연극을 보는 건 어때?
W: 아, 체육관 근처 대강당에서 하는 연극 말이지? 좋아!

Listen & Talk 2 A-1

M: _____

W: _____

M: _____

W: _____

M: _____

M: 지나야, 너 무엇을 읽고 있니?
W: '파이 이야기'라는 소설이야. 한 소년과 호랑이에 대한 이야기이지.
M: 훌륭한 책이야. 나는 그것을 영화로도 봤어. 나는 소설보다는 영화가 더 좋아.
W: 왜 영화가 더 좋은데?
M: 장면이 매우 아름다워. 그리고 호랑이가 매우 진짜같이 보이거든.

Listen & Talk 2 A-2

W: _____

M: _____

W: _____

M: _____
_____

W: 너는 Jane의 새 노래인 '여자 친구'를 들어 봤니?
M: 응, 정말 멋져. 기타 부분이 굉장하지.
W: 앨범에는 그 노래의 댄스 버전도 있어.
M: 나는 그것을 들었는데 댄스 버전보다는 기타 버전이 더 좋아. 그 버전이 그녀의 목소리와 더 잘 어울리거든.

Listen & Talk 2 B

W: _____

M: _____

W: _____

M: _____
_____

W: _____

W: 나 미술 책에서 흥미로운 그림을 봤어. 이것 봐.
M: 와, 그것은 다빈치의 '모나리자'처럼 보이는데.
W: 사실 이 그림은 페르난도 보테로의 '모나리자'야. 넌 어느 것이 더 마음에 드니?
M: 나는 보테로의 그림보다 다빈치의 모나리자가 더 좋아. 다빈치의 '모나리자'에는 흥미로운 미소가 있어. 너는 어때?
W: 음, 나는 다빈치의 모나리자보다는 보테로의 모나리자가 더 좋아. 그의 '모나리자'는 귀엽고 현대적으로 보여.

Communication

M: _____
_____

W: _____

M: _____

W: _____

M: _____

W: _____

M: _____

W: _____

M: _____

M: 안녕하세요, 저희는 학교 축제를 계획 중이고, 그래서 학생들이 어떤 종류의 공연을 좋아하는지 알고 싶습니다. 몇 가지 질문을 해도 될까요?
W: 물론이죠.
M: 어떤 종류의 공연을 가장 좋아하나요?
W: 저는 음악 공연을 가장 좋아해요.
M: 알겠습니다. 그러면 록과 힙합 중 어떤 것을 더 좋아하나요?
W: 저는 힙합보다 록을 더 좋아해요.
M: 가장 좋아하는 뮤지션은 누구인가요?
W: 제가 가장 좋아하는 뮤지션은 TJ입니다.
M: 좋습니다. 답변해 주셔서 감사합니다.

Wrap Up 1

M: _____

W: _____

M: _____

W: _____

M: _____

M: 저 좀 도와주시겠어요? 저는 기타를 하나 사고 싶어요.
W: 다양한 종류의 기타가 있어요. 어떤 종류의 음악을 연주하고 싶으신가요?
M: 저는 팝송을 연주하려고 해요.
W: 그럼 클래식 기타를 사셔야 해요.
M: 알겠습니다. 클래식 기타로 살게요.

※ 다음 우리말과 일치하도록 빈칸에 알맞은 것을 골라 쓰시오.

1 _____ _____ the World Art Museum _____.
A. tour   B. to   C. welcome

2 _____ you go to an art museum, how _____ time do you spend _____ at _____ painting?
A. much   B. looking   C. when   D. each

3 Many visitors _____ at one painting _____ only a _____ seconds before they move _____.
A. few   B. on   C. for   D. glance

4 But you _____ _____ the important details of paintings _____ it is hard to _____ them right away.
A. since   B. notice   C. miss   D. might

5 Today, we'll look _____ two paintings _____ and I'll _____ you _____ interesting details.
A. closely   B. see   C. at   D. help

6 _____ _____ this painting _____.
A. at   B. look   C. first

7 The _____ landscape is so _____ and beautiful, _____?
A. isn't   B. peaceful   C. seaside   D. it

8 The _____ of this painting _____ *Landscape* _____ *the Fall of Icarus*.
A. is   B. title   C. with

9 So, can you see _____ _____ _____?
A. Icarus   B. where   C. is

10 Do you see two legs _____ are _____ _____ of the water _____ the ship?
A. out   B. near   C. sticking   D. that

11 This is Icarus _____ the _____ _____ in Greece.
A. myth   B. famous   C. in

12 In the myth, Icarus' father made _____ for him with _____ and wax and told him to _____ _____ from the sun.
A. away   B. feathers   C. wings   D. stay

13 _____, Icarus _____ _____.
A. didn't   B. however   C. listen

14 He _____ too _____ _____ the sun.
A. close   B. flew   C. to

15 So, the wax _____ and he _____ _____ the water.
A. into   B. melted   C. fell

1 세계 미술관(the World Art Museum)에 오신 것을 환영합니다.

2 미술관에 갈 때 여러분은 각각의 그림을 보는 데 얼마나 많은 시간을 보내나요?

3 많은 방문객들은 이동하기 전에 하나의 그림을 몇 초간만 힐끗 봅니다.

4 하지만 그림의 중요한 세부 사항들을 즉시 알아채는 것은 어렵기 때문에 여러분들은 그것들을 놓칠 수 있습니다.

5 오늘 우리는 두 개의 그림을 자세히 살펴볼 것이고, 여러분이 흥미로운 세부 사항들을 볼 수 있도록 제가 도와드리겠습니다.

6 먼저 이 그림을 보세요.

7 바닷가 풍경이 매우 평화롭고 아름답죠, 그렇지 않나요?

8 이 그림의 제목은 '추락하는 이카루스가 있는 풍경'입니다.

9 그러면 이카루스가 어디에 있는지 보이나요?

10 배 근처에 물 밖으로 나와 있는 두 다리가 보이죠?

11 이것이 그리스의 유명한 신화에 나오는 이카루스입니다.

12 신화에서 이카루스의 아버지는 그를 위해 깃털과 밀랍으로 날개를 만들어 주었고 그에게 태양을 가까이 하지 말라고 말했습니다.

13 하지만 이카루스는 듣지 않았습니다.

14 그는 태양에 너무 가깝게 날았습니다.

15 그래서 밀랍이 녹았고 그는 물에 빠졌습니다.

16 Now, _____ _____ the _____ painting again.

A. at   B. entire   C. look

17 _____ the tragedy of Icarus, people are _____ _____ with their _____ activities.

A. on   B. despite   C. going   D. everyday

18 Does the painting _____ _____ _____?

A. look   B. still   C. peaceful

19 _____ do you _____ the artist is _____ to tell us?

A. trying   B. think   C. what

20 Now, let's _____ _____ _____ the next painting.

A. on   B. move   C. to

21 Do you _____ the artist _____ the _____ canvas?

A. behind   B. see   C. large

22 He is Diego Velázquez, and he _____ _____ this picture.

A. painted   B. actually

23 _____ do you _____ _____ _____ painting?

A. think   B. is   C. he   D. who

24 _____ a quick _____.

A. look   B. take

25 The young princess _____ _____ be the _____ person _____ she is in the center of the painting.

A. to   B. main   C. seems   D. because

26 But the _____ of the _____ is *The Maids of Honour*.

A. painting   B. title

27 Then, is the artist _____ the two women _____ the _____?

A. beside   B. drawing   C. princess

28 _____ a _____ look.

A. close   B. take

29 It will _____ _____ _____ about the painting more.

A. wonder   B. make   C. you

30 _____ to see _____ the artist is looking at.

A. direction   B. try   C. which

31 Can you _____ the king and the queen _____ the _____ in the _____ of the painting?

A. background   B. in   C. see   D. mirror

32 _____ do you _____ he _____ painting now?

A. is   B. think   C. who

---

16 이제, 그림 전체를 다시 보세요.

17 이카루스의 비극에도 불구하고 사람들은 일상의 활동을 계속하고 있습니다.

18 그림이 여전히 평화로워 보이나요?

19 화가가 우리에게 무엇을 말하려 한다고 생각하나요?

20 이제, 다음 그림으로 넘어갑시다.

21 커다란 캔버스 뒤에 있는 화가가 보이나요?

22 그는 Diego Velázquez이고, 그가 실제로 이 그림을 그렸습니다.

23 그가 누구를 그리고 있다고 생각하나요?

24 재빨리 봅시다.

25 어린 공주가 그림의 중앙에 있기 때문에 주인공처럼 보입니다.

26 하지만 그림의 제목은 '시녀들'입니다.

27 그렇다면 화가는 공주 옆에 있는 두 여인을 그리고 있나요?

28 자세히 보세요.

29 그림에 대해 더 궁금해하게 될 겁니다.

30 화가가 바라보고 있는 방향을 보려고 노력해 보세요.

31 그림의 배경에 있는 거울 속 왕과 왕비가 보이나요?

32 이제 여러분은 그가 누구를 그리고 있다고 생각하나요?

※ 다음 우리말과 일치하도록 빈칸에 알맞은 말을 쓰시오.

1 _____ _____ the World Art Museum _____ .

2 _____ you _____ _____ an art museum, _____ _____ _____ do you _____ _____ _____ each painting?

3 Many visitors _____ _____ one painting _____ only _____ _____ seconds before they _____ _____ .

4 But you _____ _____ the important details of paintings _____ it is hard _____ _____ _____ right away.

5 Today, we'll _____ _____ two paintings _____ and I'll _____ _____ _____ interesting _____ .

6 _____ _____ this painting _____ .

7 The _____ _____ is so _____ and beautiful, _____ _____?

8 The _____ _____ this painting _____ *Landscape with the Fall of Icarus.*

9 So, can you see _____ _____ _____ ?

10 Do you see two legs that _____ _____ _____ _____ _____ _____ _____ the ship?

11 This is Icarus _____ _____ _____ _____ in Greece.

12 In the myth, Icarus' father _____ _____ _____ _____ _____ _____ _____ and wax and told him _____ _____ _____ _____ the sun.

13 _____ , Icarus _____ _____ .

14 He _____ _____ _____ _____ to the sun.

15 So, the wax _____ and he _____ _____ the water.

1 세계 미술관(the World Art Museum)에 오신 것을 환영합니다.

2 미술관에 갈 때 여러분은 각각의 그림을 보는 데 얼마나 많은 시간을 보내나요?

3 많은 방문객들은 이동하기 전에 하나의 그림을 몇 초간만 힐끗 봅니다.

4 하지만 그림의 중요한 세부 사항들을 즉시 알아채는 것은 어렵기 때문에 여러분들은 그것들을 놓칠 수 있습니다.

5 오늘 우리는 두 개의 그림을 자세히 살펴볼 것이고, 여러분이 흥미로운 세부 사항들을 볼 수 있도록 제가 도와드리겠습니다.

6 먼저 이 그림을 보세요.

7 바닷가 풍경이 매우 평화롭고 아름답죠. 그렇지 않나요?

8 이 그림의 제목은 '추락하는 이카루스가 있는 풍경'입니다.

9 그러면 이카루스가 어디에 있는지 보이나요?

10 배 근처에 물 밖으로 나와 있는 두 다리가 보이죠?

11 이것이 그리스의 유명한 신화에 나오는 이카루스입니다.

12 신화에서 이카루스의 아버지는 그를 위해 깃털과 밀랍으로 날개를 만들어 주었고 그에게 태양을 가까이 하지 말라고 말했습니다.

13 하지만 이카루스는 듣지 않았습니다.

14 그는 태양에 너무 가깝게 날았습니다.

15 그래서 밀랍이 녹았고 그는 물에 빠졌습니다.

16 Now, _____ _____ the _____ painting again.

17 _____ the tragedy of Icarus, people are _____ _____ _____ their _____ _____.

18 Does the painting _____ _____ _____?

19 _____ _____ _____ _____ _____ the artist is _____ _____ tell us?

20 Now, let's _____ _____ _____ the next painting.

21 Do you _____ the artist _____ the large canvas?

22 He is Diego Velázquez, and he _____ _____ this picture.

23 _____ _____ _____ _____ _____ _____ _____ painting?

24 _____ a _____ _____.

25 The young princess _____ _____ _____ the main person _____ she is _____ _____ _____ of the painting.

26 But the _____ of the _____ is *The Maids of Honour*.

27 Then, is the artist _____ the two women _____ the princess?

28 _____ a _____ _____.

29 It will _____ _____ _____ about the painting more.

30 _____ _____ see _____ _____ _____ _____ _____ _____ looking at.

31 Can you _____ the king and the queen _____ _____ _____ in the _____ of the painting?

32 _____ _____ _____ _____ _____ _____ _____ _____ painting now?

---

16 이제, 그림 전체를 다시 보세요.

17 이카루스의 비극에도 불구하고 사람들은 일상의 활동을 계속하고 있습니다.

18 그림이 여전히 평화로워 보이나요?

19 화가가 우리에게 무엇을 말하려 한다고 생각하나요?

20 이제, 다음 그림으로 넘어갑시다.

21 커다란 캔버스 뒤에 있는 화가가 보이나요?

22 그는 Diego Velázquez이고, 그가 실제로 이 그림을 그렸습니다.

23 그가 누구를 그리고 있다고 생각하나요?

24 재빨리 봅시다.

25 어린 공주가 그림의 중앙에 있기 때문에 주인공처럼 보입니다.

26 하지만 그림의 제목은 '시녀들'입니다.

27 그렇다면 화가는 공주 옆에 있는 두 여인을 그리고 있나요?

28 자세히 보세요.

29 그림에 대해 더 궁금하게 될 겁니다.

30 화가가 바라보고 있는 방향을 보려고 노력해 보세요.

31 그림의 배경에 있는 거울 속 왕과 왕비가 보이나요?

32 이제 여러분은 그가 누구를 그리고 있다고 생각하나요?

※ 다음 문장을 우리말로 쓰시오.

1 Welcome to the World Art Museum tour.

➡ _____

2 When you go to an art museum, how much time do you spend looking at each painting?

➡ _____

3 Many visitors glance at one painting for only a few seconds before they move on.

➡ _____

4 But you might miss the important details of paintings since it is hard to notice them right away.

➡ _____

5 Today, we'll look at two paintings closely and I'll help you see interesting details.

➡ _____

6 Look at this painting first.

➡ _____

7 The seaside landscape is so peaceful and beautiful, isn't it?

➡ _____

8 The title of this painting is *Landscape with the Fall* of Icarus.

➡ _____

9 So, can you see where Icarus is?

➡ _____

10 Do you see two legs that are sticking out of the water near the ship?

➡ _____

11 This is Icarus in the famous myth in Greece.

➡ _____

12 In the myth, Icarus' father made wings for him with feathers and wax and told him to stay away from the sun.

➡ _____

_____

13 However, Icarus didn't listen.

➡ _____

14 He flew too close to the sun.

➡ _____

15 So, the wax melted and he fell into the water.

➡ _____

16 Now, look at the entire painting again.

➡ _____

17 Despite the tragedy of Icarus, people are going on with their everyday activities.

➡ _____

18 Does the painting still look peaceful?

➡ _____

19 What do you think the artist is trying to tell us?

➡ _____

20 Now, let's move on to the next painting.

➡ _____

21 Do you see the artist behind the large canvas?

➡ _____

22 He is Diego Velázquez, and he actually painted this picture.

➡ _____

23 Who do you think he is painting?

➡ _____

24 Take a quick look.

➡ _____

25 The young princess seems to be the main person because she is in the center of the painting.

➡ _____

26 But the title of the painting is *The Maids of Honour*.

➡ _____

27 Then, is the artist drawing the two women beside the princess?

➡ _____

28 Take a close look.

➡ _____

29 It will make you wonder about the painting more.

➡ _____

30 Try to see which direction the artist is looking at.

➡ _____

31 Can you see the king and the queen in the mirror in the background of the painting?

➡ _____

32 Who do you think he is painting now?

➡ _____

※ 다음 괄호 안의 단어들을 우리말에 맞도록 바르게 배열하시오.

1 (to / World / the / Welcome / tour. / Museum / Art)
➡ _____

2 (you / when / to / go / art / an / museum, / much / how / do / time / spend / you / at / looking / painting? / each)
➡ _____

3 (visitors / many / at / glance / painting / one / only / for / few / a / seconds / before / on. / move / they)
➡ _____

4 (you / but / miss / might / important / the / of / paintings / details / it / since / is / to / hard / them / notice / away. / right)
➡ _____

5 (today, / look / we'll / two / at / closely / paintings / and / help / I'll / see / you / details. / interesting)
➡ _____
_____

6 (at / look / first. / painting / this)
➡ _____

7 (seaside / the / is / landscape / peaceful / so / and / isn't / beautiful / it?)
➡ _____

8 (title / the / this / of / painting / is / *with* / *Landscape* / *the* / *Icarus.* / *of* / *Fall*)
➡ _____

9 (so, / you / can / see / Icarus / is? / where)
➡ _____

10 (you / do / see / legs / two / are / that / out / sticking / of / water / the / near / ship? / the)
➡ _____

11 (is / this / Icarus / in / famous / the / Greece. / in / myth)
➡ _____

12 (the / in / myth, / father / Icarus' / wings / made / him / for / feathers / with / wax / and / told / to / him / away / stay / from / sun. / the)
➡ _____

13 (Icarus / however, / listen. / didn't)
➡ _____

14 (flew / he / close / too / sun. / the / to)
➡ _____

15 (so, / wax / the / melted / and / fell / he / into / water. / the)
➡ _____

1 세계 미술관(the World Art Museum)에 오신 것을 환영합니다.

2 미술관에 갈 때 여러분은 각각의 그림을 보는 데 얼마나 많은 시간을 보내나요?

3 많은 방문객들은 이동하기 전에 하나의 그림을 몇 초간만 힐끗 봅니다.

4 하지만 그림의 중요한 세부 사항들을 즉시 알아채는 것은 어렵기 때문에 여러분들은 그것들을 놓칠 수 있습니다.

5 오늘 우리는 두 개의 그림을 자세히 살펴볼 것이고, 여러분이 흥미로운 세부 사항들을 볼 수 있도록 제가 도와드리겠습니다.

6 먼저 이 그림을 보세요.

7 바닷가 풍경이 매우 평화롭고 아름답죠, 그렇지 않나요?

8 이 그림의 제목은 '추락하는 이카루스가 있는 풍경'입니다.

9 그러면 이카루스가 어디에 있는지 보이나요?

10 배 근처에 물 밖으로 나와 있는 두 다리가 보이죠?

11 이것이 그리스의 유명한 신화에 나오는 이카루스입니다.

12 신화에서 이카루스의 아버지는 그를 위해 깃털과 밀랍으로 날개를 만들어 주었고 그에게 태양을 가까이 하지 말라고 말했습니다.

13 하지만 이카루스는 듣지 않았습니다.

14 그는 태양에 너무 가깝게 날았습니다.

15 그래서 밀랍이 녹았고 그는 물에 빠졌습니다.

16 (now, / at / look / entire / the / again. / painting)
➡ _____

17 (the / despite / tragedy / Icarus, / of / are / people / going / with / on / everyday / their / activities.)
➡ _____

18 (the / does / still / painting / peaceful? / look)
➡ _____

19 (do / what / think / you / artist / the / trying / is / us? / tell / to)
➡ _____

20 (now, / move / let's / to / on / painting. / next / the)
➡ _____

21 (you / do / see / artist / the / the / behind / canvas? / large)
➡ _____

22 (is / he / Velázquez, / Diego / and / actually / he / this / picture. / painted)
➡ _____

23 (do / who / think / you / painting? / is / he)
➡ _____

24 (a / take / look. / quick)
➡ _____

25 (young / the / seems / princess / be / to / main / the / because / person / is / she / the / in / center / the / painting. / of)
➡ _____

26 (the / but / of / title / painting / the / is / *of* / *Maids* / *Honour.* / *The*)
➡ _____

27 (then, / the / is / drawing / artist / the / women / two / princess? / the / beside)
➡ _____

28 (a / take / look. / close)
➡ _____

29 (will / it / you / make / about / wonder / the / more. / about / painting)
➡ _____

30 (to / try / which / direction / see / the / artist / at. / looking / is)
➡ _____

31 (you / can / the / see / king / the / and / queen / the / in / mirror / the / in / background / painting? / the / of)
➡ _____
_____

32 (do / who / think / you / is / he / now? / painting)
➡ _____

16 이제, 그림 전체를 다시 보세요.

17 이카루스의 비극에도 불구하고 사람들은 일상의 활동을 계속하고 있습니다.

18 그림이 여전히 평화로워 보이나요?

19 화가가 우리에게 무엇을 말하려 한다고 생각하나요?

20 이제, 다음 그림으로 넘어갑시다.

21 커다란 캔버스 뒤에 있는 화가가 보이나요?

22 그는 Diego Velázquez이고, 그가 실제로 이 그림을 그렸습니다.

23 그가 누구를 그리고 있다고 생각하나요?

24 재빨리 봅시다.

25 어린 공주가 그림의 중앙에 있기 때문에 주인공처럼 보입니다.

26 하지만 그림의 제목은 '시녀들'입니다.

27 그렇다면 화가는 공주 옆에 있는 두 여인을 그리고 있나요?

28 자세히 보세요.

29 그림에 대해 더 궁금해하게 될 겁니다.

30 화가가 바라보고 있는 방향을 보려고 노력해 보세요.

31 그림의 배경에 있는 거울 속 왕과 왕비가 보이나요?

32 이제 여러분은 그가 누구를 그리고 있다고 생각하나요?

※ 다음 우리말을 영어로 쓰시오.

1 세계 미술관(the World Art Museum)에 오신 것을 환영합니다.

➡ _____

2 미술관에 갈 때 여러분은 각각의 그림을 보는 데 얼마나 많은 시간을 보내나요?

➡ _____

3 많은 방문객들은 이동하기 전에 하나의 그림을 몇 초간만 힐끗 봅니다.

➡ _____

4 하지만 그림의 중요한 세부 사항들을 즉시 알아채는 것은 어렵기 때문에 여러분들은 그것들을 놓칠 수 있습니다.

➡ _____

5 오늘 우리는 두 개의 그림을 자세히 살펴볼 것이고, 여러분이 흥미로운 세부 사항들을 볼 수 있도록 제가 도와드리겠습니다.

➡ _____

6 먼저 이 그림을 보세요.

➡ _____

7 바닷가 풍경이 매우 평화롭고 아름답죠, 그렇지 않나요?

➡ _____

8 이 그림의 제목은 '추락하는 이카루스가 있는 풍경'입니다.

➡ _____

9 그러면 이카루스가 어디에 있는지 보이나요?

➡ _____

10 배 근처에 물 밖으로 나와 있는 두 다리가 보이죠?

➡ _____

11 이것이 그리스의 유명한 신화에 나오는 이카루스입니다.

➡ _____

12 신화에서 이카루스의 아버지는 그를 위해 깃털과 밀랍으로 날개를 만들어 주었고 그에게 태양을 가까이 하지 말라고 말했습니다.

➡ _____

➡ _____

13 하지만 이카루스는 듣지 않았습니다.

➡ _____

14 그는 태양에 너무 가깝게 날았습니다.

➡ _____

15 그래서 밀랍이 녹았고 그는 물에 빠졌습니다.

➡ _____

16 이제, 그림 전체를 다시 보세요.

➡ _____

17 이카루스의 비극에도 불구하고 사람들은 일상의 활동을 계속하고 있습니다.

➡ _____

18 그림이 여전히 평화로워 보이나요?

➡ _____

19 화가가 우리에게 무엇을 말하려 한다고 생각하나요?

➡ _____

20 이제, 다음 그림으로 넘어갑시다.

➡ _____

21 커다란 캔버스 뒤에 있는 화가가 보이나요?

➡ _____

22 그는 Diego Velázquez이고, 그가 실제로 이 그림을 그렸습니다.

➡ _____

23 그가 누구를 그리고 있다고 생각하나요?

➡ _____

24 재빨리 봅시다.

➡ _____

25 어린 공주가 그림의 중앙에 있기 때문에 주인공처럼 보입니다.

➡ _____

26 하지만 그림의 제목은 '시녀들'입니다.

➡ _____

27 그렇다면 화가는 공주 옆에 있는 두 여인을 그리고 있나요?

➡ _____

28 자세히 보세요.

➡ _____

29 그림에 대해 더 궁금해하게 될 겁니다.

➡ _____

30 화가가 바라보고 있는 방향을 보려고 노력해 보세요.

➡ _____

31 그림의 배경에 있는 거울 속 왕과 왕비가 보이나요?

➡ _____

32 이제 여러분은 그가 누구를 그리고 있다고 생각하나요?

➡ _____

※ 다음 우리말과 일치하도록 빈칸에 알맞은 말을 쓰시오.

Listen & Talk

1. M: What _____ you _____, Sally?

2 W: I'm _____ *The Maze Runner*. It's about boys _____ are put _____ _____ _____.

3 M: It's a great story. I've _____ the movie of it, _____. I _____ the novel _____ the movie.

4 W: _____ do you _____ it _____?

5 M: The novel has _____ _____. But the movie didn't _____ some _____ _____ of the story.

Grammar in Real Life

1. Princess, please _____ me _____.

2. _____ are _____?

3. The princess _____ _____, "If you help me, I'll _____ _____ _____ the palace and _____ my friend."

4. Come here. I'll have people _____ _____ some _____ and _____.

5. No! _____ _____ him _____. I don't like him.

6. Don't _____, Frog. I'll _____ _____ _____ _____ her promise.

Think and Write C

1. Today, I went to the _____ _____ _____.

2. At the exhibition, I saw many _____ _____ _____ _____.

3. _____ them, I liked the piece _____ *Moon Tree*.

4. It _____ _____ _____ French artist, David Myriam.

5. _____, sand _____ _____ in this painting.

6. I like it _____ a tree in the moon _____ _____ _____ _____.

7. Now I know that anything _____ _____ _____ _____ make art.

8. _____ is _____!

---

1. M: Sally, 너는 무엇을 읽고 있니?
2. W: 나는 '미로를 달리는 사람'을 읽고 있어. 미로에 갇힌 소년들에 관한 내용이야.
3. M: 그건 대단한 이야기이지. 나는 그것을 영화로도 봤어. 나는 영화보다는 소설이 더 좋아.
4. W: 왜 소설이 더 좋은데?
5. M: 소설에는 다양한 이야기가 담겨 있어. 하지만 영화에서는 이야기의 중요한 몇 부분이 나오지 않았어.

---

1. 공주님, 저를 들어가게 해 주세요.
2. 그대는 누군가?
3. 공주님은 제게 "네가 날 도와준다면, 나는 너를 궁전에 들어오게 하고 내 친구가 되게 해 주겠어."라고 약속하셨어요.
4. 이쪽으로 오게. 내가 사람들을 시켜 자네에게 과자와 차를 가져다 주게 하겠네.
5. 안 돼요! 그를 들어오게 하지 마세요. 저는 그를 좋아하지 않아요.
6. 걱정 말게, 개구리. 나는 공주가 그녀의 약속을 지키게 하겠네.

---

1. 오늘 나는 놀라운 미술 전시회에 갔다.
2. 전시회에서, 나는 많은 흥미로운 예술 작품들을 보았다.
3. 그 중에서, 나는 Moon Tree라고 불리는 작품이 좋았다.
4. 그것은 프랑스 예술가 David Myriam에 의해 만들어졌다.
5. 흥미롭게도, 모래가 이 미술품에 사용되었다.
6. 달 속에 있는 나무 한그루가 내 마음을 고요하게 만들기 때문에 나는 그것이 좋다.
7. 이제 나는 어떠한 것이든 미술을 만들기 위해 사용될 수 있다는 사실을 안다.
8. 무엇이든 가능하다!

※ 다음 우리말을 영어로 쓰시오.

Listen & Talk

1. M: Sally, 너는 무엇을 읽고 있니?
➡ _____

2. W: 나는 '미로를 달리는 사람'을 읽고 있어. 미로에 갇힌 소년들에 관한 내용이야.
➡ _____

3. M: 그건 대단한 이야기이지. 나는 그것을 영화로도 봤어. 나는 영화보다는 소설이 더 좋아.
➡ _____

4. W: 왜 소설이 더 좋은데?
➡ _____

5. M: 소설에는 다양한 이야기가 담겨 있어. 하지만 영화에서는 이야기의 중요한 몇 부분이 나오지 않았어.
➡ _____

Grammar in Real Life

1. 공주님, 저를 들어가게 해 주세요.
➡ _____

2. 그대는 누군가?
➡ _____

3. 공주님은 제게 "네가 날 도와준다면, 나는 너를 궁전에 들어오게 하고 내 친구가 되게 해 주겠어."라고 약속하셨어요.
➡ _____

4. 이쪽으로 오게. 내가 사람들을 시켜 자네에게 과자와 차를 가져다 주게 하겠네.
➡ _____

5. 안 돼요! 그를 들어오게 하지 마세요. 저는 그를 좋아하지 않아요.
➡ _____

6. 걱정 말게, 개구리. 나는 공주가 그녀의 약속을 지키게 하겠네.
➡ _____

Think and Write C

1. 오늘 나는 놀라운 미술 전시회에 갔다.
➡ _____

2. 전시회에서, 나는 많은 흥미로운 예술 작품들을 보았다.
➡ _____

3. 그 중에서, 나는 Moon Tree라고 불리는 작품이 좋았다.
➡ _____

4. 그것은 프랑스 예술가 David Myriam에 의해 만들어졌다.
➡ _____

5. 흥미롭게도, 모래가 이 미술품에 사용되었다.
➡ _____

6. 달 속에 있는 나무 한그루가 내 마음을 고요하게 만들기 때문에 나는 그것이 좋다.
➡ _____

7. 이제 나는 어떠한 것이든 미술을 만들기 위해 사용될 수 있다는 사실을 안다.
➡ _____

8. 무엇이든 가능하다!
➡ _____

※ 다음 영어를 우리말로 쓰시오.

01 balance

02 counter

03 mixture

04 sugar-free

05 deliver

06 thought

07 effect

08 guidebook

09 handwritten

10 fry

11 bakery

12 presence

13 hundred

14 suggest

15 importance

16 dependence

17 post

18 local

19 machine

20 experience

21 moment

22 nearby

23 trendy

24 opinion

25 downtown

26 creative

27 debate

28 price

29 remain

30 scared

31 elderly

32 donate

33 technology

34 wisely

35 throw away

36 can't wait to

37 rely on

38 even though

39 get attention

40 pay for

41 fall asleep

42 keep -ing

43 be busy -ing

※ 다음 우리말을 영어로 쓰시오.

01 계산대, 판매대 _____

02 (과학) 기술 _____

03 제안하다 _____

04 토론, 논의 _____

05 기계 _____

06 기부하다 _____

07 시내의 _____

08 효과 _____

09 무가당의 _____

10 경험 _____

11 튀기다 _____

12 존재 _____

13 가격 _____

14 손으로 쓴 _____

15 균형을 잡다 _____

16 백, 100 _____

17 중요함 _____

18 생각 _____

19 지역의; 현지인 _____

20 창의적인 _____

21 전달하다, 배달하다 _____

22 근처에 _____

23 최신 유행의 _____

24 의견 _____

25 (웹사이트에 정보, 사진을) 올리다 _____

26 혼합물, 혼합 _____

27 동의하다 _____

28 남아 있다, 남다 _____

29 의존, 의지 _____

30 현명하게 _____

31 순간 _____

32 무서워하는, 겁먹은 _____

33 (여행자 등의) 숙소, 여관 _____

34 나이가 지긋한 _____

35 계속해서 ~하다 _____

36 대금을 지불하다 _____

37 ~하느라 바쁘다 _____

38 ~을 버리다 _____

39 ~에 의존하다 _____

40 비록 ~할지라도 _____

41 잠들다 _____

42 주목을 받다 _____

43 길을 잃다 _____

※ 다음 영영풀이에 알맞은 단어를 <보기>에서 골라 쓴 후, 우리말 뜻을 쓰시오.

1 _____ : to cook something in hot oil: _____

2 _____ : a book of directions and information for travelers: _____

3 _____ : relating to the particular area you live in: _____

4 _____ : a place where bread and cakes are made or sold: _____

5 _____ : to continue to exist or be left after others have gone: _____

6 _____ : a particular point in time: _____

7 _____ : to be in a steady position without falling to one side: _____

8 _____ : knowledge or skill that you gain from doing a job or activity: _____

9 _____ : to put a message or computer document on the Internet: _____

10 _____ : in a way that show experience, knowledge, and good judgment: _____

11 _____ : relating to or located in the center of a town or city: _____

12 _____ : a private house where people can pay to stay and have meals: _____

13 _____ : to give money, food, clothes, etc. to someone or something, especially a charity: _____

14 _____ : new machines, equipment, and ways of doing things that are based on modern scientific knowledge: _____

15 _____ : to tell someone your ideas about what they should do, where they should go, etc.: _____

16 _____ : the state of needing the help and support of somebody/something in order to survive or be successful: _____

suggest	fry	wisely	experience
post	technology	guesthouse	donate
local	remain	balance	moment
downtown	dependence	guidebook	bakery

※ 다음 우리말과 일치하도록 빈칸에 알맞은 말을 쓰시오.

Listen & Talk 1 A-1

Jane: Look, Dad. This is Mom's _____ _____.

Dad: Oh, you're _____ her a _____ _____?

Jane: Yeah, I've made a family _____ _____ for Mom and _____ it on this stick. What do you _____ about the _____?

Dad: I think it's really _____. She'll love it.

Listen & Talk 1 A-2

Mike: Jenny, _____ _____ _____ _____ the new online comic *Scary Night*?

Jenny: I didn't like it. I _____ it had too many _____ _____.

Mike: Really? I thought they _____ the story more _____.

Jenny: Not me. I _____ _____ because I was too _____.

Listen & Talk 1 B

Tony: Hey, Julie! _____ you _____ about the *Quiz & Rice* game?

Julie: Yeah, isn't it the one that _____ rice when you get a _____ _____?

Tony: Yeah, _____ do you _____ _____ the game?

Julie: I think it's a _____ game. You can _____ _____ and _____ _____ hungry people. _____ you _____ it yet?

Tony: No, but I'm _____ _____ _____ it _____ this weekend.

Listen & Talk 2 A-1

Jack: Sally, did you watch *Super Voice's* Top 10 finalists yesterday?

Sally: Yeah. They all sang much _____ _____ _____.

Jack: Yeah, they did. I think this _____ _____ helps them _____ _____ to their dreams.

Sally: I'm _____ _____ _____ _____. I can't _____ _____ _____ their _____ _____.

Jane: 보세요, 아빠. 이거 엄마의 생신 선물이에요.

Dad: 오, 너는 엄마에게 막대 기억 장치 (메모리 스틱)를 준다는 거지?

Jane: 네, 엄마를 위한 가족 동영상을 만들어서, 그것을 이 막대 기억 장치에 저장했어요. 이 선물에 대해 어떻게 생각하세요?

Dad: 정말 감동적인 것 같구나. 엄마가 그걸 정말 좋아할 거 같아.

Mike: Jenny, 너는 새로운 온라인 만화 '무서운 밤'에 대해 어떻게 생각하니?

Jenny: 난 그거 별로였어. 거기에 음향 효과가 너무 많다고 생각했어.

Mike: 정말? 나는 그것이 이야기를 더욱 흥미진진하게 만들어 준다고 생각했는데.

Jenny: 난 아니야. 난 너무 무서워서 집중할 수가 없었거든.

Tony: 저기, Julie! 너 '퀴즈와 쌀'이라는 게임에 대해 들어봤니?

Julie: 응, 정답을 맞히면 쌀을 기부하는 게임 아니야?

Tony: 맞아, 넌 그 게임에 대해 어떻게 생각하니?

Julie: 난 그것이 창의적인 게임이라고 생각해. 재미있게 놀면서 배고픈 사람들을 도울 수 있잖아. 너 그거 이미 해 봤니?

Tony: 아니, 하지만 이번 주말에 해 보려고 해.

Jack: Sally, 너 어제 '슈퍼 보이스'의 상위 10위 결정전을 봤니?

Sally: 응. 그들은 모두 전보다 훨씬 더 노래를 잘 불렀어.

Jack: 맞아, 그랬어. 나는 이 노래 경연 대회가 그들이 자신의 꿈에 더 가까워지도록 도와준다고 생각해.

Sally: 나도 그 말에 동의해. 그들의 다음 공연을 보는 것이 너무 기다려진다.

Listen & Talk 2 A-2

Steve: Hey, Lisa. I've got over a hundred _____ on my SNS posts.

Lisa: Oh, I wouldn't feel _____ _____ my posts with so many people.

Steve: Really? I think it's great _____ a lot of people see my _____.

Lisa: I'm _____ _____ _____ _____ _____. I only want to _____ my posts with my _____ _____.

Listen & Talk 2 B

Emma: Excuse me. Can you _____ me _____ with this machine?

Tom: Sure. First, _____ the Hot Dog button and _____ your hot dog and drink.

Emma: Okay. _____ do I _____ _____ _____ _____?

Tom: Touch the Done button at the _____ and _____ for them.

Emma: Wow, it's so _____. This machine is _____ _____ _____ ordering at the _____.

Tom: I'm _____ _____ on that. It really _____ a lot of _____ _____ there's a long _____.

Communication

Sujin: Now, we will start the three-minute _____. Today's _____ _____ is fast fashion. _____ do you _____ about it? Please, begin, James.

James: I think fast fashion is good. We can wear _____ clothes _____ _____ _____ _____.

Wendy: I'm not _____ you _____ _____. It makes us _____ too much money and _____ _____ clothes too often.

Sujin: It looks like the two of you have different _____ on the first topic. Now, let's _____ _____ to the second topic.

Wrap Up 1

Alex: I've just _____ _____ _____ _____ for Leon, Mom. _____ _____ _____ _____ _____ _____ _____?

Mom: Oh, the title "LOST CAT" in big letters at the top is easy to see.

Alex: Yeah, I did it to _____ _____. _____ _____ these photos _____ the title?

Mom: Hmm... the _____ on the _____ doesn't show Leon's face well.

Alex: Okay, I'll _____ the photo.

Mom: Oh, I _____ we can _____ Leon.

Steve: 저기, Lisa. 나 내 SNS 게시물들에 100개가 넘는 댓글을 받았어.

Lisa: 아, 나는 내 게시물들을 너무 많은 사람들과 공유하는 게 편하지 않을 거야.

Steve: 정말? 나는 많은 사람들이 내 게시물들을 보는 게 정말 좋다고 생각해.

Lisa: 나는 그 점에 있어서 너랑 생각이 달라. 나는 그냥 가까운 친구들하고만 내 게시물들을 공유하고 싶어.

Emma: 실례합니다. 제가 이 기계로 주문하는 것을 좀 도와주실 수 있나요?

Tom: 물론이죠. 먼저 '핫도그' 버튼을 누르시고, 드시고 싶은 핫도그와 음료를 고르세요.

Emma: 알겠습니다. 주문한 것에 대한 지불을 어떻게 하나요?

Tom: 맨 아래에 있는 '완료' 버튼을 누르시고 그것들에 대해 지불하세요.

Emma: 와, 정말 간단하네요. 이 기계가 계산대에서 주문하는 것보다 훨씬 더 빨라요.

Tom: 저도 그렇게 생각해요. 줄이 길 때, 그것은 정말 많은 시간을 절약해 줘요.

Sujin: 자, 3분 토론을 시작하겠습니다. 오늘의 첫 번째 주제는 '패스트 패션'입니다. 여러분들은 그것에 대해 어떻게 생각하십니까? 시작해 주세요, James.

James: 저는 '패스트 패션'이 좋다고 생각합니다. 우리는 보다 저렴한 가격으로 최신 유행의 옷들을 입을 수 있습니다.

Wendy: 저는 그 의견에 동의하지 않습니다. 그것은 우리가 너무 많은 돈을 쓰고 너무 자주 옷을 버리게 합니다.

Sujin: 첫 번째 주제에 대해서는 두 사람이 다른 의견을 갖고 있는 것 같습니다. 이제 두 번째 주제로 넘어가 보도록 하겠습니다.

Alex: 엄마, Leon을 위한 인터넷 게시물 만드는 걸 막 끝냈어요. 이것에 대해 어떻게 생각하세요?

Mom: 오, 맨 위에 큰 글자로 된 제목 "LOST CAT"이 잘 보이는구나.

Alex: 네, 주목을 끌기 위해 그렇게 했어요. 제목 밑에 있는 이 사진들은 어때요?

Mom: 흠… 오른쪽에 있는 사진에서 Leon의 얼굴이 잘 보이지 않아.

Alex: 알겠어요, 그 사진을 바꿀게요.

Mom: 오, 우리가 Leon을 찾을 수 있으면 좋겠구나.

대화문 Test

※ 다음 우리말에 맞도록 대화를 영어로 쓰시오.

Listen & Talk 1 A-1

Jane: _____

Dad: _____

Jane: _____

_____

Dad: _____

Listen & Talk 1 A-2

Mike: _____

Jenny: _____

Mike: _____

Jenny: _____

Listen & Talk 1 B

Tony: _____

Julie: _____

Tony: _____

Julie: _____

_____

Tony: _____

Listen & Talk 2 A-1

Jack: _____

Sally: _____

Jack: _____

_____

Sally: _____

Jane: 보세요, 아빠. 이거 엄마의 생신 선물이에요.

Dad: 오, 너는 엄마에게 막대 기억 장치 (메모리 스틱)를 준다는 거지?

Jane: 네, 엄마를 위한 가족 동영상을 만들어서, 그것을 이 막대 기억 장치에 저장했어요. 이 선물에 대해 어떻게 생각하세요?

Dad: 정말 감동적인 것 같구나. 엄마가 그걸 정말 좋아할 거 같아.

Mike: Jenny, 너는 새로운 온라인 만화 '무서운 밤'에 대해 어떻게 생각하니?

Jenny: 난 그거 별로였어. 거기에 음향 효과가 너무 많다고 생각했어.

Mike: 정말? 나는 그것이 이야기를 더욱 흥미진진하게 만들어 준다고 생각했는데.

Jenny: 난 아니야. 난 너무 무서워서 집중할 수가 없었거든.

Tony: 저기, Julie! 너 '퀴즈와 쌀'이라는 게임에 대해 들어봤니?

Julie: 응, 정답을 맞히면 쌀을 기부하는 게임 아니야?

Tony: 맞아, 넌 그 게임에 대해 어떻게 생각하니?

Julie: 난 그것이 창의적인 게임이라고 생각해. 재미있게 놀면서 배고픈 사람들을 도울 수 있잖아. 너 그거 이미 해 봤니?

Tony: 아니, 하지만 이번 주말에 해 보려고 해.

Jack: Sally, 너 어제 '슈퍼 보이스'의 상위 10위 결정전을 봤니?

Sally: 응. 그들은 모두 전보다 훨씬 더 노래를 잘 불렀어.

Jack: 맞아, 그랬어. 나는 이 노래 경연 대회가 그들이 자신의 꿈에 더 가까워지도록 도와준다고 생각해.

Sally: 나도 그 말에 동의해. 그들의 다음 공연을 보는 것이 너무 기다려진다.

Listen & Talk 2 A-2

Steve: _____

Lisa: _____

Steve: _____

Lisa: _____

Listen & Talk 2 B

Emma: _____

Tom: _____

Emma: _____

Tom: _____

Emma: _____

Tom: _____

Communication

Sujin: _____
_____

James: _____

Wendy: _____
_____

Sujin: _____
_____

Wrap Up 1

Alex: _____

Mom: _____

Alex: _____

Mom: _____

Alex: _____

Mom: _____

Steve: 저기, Lisa. 나 내 SNS 게시물들에 100개가 넘는 댓글을 받았어.

Lisa: 아, 나는 내 게시물들을 너무 많은 사람들과 공유하는 게 편하지 않을 거야.

Steve: 정말? 나는 많은 사람들이 내 게시물들을 보는 게 정말 좋다고 생각해.

Lisa: 나는 그 점에 있어서 너랑 생각이 달라. 나는 그냥 가까운 친구들하고만 내 게시물들을 공유하고 싶어.

Emma: 실례합니다. 제가 이 기계로 주문하는 것을 좀 도와주실 수 있나요?

Tom: 물론이죠. 먼저 '핫도그' 버튼을 누르시고, 드시고 싶은 핫도그와 음료를 고르세요.

Emma: 알겠습니다. 주문한 것에 대한 지불을 어떻게 하나요?

Tom: 맨 아래에 있는 '완료' 버튼을 누르시고 그것들에 대해 지불하세요.

Emma: 와, 정말 간단하네요. 이 기계가 계산대에서 주문하는 것보다 훨씬 더 빨라요.

Tom: 저도 그렇게 생각해요. 줄이 길 때, 그것은 정말 많은 시간을 절약해 줘요.

Sujin: 자, 3분 토론을 시작하겠습니다. 오늘의 첫 번째 주제는 '패스트 패션'입니다. 여러분들은 그것에 대해 어떻게 생각하십니까? 시작해 주세요, James.

James: 저는 '패스트 패션'이 좋다고 생각합니다. 우리는 보다 저렴한 가격으로 최신 유행의 옷들을 입을 수 있습니다.

Wendy: 저는 그 의견에 동의하지 않습니다. 그것은 우리가 너무 많은 돈을 쓰고 너무 자주 옷을 버리게 합니다.

Sujin: 첫 번째 주제에 대해서는 두 사람이 다른 의견을 갖고 있는 것 같습니다. 이제 두 번째 주제로 넘어가 보도록 하겠습니다.

Alex: 엄마, Leon을 위한 인터넷 게시물 만드는 걸 막 끝냈어요. 이것에 대해 어떻게 생각하세요?

Mom: 오, 맨 위에 큰 글자로 된 제목 "LOST CAT"이 잘 보이는구나.

Alex: 네, 주목을 끌기 위해 그렇게 했어요. 제목 밑에 있는 이 사진들은 어때요?

Mom: 흠… 오른쪽에 있는 사진에서 Leon의 얼굴이 잘 보이지 않아.

Alex: 알겠어요, 그 사진을 바꿀게요.

Mom: 오, 우리가 Leon을 찾을 수 있으면 좋겠구나.

※ 다음 우리말과 일치하도록 빈칸에 알맞은 것을 골라 쓰시오.

1 Last summer, my father _____ a _____ event: a family trip _____ smartphones!

    A. surprising   B. without   C. suggested

2 He said, "I hate _____ see you _____ together and only _____ _____ your smartphones."

    A. looking   B. to   C. at   D. sitting

3 My sister and I _____ the need for smartphones, but he _____ _____ that we could not _____ enjoy the trip with them.

    A. saying   B. kept   C. explained   D. fully

4 So we _____ a technology-free _____ _____ a new city, Barcelona, Spain.

    A. trip   B. to   C. started

5 Our _____ day was _____ .

    A. terrible   B. first

6 On the _____ to our guesthouse _____ Plaza Reial, we got _____ in _____ Barcelona.

    A. lost   B. way   C. downtown   D. around

7 Dad was _____ _____ at the map and _____ for directions with a _____ Spanish words he got _____ a tour guidebook.

    A. few   B. looking   C. asking   D. busy

8 _____ _____ our guesthouse was _____ next to the Plaza, it took us about two hours to _____ there.

    A. get   B. though   C. right   D. even

9 We were _____ _____ _____ we could not go _____ for dinner.

    A. out   B. tired   C. that   D. so

10 I went to bed but couldn't _____ _____ because I was _____ about what would _____ the next day.

    A. asleep   B. happen   C. worried   D. fall

11 After _____ _____ Gaudi's Park Guell, we decided to _____ seafood _____ rice for lunch.

    A. looking   B. fried   C. have   D. around

12 _____ , we didn't know _____ restaurant to go _____ .

    A. which   B. to   C. however

13 We needed help, so Mom went _____ to an _____ lady and _____ to ask for _____ to a popular seafood restaurant.

    A. directions   B. elderly   C. up   D. tried

1 지난여름, 아빠가 깜짝 놀랄 만한 이벤트로 스마트폰 없는 가족 여행을 제안하셨다!

2 아빠는 "나는 우리 가족이 함께 앉아서 각자의 스마트폰만 보고 있는 걸 보는 게 참 싫구나."라고 말씀하셨다.

3 여동생과 내가 스마트폰이 필요하다고 설명했지만, 아빠는 스마트폰이 있으면 여행을 충분히 즐길 수 없을 거라고 계속해서 말씀하셨다.

4 그래서 우리는 새로운 도시인 스페인의 바르셀로나로 '첨단 과학 기술 없는 여행'을 시작했다.

5 우리의 첫째 날은 엉망이었다.

6 레이알 광장 주변에 있는 여행자 숙소로 가는 길에 우리는 바르셀로나 시내에서 길을 잃었다.

7 아빠는 지도를 보며 여행안내 책자에서 배운 스페인어 몇 마디로 길을 묻느라 분주하셨다.

8 우리의 숙소가 광장 바로 옆에 있었음에도 불구하고, 우리가 그곳에 도착하는 데는 거의 두 시간이 걸렸다.

9 우리는 너무 피곤해서 저녁을 먹으러 나갈 수가 없었다.

10 나는 잠자리에 들었지만 내일 무슨 일이 일어날지 걱정이 되어서 잠들 수가 없었다.

11 가우디가 지은 구엘 공원을 둘러본 후, 우리는 점심으로 해산물 볶음밥을 먹기로 했다.

12 그러나 우리는 어떤 식당으로 가야 할지 몰랐다.

13 우리는 도움이 필요해서, 엄마가 한 노부인에게 가서 인기 있는 해산물 식당으로 가는 길을 물어보려고 애쓰셨다.

14 Luckily, she _____ to _____ Mom's few Spanish _____.
    A. understand   B. words   C. seemed

15 She _____ us to a small _____ restaurant _____.
    A. local   B. took   C. nearby

16 The seafood _____ _____ was _____.
    A. rice   B. amazing   C. fried

17 I really wanted to _____ picture of the food and _____ them on my _____.
    A. post   B. take   C. blog

18 But _____ my phone, I just _____ to _____ the _____.
    A. enjoy   B. without   C. moment   D. decided

19 During the _____ days, we _____ more and more _____ the locals.
    A. on   B. remaining   C. relied

20 We were _____ to meet and talk with _____ people _____ the _____, in the bakeries, and in the parks.
    A. various   B. able   C. streets   D. on

21 They were always _____ _____ to show us different _____ of Barcelona with a smile.
    A. sides   B. enough   C. kind

22 Also, our family _____ a lot _____ each _____.
    A. other   B. with   C. talked

23 We spent _____ of our time _____ _____ the Spanish train, on the bus, and at the restaurants.
    A. together   B. much   C. on

24 Our technology-free _____ was a new and _____.
    A. different   B. trip   C. experience

25 Before the trip, I was so _____ _____ my smartphone _____ I couldn't do anything _____ it.
    A. without   B. dependent   C. that   D. on

26 But now I see _____ I can enjoy the _____ _____ it.
    A. without   B. that   C. moment

27 _____ the experience, I have _____ the _____ of a _____ use of the smartphone.
    A. importance   B. balanced   C. learned   D. from

28 _____, next time, _____ I _____ without a smartphone?
    A. travel   B. would   C. so

29 _____ not. But I will _____ to use it more _____.
    A. wisely   B. probably   C. try

---

14 운이 좋게도 그녀는 몇 마디 안 되는 엄마의 스페인어를 이해하는 듯했다.

15 그녀는 우리를 근처에 있는 작은 현지 식당으로 데려다 주었다.

16 그 해산물 볶음밥은 놀랍도록 맛있었다.

17 나는 음식 사진을 찍어 그것을 내 블로그에 올리고 싶은 마음이 정말 간절했다.

18 그러나 스마트폰이 없었기 때문에 나는 그냥 그 순간을 즐기기로 했다.

19 (여행의) 남아 있는 날들 동안, 우리는 점점 더 현지 사람들에게 의존하게 되었다.

20 우리는 거리에서, 빵집에서, 공원에서 다양한 사람들을 만나 이야기할 수 있었다.

21 그들은 항상 웃으면서 너무나 친절히도 바르셀로나의 다양한 면을 우리에게 보여 주었다.

22 또한 우리 가족은 서로 많은 대화를 나누었다.

23 우리는 스페인의 기차에서, 버스에서, 그리고 식당에서 많은 시간을 함께 보냈다.

24 우리의 '첨단 과학 기술 없는' 여행은 새롭고 색다른 경험이었다.

25 여행 전에 나는 내 스마트폰에 너무 의존해서 그것 없이는 아무것도 할 수 없었다.

26 하지만 지금은 내가 스마트폰 없이도 그 순간을 즐길 수 있음을 알고 있다.

27 그 경험을 통해, 나는 스마트폰을 균형 있게 사용하는 것이 중요함을 배우게 되었다.

28 그러면, 다음번에 나는 스마트폰 없이 여행을 하게 될까?

29 아마도 그렇지는 않을 것이다. 하지만 나는 그것을 좀 더 현명하게 사용하기 위해 노력할 것이다.

※ 다음 우리말과 일치하도록 빈칸에 알맞은 말을 쓰시오.

1 Last summer, my father _____ a _____ event: a _____ _____ _____ smartphones!

2 He said, "I _____ _____ _____ you _____ _____ and only _____ _____ your smartphones."

3 My sister and I _____ the need for smartphones, but he _____ _____ _____ we could _____ _____ _____ the trip with them.

4 So we _____ a technology-free _____ _____ a new city, Barcelona, Spain.

5 Our _____ _____ was _____.

6 _____ _____ _____ _____ _____ our guesthouse _____ Plaza Reial, we _____ _____ _____ _____ _____ Barcelona.

7 Dad _____ _____ _____ at the map and _____ _____ directions _____ _____ _____ Spanish words he got _____ a tour guidebook.

8 _____ _____ our guesthouse was _____ _____ _____ the Plaza, _____ _____ us about two hours _____ _____ there.

9 We _____ _____ _____ _____ _____ _____ we _____ _____ _____ for dinner.

10 I _____ _____ _____ but couldn't _____ _____ because I was _____ about _____ _____ _____ the next day.

11 _____ _____ _____ Gaudi's Park Guell, we decided _____ _____ seafood _____ rice for lunch.

12 However, we didn't know _____ _____ _____ _____ _____.

13 We needed help, so Mom _____ _____ _____ an elderly lady and _____ _____ _____ _____ _____ to a popular seafood restaurant.

1 지난여름, 아빠가 깜짝 놀랄 만한 이벤트로 스마트폰 없는 가족 여행을 제안하셨다!

2 아빠는 "나는 우리 가족이 함께 앉아서 각자의 스마트폰만 보고 있는 걸 보는 게 참 싫구나."라고 말씀하셨다.

3 여동생과 내가 스마트폰이 필요하다고 설명했지만, 아빠는 스마트폰이 있으면 여행을 충분히 즐길 수 없을 거라고 계속해서 말씀하셨다.

4 그래서 우리는 새로운 도시인 스페인의 바르셀로나로 '첨단 과학 기술 없는 여행'을 시작했다.

5 우리의 첫째 날은 엉망이었다.

6 레이알 광장 주변에 있는 여행자 숙소로 가는 길에 우리는 바르셀로나 시내에서 길을 잃었다.

7 아빠는 지도를 보며 여행안내 책자에서 배운 스페인어 몇 마디로 길을 묻느라 분주하셨다.

8 우리의 숙소가 광장 바로 옆에 있었음에도 불구하고, 우리가 그곳에 도착하는 데는 거의 두 시간이 걸렸다.

9 우리는 너무 피곤해서 저녁을 먹으러 나갈 수가 없었다.

10 나는 잠자리에 들었지만 내일 무슨 일이 일어날지 걱정이 되어서 잠들 수가 없었다.

11 가우디가 지은 구엘 공원을 둘러본 후, 우리는 점심으로 해산물 볶음밥을 먹기로 했다.

12 그러나 우리는 어떤 식당으로 가야 할지 몰랐다.

13 우리는 도움이 필요해서, 엄마가 한 노부인에게 가서 인기 있는 해산물 식당으로 가는 길을 물어보려고 애쓰셨다.

14 Luckily, she _____ _____ _____ Mom's few Spanish _____.

15 She _____ _____ to a small local restaurant _____.

16 The seafood _____ _____ was _____.

17 I really wanted to _____ _____ _____ the food and _____ _____ on my blog.

18 But _____ my phone, I just _____ _____ _____ the moment.

19 _____ the _____ days, we _____ more and more _____ the locals.

20 We _____ _____ _____ _____ _____ and _____ _____ various people on the streets, in the bakeries, and in the parks.

21 They were always _____ _____ _____ _____ us different sides of Barcelona _____ _____ _____.

22 Also, our family _____ a lot _____ _____.

23 We spent _____ _____ _____ _____ _____ on the Spanish train, on the bus, and at the restaurants.

24 Our technology-free trip was a _____ _____ _____ _____.

25 Before the trip, I was _____ _____ _____ my smartphone _____ I _____ do anything _____ it.

26 But now I see _____ I can enjoy the moment _____ _____.

27 _____ the experience, I _____ _____ the _____ of a _____ _____ of the smartphone.

28 So, next time, _____ _____ _____ without a smartphone?

29 Probably not. But I will _____ _____ _____ _____ more _____.

14 운이 좋게도 그녀는 몇 마디 안 되는 엄마의 스페인어를 이해하는 듯했다.

15 그녀는 우리를 근처에 있는 작은 현지 식당으로 데려다 주었다.

16 그 해산물 볶음밥은 놀랍도록 맛있었다.

17 나는 음식 사진을 찍어 그것을 내 블로그에 올리고 싶은 마음이 정말 간절했다.

18 그러나 스마트폰이 없었기 때문에 나는 그냥 그 순간을 즐기기로 했다.

19 (여행의) 남아 있는 날들 동안, 우리는 점점 더 현지 사람들에게 의존하게 되었다.

20 우리는 거리에서, 빵집에서, 공원에서 다양한 사람들을 만나 이야기할 수 있었다.

21 그들은 항상 웃으면서 너무나 친절히도 바르셀로나의 다양한 면을 우리에게 보여 주었다.

22 또한 우리 가족은 서로 많은 대화를 나누었다.

23 우리는 스페인의 기차에서, 버스에서, 그리고 식당에서 많은 시간을 함께 보냈다.

24 우리의 '첨단 과학 기술 없는' 여행은 새롭고 색다른 경험이었다.

25 여행 전에 나는 내 스마트폰에 너무 의존해서 그것 없이는 아무것도 할 수 없었다.

26 하지만 지금은 내가 스마트폰 없이도 그 순간을 즐길 수 있음을 알고 있다.

27 그 경험을 통해, 나는 스마트폰을 균형 있게 사용하는 것이 중요함을 배우게 되었다.

28 그러면, 다음번에 나는 스마트폰 없이 여행을 하게 될까?

29 아마도 그렇지는 않을 것이다. 하지만 나는 그것을 좀 더 현명하게 사용하기 위해 노력할 것이다.

※ 다음 문장을 우리말로 쓰시오.

1 Last summer, my father suggested a surprising event: a family trip without smartphones!

➡ _____

2 He said, "I hate to see you sitting together and only looking at your smartphones."

➡ _____

3 My sister and I explained the need for smartphones, but he kept saying that we could not fully enjoy the trip with them.

➡ _____

_____

4 So we started a technology-free trip to a new city, Barcelona, Spain.

➡ _____

5 Our first day was terrible.

➡ _____

6 On the way to our guesthouse around Plaza Reial, we got lost in downtown Barcelona.

➡ _____

7 Dad was busy looking at the map and asking for directions with a few Spanish words he got from a tour guidebook.

➡ _____

8 Even though our guesthouse was right next to the Plaza, it took us about two hours to get there.

➡ _____

9 We were so tired that we could not go out for dinner.

➡ _____

10 I went to bed but couldn't fall asleep because I was worried about what would happen the next day.

➡ _____

11 After looking around Gaudi's Park Guell, we decided to have seafood fried rice for lunch.

➡ _____

12 However, we didn't know which restaurant to go to.

➡ _____

13 We needed help, so Mom went up to an elderly lady and tried to ask for directions to a popular seafood restaurant.

➡ _____

14 ▷ Luckily, she seemed to understand Mom's few Spanish words.

➡ _____

15 ▷ She took us to a small local restaurant nearby.

➡ _____

16 ▷ The seafood fried rice was amazing.

➡ _____

17 ▷ I really wanted to take pictures of the food and post them on my blog.

➡ _____

18 ▷ But without my phone, I just decided to enjoy the moment.

➡ _____

19 ▷ During the remaining days, we relied more and more on the locals.

➡ _____

20 ▷ We were able to meet and talk with various people on the streets, in the bakeries, and in the parks.

➡ _____

21 ▷ They were always kind enough to show us different sides of Barcelona with a smile.

➡ _____

22 ▷ Also, our family talked a lot with each other.

➡ _____

23 ▷ We spent much of our time together on the Spanish train, on the bus, and at the restaurants.

➡ _____

24 ▷ Our technology-free trip was a new and different experience.

➡ _____

25 ▷ Before the trip, I was so dependent on my smartphone that I couldn't do anything without it.

➡ _____

26 ▷ But now I see that I can enjoy the moment without it.

➡ _____

27 ▷ From the experience, I have learned the importance of a balanced use of the smartphone.

➡ _____

28 ▷ So, next time, would I travel without a smartphone?

➡ _____

29 ▷ Probably not. But I will try to use it more wisely.

➡ _____

※ 다음 괄호 안의 단어들을 우리말에 맞도록 바르게 배열하시오.

1 (summer, / last / father / my / suggested / surprising / a / event: / family / a / trip / smartphones! / without)
➡ _____
_____

2 (said, / he / hate / "I / see / to / sitting / you / and / together / only / at / looking / smarphones." / your)
➡ _____
_____

3 (sister / my / I / and / the / explained / need / smartphones, / for / but / he / saying / kept / that / could / we / not / enjoy / fully / trip / them. / with / the)
➡ _____
_____

4 (we / so / a / started / technology-free / to / trip / new / a / city, / Spain. / Barcelona,)
➡ _____

5 (first / our / day / terrible. / was)
➡ _____

6 (the / on / way / our / to / around / guesthouse / Reial, / Plaza / got / we / lost / in / Barcelona. / downtown)
➡ _____
_____

7 (was / Dad / looking / busy / at / map / the / and / for / asking / with / directions / a / few / words / Spanish / got / he / from / guidebook. / tour / a)
➡ _____
_____

8 (though / even / guesthouse / our / was / next / right / the / to / Plaza, / took / it / us / two / about / hours / there. / to / get)
➡ _____
_____

9 (were / we / tired / so / that / could / we / go / not / dinner. / for / out)
➡ _____

10 (went / I / bed / to / couldn't / but / asleep / fall / because / was / I / worried / about / would / what / happen / day. / the / next)
➡ _____
_____

11 (looking / after / Gaudi's / around / Guell, / Park / decided / we / have / to / seafood / fried / for / lunch. / rice)
➡ _____
_____

12 (we / however, / know / didn't / which / to / resturant. / to. / go)
➡ _____

13 (needed / we / help, / Mom / so / went / to / up / an / lady / elderly / and / to / tired / ask / to / directions / for / popular / a / restaurant. / seafood)
➡ _____
_____

1 지난여름, 아빠가 깜짝 놀랄 만한 이벤트로 스마트폰 없는 가족 여행을 제안하셨다!

2 아빠는 "나는 우리 가족이 함께 앉아서 각자의 스마트폰만 보고 있는 걸 보는 게 참 싫구나."라고 말씀하셨다.

3 여동생과 내가 스마트폰이 필요하다고 설명했지만, 아빠는 스마트폰이 있으면 여행을 충분히 즐길 수 없을 거라고 계속해서 말씀하셨다.

4 그래서 우리는 새로운 도시인 스페인의 바르셀로나로 '첨단 과학 기술 없는 여행'을 시작했다.

5 우리의 첫째 날은 엉망이었다.

6 레이알 광장 주변에 있는 여행자 숙소로 가는 길에 우리는 바르셀로나 시내에서 길을 잃었다.

7 아빠는 지도를 보며 여행안내 책자에서 배운 스페인어 몇 마디로 길을 묻느라 분주하셨다.

8 우리의 숙소가 광장 바로 옆에 있었음에도 불구하고, 우리가 그곳에 도착하는 데는 거의 두 시간이 걸렸다.

9 우리는 너무 피곤해서 저녁을 먹으러 나갈 수가 없었다.

10 나는 잠자리에 들었지만 내일 무슨 일이 일어날지 걱정이 되어서 잠들 수가 없었다.

11 가우디가 지은 구엘 공원을 둘러본 후, 우리는 점심으로 해산물 볶음밥을 먹기로 했다.

12 그러나 우리는 어떤 식당으로 가야 할지 몰랐다.

13 우리는 도움이 필요해서, 엄마가 한 노부인에게 가서 인기 있는 해산물 식당으로 가는 길을 물어보려고 애쓰셨다.

14 (she / luckily, / to / seemed / understand / Mom's / Spanish / few / words.)

➡ _____

15 (took / she / to / us / a / local / small / nearby. / restaurant)

➡ _____

16 (seafood / the / rice / fried / amazing. / was)

➡ _____

17 (really / I / to / wanted / pictures / take / the / of / food / and / them / post / on / blog. / my)

➡ _____

18 (without / but / phone, / my / just / I / to / decided / enjoy / moment. / the)

➡ _____

19 (the / during / days, / remaining / relied / we / and / more / on / more / locals. / the)

➡ _____

20 (were / we / to / able / meet / and / with / talk / people / various / on / streets, / the / in / bakeries, / the / and / parks. / the / in)

➡ _____

21 (were / they / kind / always / enough / show / to / us / sides / different / of / with / Barcelona / smile. / a)

➡ _____

22 (our / also, / family / a / talked / lot / with / other. / each)

➡ _____

23 (spent / we / of / much / our / together / time / the / Spanish / on / train, / the / on / bus, / and / the / restaurants. / at)

➡ _____

24 (technology-free / our / trip / was / new / a / and / experience. / different)

➡ _____

25 (the / before / trip, / I / so / was / dependent / my / on / that / smartphone / I / do / couldn't / anything / it. / without)

➡ _____

26 (now / but / see / I / that / can / I / enjoy / moment / the / it. / without)

➡ _____

27 (the / from / experience, / have / I / learned / importance / the / of / balanced / a / use / of / smartphone. / the)

➡ _____

28 (next / so, / time, / I / would / without / travel / smartphone? / a)

➡ _____

29 (not. / probably // but / will / I / to / try / it / use / wisely. / more)

➡ _____

14 운이 좋게도 그녀는 몇 마디 안 되는 엄마의 스페인어를 이해하는 듯했다.

15 그녀는 우리를 근처에 있는 작은 현지 식당으로 데려다 주었다.

16 그 해산물 볶음밥은 놀랍도록 맛있었다.

17 나는 음식 사진을 찍어 그것을 내 블로그에 올리고 싶은 마음이 정말 간절했다.

18 그러나 스마트폰이 없었기 때문에 나는 그냥 그 순간을 즐기기로 했다.

19 (여행의) 남아 있는 날들 동안, 우리는 점점 더 현지 사람들에게 의존하게 되었다.

20 우리는 거리에서, 빵집에서, 공원에서 다양한 사람들을 만나 이야기할 수 있었다.

21 그들은 항상 웃으면서 너무나 친절히도 바르셀로나의 다양한 면을 우리에게 보여 주었다.

22 또한 우리 가족은 서로 많은 대화를 나누었다.

23 우리는 스페인의 기차에서, 버스에서, 그리고 식당에서 많은 시간을 함께 보냈다.

24 우리의 '첨단 과학 기술 없는' 여행은 새롭고 색다른 경험이었다.

25 여행 전에 나는 내 스마트폰에 너무 의존해서 그것 없이는 아무것도 할 수 없었다.

26 하지만 지금은 내가 스마트폰 없이도 그 순간을 즐길 수 있음을 알고 있다.

27 그 경험을 통해, 나는 스마트폰을 균형 있게 사용하는 것이 중요함을 배우게 되었다.

28 그러면, 다음번에 나는 스마트폰 없이 여행을 하게 될까?

29 아마도 그렇지는 않을 것이다. 하지만 나는 그것을 좀 더 현명하게 사용하기 위해 노력할 것이다.

※ 다음 우리말을 영어로 쓰시오.

1 지난여름, 아빠가 깜짝 놀랄 만한 이벤트로 스마트폰 없는 가족 여행을 제안하셨다!

➡ _____

2 아빠는 "나는 우리 가족이 함께 앉아서 각자의 스마트폰만 보고 있는 걸 보는 게 참 싫구나."라고 말씀하셨다.

➡ _____

3 여동생과 내가 스마트폰이 필요하다고 설명했지만, 아빠는 스마트폰이 있으면 여행을 충분히 즐길 수 없을 거라고 계속해서 말씀하셨다.

➡ _____

4 그래서 우리는 새로운 도시인 스페인의 바르셀로나로 '첨단 과학 기술 없는 여행'을 시작했다.

➡ _____

5 우리의 첫째 날은 엉망이었다.

➡ _____

6 레이알 광장 주변에 있는 여행자 숙소로 가는 길에 우리는 바르셀로나 시내에서 길을 잃었다.

➡ _____

7 아빠는 지도를 보며 여행안내 책자에서 배운 스페인어 몇 마디로 길을 묻느라 분주하셨다.

➡ _____

8 우리의 숙소가 광장 바로 옆에 있었음에도 불구하고, 우리가 그곳에 도착하는 데는 거의 두 시간이 걸렸다.

➡ _____

9 우리는 너무 피곤해서 저녁을 먹으러 나갈 수가 없었다.

➡ _____

10 나는 잠자리에 들었지만 내일 무슨 일이 일어날지 걱정이 되어서 잠들 수가 없었다.

➡ _____

11 가우디가 지은 구엘 공원을 둘러본 후, 우리는 점심으로 해산물 볶음밥을 먹기로 했다.

➡ _____

12 그러나 우리는 어떤 식당으로 가야 할지 몰랐다.

➡ _____

13 우리는 도움이 필요해서, 엄마가 한 노부인에게 가서 인기 있는 해산물 식당으로 가는 길을 물어보려고 애쓰셨다.

➡ _____

14 운이 좋게도 그녀는 몇 마디 안 되는 엄마의 스페인어를 이해하는 듯했다.

➡ _____

15 그녀는 우리를 근처에 있는 작은 현지 식당으로 데려다 주었다.

➡ _____

16 그 해산물 볶음밥은 놀랍도록 맛있었다.

➡ _____

17 나는 음식 사진을 찍어 그것을 내 블로그에 올리고 싶은 마음이 정말 간절했다.

➡ _____

18 그러나 스마트폰이 없었기 때문에 나는 그냥 그 순간을 즐기기로 했다.

➡ _____

19 (여행의) 남아 있는 날들 동안, 우리는 점점 더 현지 사람들에게 의존하게 되었다.

➡ _____

20 우리는 거리에서, 빵집에서, 공원에서 다양한 사람들을 만나 이야기할 수 있었다.

➡ _____

21 그들은 항상 웃으면서 너무나 친절히도 바르셀로나의 다양한 면을 우리에게 보여 주었다.

➡ _____

22 또한 우리 가족은 서로 많은 대화를 나누었다.

➡ _____

23 우리는 스페인의 기차에서, 버스에서, 그리고 식당에서 많은 시간을 함께 보냈다.

➡ _____

24 우리의 '첨단 과학 기술 없는' 여행은 새롭고 색다른 경험이었다.

➡ _____

25 여행 전에 나는 내 스마트폰에 너무 의존해서 그것 없이는 아무것도 할 수 없었다.

➡ _____

26 하지만 지금은 내가 스마트폰 없이도 그 순간을 즐길 수 있음을 알고 있다.

➡ _____

27 그 경험을 통해, 나는 스마트폰을 균형 있게 사용하는 것이 중요함을 배우게 되었다.

➡ _____

28 그러면, 다음번에 나는 스마트폰 없이 여행을 하게 될까?

➡ _____

29 아마도 그렇지는 않을 것이다. 하지만 나는 그것을 좀 더 현명하게 사용하기 위해 노력할 것이다.

➡ _____

※ 다음 우리말과 일치하도록 빈칸에 알맞은 말을 쓰시오.

Read and Think

1. _____ _____ to Barcelona

2. Last summer, I had a _____ and _____ _____: a family trip _____ smartphones.

3. _____

4. _____ the first day, we got lost _____ _____ _____ _____ the guesthouse.

5. I couldn't _____ _____ _____ the food and _____ them _____ my blog.

6. _____

7. I _____ the places and the people _____ me.

8. I talked _____ _____ with my family _____ _____ _____ and everywhere.

9. Changes _____ the Trip

10. My _____ on _____ a smartphone

11. Before: I _____ _____ _____ without it.

12. Now: I understand the _____ of a _____ _____ of it.

Grammar in Real Life B

1. _____ one apple under _____ water and _____ it _____ small _____.

2. Cook the _____ apple pieces _____ brown sugar on _____ _____.

3. _____ salt, milk, and a beaten egg _____ _____ the egg _____.

4. _____ the bread _____ and _____ the cooked apple _____ on it.

5. Put the _____ _____ in the egg mixture and _____ _____ _____ quickly. Then _____ it for 3 _____.

6. _____ a dish with the bread rolls and the _____ _____ _____.

1. 바르셀로나로의 첨단 과학 기술 없는 여행
2. 지난여름, 나는 새롭고 색다른 경험으로 '스마트폰 없는 가족 여행'을 갔다.
3. 힘들었던 점
4. 첫째 날, 우리는 숙소로 가는 도중에 길을 잃었다.
5. 나는 음식 사진을 찍어 블로그에 올릴 수 없었다.
6. 좋았던 점
7. 나는 내 주위에 있는 장소들과 사람들을 즐겼다.
8. 나는 가족들과 언제 어디서든 많은 대화를 나누었다.
9. 여행 후 달라진 점
10. 스마트폰 사용에 대한 나의 생각
11. 이전: 나는 그것 없이는 아무것도 할 수 없었다.
12. 지금: 나는 그것을 균형 있게 사용하는 것이 중요함을 이해한다.

1. 사과 한 개를 흐르는 물에 씻어 작은 조각으로 자르세요.
2. 잘라진 사과 조각들을 노란 설탕과 함께 약한 불에서 조리세요.
3. 계란 혼합물을 만들기 위해 소금, 우유, 그리고 휘저은 계란을 더하세요.
4. 식빵을 얇게 밀어서 펴고 그 위에 조린 사과 소를 올리세요.
5. 돌돌 말은 빵을 계란 혼합물에 넣었다가 빠르게 꺼내세요. 그러고 나서 그 것을 3분간 구우세요.
6. 돌돌 말은 빵과 남아 있는 사과 소로 접시를 장식하세요.

※ 다음 우리말을 영어로 쓰시오.

Read and Think

1. 바르셀로나로의 첨단 과학 기술 없는 여행
➡ _____

2. 지난여름, 나는 새롭고 색다른 경험으로 '스마트폰 없는 가족 여행'을 갔다.
➡ _____

3. 힘들었던 점
➡ _____

4. 첫째 날, 우리는 숙소로 가는 도중에 길을 잃었다.
➡ _____

5. 나는 음식 사진을 찍어 블로그에 올릴 수 없었다.
➡ _____

6. 좋았던 점
➡ _____

7. 나는 내 주위에 있는 장소들과 사람들을 즐겼다.
➡ _____

8. 나는 가족들과 언제 어디서든 많은 대화를 나누었다.
➡ _____

9. 여행 후 달라진 점
➡ _____

10. 스마트폰 사용에 대한 나의 생각
➡ _____

11. 이전: 나는 그것 없이는 아무것도 할 수 없었다.
➡ _____

12. 지금: 나는 그것을 균형 있게 사용하는 것이 중요함을 이해한다.
➡ _____

Grammar in Real Life B

1. 사과 한 개를 흐르는 물에 씻어 작은 조각으로 자르세요.
➡ _____

2. 잘라진 사과 조각들을 노란 설탕과 함께 약한 불에서 조리세요.
➡ _____

3. 계란 혼합물을 만들기 위해 소금, 우유, 그리고 휘저은 계란을 더하세요.
➡ _____

4. 식빵을 얇게 밀어서 펴고 그 위에 조린 사과 소를 올리세요.
➡ _____

5. 돌돌 말은 빵을 계란 혼합물에 넣었다가 빠르게 꺼내세요. 그러고 나서 그것을 3분간 구우세요.
➡ _____

6. 돌돌 말은 빵과 남아 있는 사과 소로 접시를 장식하세요.
➡ _____

※ 다음 영어를 우리말로 쓰시오.

01	beard		21	decide	
02	cart		22	season	
03	grandchild		23	dwarf	
04	wife		24	explain	
05	ground		25	field	
06	stone		26	tooth	
07	trouble		27	unless	
08	destroy		28	go by	
09	glad		29	look forward to	
10	hand		30	get rid of	
11	arrive		31	throw away	
12	bear		32	be proud of	
13	warn		33	change into	
14	log		34	far from	
15	magic		35	try to	
16	cow		36	give birth	
17	delight		37	go away	
18	nothing		38	keep ~ from -ing	
19	reward		39	on one's way to	
20	free		40	worry about	
			41	keep -ing	

※ 다음 우리말을 영어로 쓰시오.

01 도착하다

02 계절

03 기쁨

04 빼내다, 풀어 주다

05 땅, 지면

06 결심하다, 결정하다

07 경고하다

08 설명하다

09 ~하지 않는 한

10 들판

11 수염

12 아내, 부인

13 기쁜

14 건네주다

15 통나무

16 마술의

17 파괴하다, 없애다

18 이, 치아

19 손주

20 아무것도 ~아닌 것

21 수레, 우마차

22 돌

23 (새끼를) 낳다

24 소, 암소

25 보상, 보답

26 난쟁이

27 문제

28 ~에서 멀리

29 ~을 자랑스러워하다

30 ~가 …하지 못하게 하다

31 ~하려고 노력하다

32 ~을 없애다

33 떠나가다

34 ~으로 바꾸다

35 계속 ~하다

36 ~을 기대하다, ~을 고대하다

37 ~로 가는 길에

38 흐르다, 지나가다

39 ~을 버리다

40 ~에 대해 걱정하다

41 새끼를 낳다, 출산하다

※ 다음 영영풀이에 알맞은 단어를 <보기>에서 골라 쓴 후, 우리말 뜻을 쓰시오.

1 _____ : a small piece of rock of any shape: _____

2 _____ : to pass or give something to somebody: _____

3 _____ : to give birth to a child: _____

4 _____ : a child of your son or daughter: _____

5 _____ : hair that grows on the chin and cheeks of a man's face: _____

6 _____ : the woman that somebody is married to: _____

7 _____ : to get to a place, especially at the end of a journey: _____

8 _____ : to damage something so badly that it no longer exists, works, etc.: _____

9 _____ : a thick piece of wood that is cut from or has fallen from a tree: _____

10 _____ : a large animal that is raised by people for milk or meat usually on a farm: _____

11 _____ : any of the four main periods of the year: spring, summer, fall, and winter: _____

12 _____ : an area of land in the country, especially one where crops are grown or animals feed on grass: _____

13 _____ : a vehicle with two or four wheels that is pulled by a horse and used for carrying loads: _____

14 _____ : a thing that you are given because you have done something good, worked hard, etc.: _____

15 _____ : to tell somebody about something, especially something dangerous or unpleasant that is likely to happen, so that they can avoid it: _____

16 _____ : to remove something that is unpleasant or not wanted from somebody/ something: _____

보기			
arrive	stone	bear	log
warn	free	reward	grandchild
beard	hand	wife	destroy
field	season	cow	cart

※ 다음 우리말과 일치하도록 빈칸에 알맞은 것을 골라 쓰시오.

1 _____ day, Maibon was _____ _____ the road on his horse and cart _____ he saw an old man.

A. when   B. down   C. one   D. driving

2 The old man _____ very _____. Maibon began to _____ _____ growing old.

A. sick   B. about   C. looked   D. worry

3 _____ that day, he _____ a dwarf, Doli, in the _____.

A. field   B. saw   C. later

4 He was trying to _____ his leg _____ from _____ a log.

A. out   B. get   C. under

5 Maibon _____ the log _____ and _____ the dwarf.

A. away   B. pulled   C. freed

6 "You'll _____ your _____. What do you _____?"

A. reward   B. have   C. want

7 "I've _____ that you have magic stones _____ can _____ a man _____. I want one."

A. keep   B. that   C. heard   D. young

8 "Oh, you _____ have it all _____. Those stones don't make you young again. They only _____ you _____ getting older."

A. wrong   B. from   C. humans   D. keep

9 "Just as good!" Doli _____ to _____ the problem _____ the stones, but Maibon didn't _____.

A. explain   B. with   C. listen   D. tried

10 So Doli _____ him a magic stone and _____ _____.

A. away   B. handed   C. went

11 After _____ _____ days, Maibon saw that his beard didn't _____ at _____.

A. few   B. grow   C. all   D. a

12 He _____ happy, but his wife, Modrona, _____ _____.

A. got   B. became   C. upset

13 The eggs don't _____ _____ chickens!" "Oh, the season's _____, that's all."

A. into   B. slow   C. change

14 But she was not happy. "The cow doesn't give _____!" Maibon, then, told her about the stone, and she _____ very angry and told him to _____ it _____.

A. away   B. birth   C. throw   D. got

15 He didn't want to, but he _____ _____ his wife and _____ the stone _____ the window.

A. to   B. out   C. listened   D. threw

16 However, the next morning, he _____ the stone _____ the window!

A. sitting   B. found   C. by

1 어느 날, Maibon이 한 노인을 보았을 때, 그는 마차를 타고 길을 내려가고 있던 중이었다.

2 그 노인은 매우 아파 보였다. Maibon은 늙어 가는 것이 걱정되기 시작했다.

3 그날 오후, 그는 들판에서 Doli라는 난쟁이를 보았다.

4 그는 통나무 아래에 깔린 그의 다리를 빼내려고 하고 있었다.

5 Maibon은 통나무를 잡아당겨서 난쟁이를 풀어주었다.

6 "너는 보상을 받게 될 거야. 원하는게 뭐니?"

7 "나는 네가 사람의 젊음을 유지해 주는 마법의 돌들을 가지고 있다고 들었어. 나는 그것을 원해."

8 "오, 너희 인간들은 잘못 알고 있어. 그 돌들은 너희들이 다시 젊어지게 해 주지 않아. 단지 더 늙지 않게 막아 줄 뿐이라고."

9 "그것대로 좋아!" Doli는 그 돌에 관한 문제를 설명하려고 했지만, Maibon은 듣지 않았다.

10 그래서 Doli는 그에게 마법의 돌을 건네고는 가버렸다.

11 며칠이 지나서, Maibon은 그의 수염이 전혀 자라지 않았음을 알았다.

12 그는 행복해졌지만, 그의 아내 Modrona는 화가 났다.

13 "달걀이 닭이 되지 않아요!" "아, 시기가 더딘 거예요. 그 뿐이에요."

14 하지만 그녀는 탐탁해하지 않았다. "소가 새끼를 낳지 않아요!" 그때 Maibon은 그 돌에 대해 그녀에게 이야기를 했고 그녀는 매우 화를 내며 그에게 그것을 버리라고 말했다.

15 그는 원하지 않았지만, 아내의 말을 듣고 창밖으로 돌을 던졌다.

16 그러나 다음날 아침 그는 창가에 그 돌이 있는 것을 발견했다!

17 Maibon was _____ _____ the animals, but he was glad _____ he was _____ young.

    A. about   B. that   C. worried   D. still

18 Now Maibon's baby was _____ _____. No _____ was _____ in his mouth.

    A. seen   B. trouble   C. having   D. tooth

19 His wife told him to _____ _____ the stone and this time, Maibon _____ the stone _____ the ground.

    A. put   B. away   C. under   D. throw

20 But, the next day, the stone came _____! Time _____ and nothing _____ or changed.

    A. by   B. back   C. grew   D. went

21 Maibon began to _____. "There's nothing to _____ to, _____ to show for my work."

    A. forward   B. nothing   C. worry   D. look

22 Maibon tried to _____ the stone, but it _____ coming _____.

    A. destroy   B. back   C. kept

23 Maibon decided to _____ _____ the stone _____ his house.

    A. far   B. throw   C. from   D. away

24 _____ his _____ to the field, he saw the dwarf. Maibon _____ with him.

    A. got   B. on   C. angry   D. way

25 "Why _____ you _____ me _____ the stone?"

    A. warn   B. didn't   C. about

26 "I _____ to, but you _____ _____."

    A. listen   B. tried   C. wouldn't

27 Doli _____ that Maibon couldn't get _____ _____ the stone _____ he really wanted to.

    A. rid   B. explained   C. unless   D. of

28 "I want no _____ of it. _____ may happen, _____ it _____!"

    A. let   B. more   C. whatever   D. happen

29 Doli told him to _____ the stone _____ the ground and go _____ home.

    A. onto   B. back   D. throw

30 Maibon did _____ Doli said. When he _____ home, Modrona told him the good news — the eggs _____ into chickens and the cow _____ her baby.

    A. changed   B. as   C. bore   D. arrived

31 And Maibon laughed _____ _____ when he saw the first _____ in his baby's _____.

    A. delight   B. tooth   C. with   D. mouth

32 Maibon, Modrona and _____ children and grandchildren _____ many _____.

    A. for   B. years   C. lived   D. their

33 Maibon was _____ _____ his white hair and long _____.

    A. of   B. proud   C. beard

---

17 Maibon은 동물들이 걱정되긴 했지만, 자신이 여전히 젊어서 기뻤다.

18 이제 Maibon의 아기에게 문제가 생겼다. 아기의 입에서 이가 보이지 않았다.

19 그의 아내는 그에게 그 돌을 버리라고 말했고 Maibon은 이번엔 그 돌을 땅속에 묻었다.

20 그런데 그 다음날 그 돌은 다시 돌아왔다! 시간이 흘렀고 어떤 것도 자라거나 변하지 않았다.

21 Maibon은 걱정이 되기 시작했다. "기대할 것도 내 일의 결과를 보여 줄 것도 아무것도 없어."

22 Maibon은 그 돌을 없애려고 노력했지만 돌은 계속 되돌아왔다.

23 Maibon은 그 돌을 그의 집에서 멀리 떨어진 곳에 버리기로 결심했다.

24 그는 들판으로 가는 길에 난쟁이를 보았다. Maibon은 그에게 화를 냈다.

25 "너는 왜 내게 그 돌에 대해 경고하지 않았어?"

26 "나는 하려고 했지만, 너는 들으려 하지 않았어."

27 Doli는 Maibon이 진심으로 원하지 않는 한 그 돌을 없앨 수 없다고 설명했다.

28 "나는 그것을 더 이상 원하지 않아. 무슨 일이 있어도 일어나게 해!"

29 Doli는 그에게 그 돌을 땅에 던지고 집으로 돌아가라고 말했다.

30 Maibon은 Doli가 말한 대로 했다. 그가 집에 도착했을 때, Modrona는 그에게 달걀이 닭이 되고 소가 새끼를 낳았다는 좋은 소식을 말해 주었다.

31 그리고 Maibon은 아기의 입에 첫 이가 난 것을 보고 기뻐서 웃었다.

32 Maibon과 Modrona, 그리고 그들의 자녀들과 손주들은 오랫동안 살았다.

33 Maibon은 그의 흰 머리와 긴 수염을 자랑스러워했다.

※ 다음 우리말과 일치하도록 빈칸에 알맞은 말을 쓰시오.

1 One day, Maibon was _____ _____ the road _____ _____ _____ and cart _____ he saw an old man.

2 The old man _____ very _____. Maibon began _____ _____ _____ _____ _____.

3 _____ _____ _____, he saw a _____, Doli, in the field.

4 He was _____ _____ _____ his leg _____ _____ under a log.

5 Maibon _____ the log _____ and _____ the dwarf.

6 "You'll have your _____. What _____ you _____?"

7 "I've _____ that you have magic stones _____ can _____ a man _____. I want one."

8 "Oh, you humans have _____ _____ _____. Those stones don't make you _____ _____. They only _____ you _____ _____ _____."

9 "Just as good!" Doli _____ _____ _____ the problem with the stones, but Maibon _____ _____.

10 So Doli _____ _____ a magic stone and went away.

11 After _____ _____ _____, Maibon saw that his beard didn't _____ _____ _____.

12 He _____ happy, but his wife, Modrona, _____ _____.

13 The eggs don't _____ _____ _____!" "Oh, the season's _____, that's all."

14 But she was not happy. "The cow doesn't _____ _____!" Maibon, then, told her about the stone, and she _____ very _____ and told him _____ _____ _____ _____.

15 He didn't want to, but he _____ _____ his wife and the stone _____ the window.

16 _____, the next morning, he _____ the stone _____ _____ the window!

1 어느 날, Maibon이 한 노인을 보았을 때, 그는 마차를 타고 길을 내려가고 있던 중이었다.

2 그 노인은 매우 아파 보였다. Maibon은 늙어 가는 것이 걱정되기 시작했다.

3 그날 오후, 그는 들판에서 Doli라는 난쟁이를 보았다.

4 그는 통나무 아래에 깔린 그의 다리를 빼내려고 하고 있었다.

5 Maibon은 통나무를 잡아당겨서 난쟁이를 풀어주었다.

6 "너는 보상을 받게 될 거야. 원하는게 뭐니?"

7 "나는 네가 사람의 젊음을 유지해 주는 마법의 돌들을 가지고 있다고 들었어. 나는 그것을 원해."

8 "오, 너희 인간들은 잘못 알고 있어. 그 돌들은 너희들이 다시 젊어지게 해 주지 않아. 단지 더 늙지 않게 막아 줄 뿐이라고."

9 "그것대로 좋아!" Doli는 그 돌에 관한 문제를 설명하려고 했지만, Maibon은 듣지 않았다.

10 그래서 Doli는 그에게 마법의 돌을 건네고는 가버렸다.

11 며칠이 지나서, Maibon은 그의 수염이 전혀 자라지 않았음을 알았다.

12 그는 행복해졌지만, 그의 아내 Modrona는 화가 났다.

13 "달걀이 닭이 되지 않아요!" "아, 시기가 더딘 거예요. 그 뿐이에요."

14 하지만 그녀는 탐탁해하지 않았다. "소가 새끼를 낳지 않아요!" 그때 Maibon은 그 돌에 대해 그녀에게 이야기를 했고 그녀는 매우 화를 내며 그에게 그것을 버리라고 말했다.

15 그는 원하지 않았지만, 아내의 말을 듣고 창밖으로 돌을 던졌다.

16 그러나 다음날 아침 그는 창가에 그 돌이 있는 것을 발견했다!

17 Maibon was _____ _____ the animals, but he was _____ _____ he was _____ _____ .

18 Now Maibon's baby was _____ _____ . _____ _____ _____ was _____ in his mouth.

19 His wife told him _____ _____ _____ the stone and this time, Maibon _____ the stone _____ _____ _____ .

20 But, the next day, the stone _____ _____ ! Time _____ _____ and _____ _____ or _____ .

21 Maibon began _____ _____ . "There's _____ _____ _____ _____ , nothing to show for my work."

22 Maibon _____ _____ _____ the stone, but it _____ _____ _____ .

23 Maibon _____ _____ _____ _____ the stone _____ _____ his house.

24 _____ _____ _____ _____ the field, he saw the dwarf. Maibon _____ _____ with him.

25 "Why _____ _____ _____ me about the stone?"

26 "I _____ _____ , but you wouldn't _____ ."

27 Doli _____ that Maibon couldn't _____ _____ _____ the stone _____ he really _____ _____ .

28 "I want _____ _____ _____ it. _____ may happen, _____ it _____ !"

29 Doli told him _____ _____ the stone _____ the ground and _____ _____ _____ .

30 Maibon _____ as Doli _____ . When he _____ home, Modrona told him the good news — the eggs _____ _____ chickens and the cow _____ her baby.

31 And Maibon _____ _____ _____ when he saw the first tooth in _____ _____ _____ .

32 Maibon, Modrona and their children and grandchildren _____ _____ _____ .

33 Maibon _____ _____ _____ his white hair and long beard.

17 Maibon은 동물들이 걱정되긴 했지만, 자신이 여전히 젊어서 기뻤다.

18 이제 Maibon의 아기에게 문제가 생겼다. 아기의 입에서 이가 보이지 않았다.

19 그의 아내는 그에게 그 돌을 버리라고 말했고 Maibon은 이번엔 그 돌을 땅속에 묻었다.

20 그런데 그 다음날 그 돌은 다시 돌아왔다! 시간이 흘렀고 어떤 것도 자라거나 변하지 않았다.

21 Maibon은 걱정이 되기 시작했다. "기대할 것도 내 일의 결과를 보여 줄 것도 아무것도 없어."

22 Maibon은 그 돌을 없애려고 노력했지만 돌은 계속 되돌아왔다.

23 Maibon은 그 돌을 그의 집에서 멀리 떨어진 곳에 버리기로 결심했다.

24 그는 들판으로 가는 길에 난쟁이를 보았다. Maibon은 그에게 화를 냈다.

25 "너는 왜 내게 그 돌에 대해 경고하지 않았어?"

26 "나는 하려고 했지만, 너는 들으려 하지 않았어."

27 Doli는 Maibon이 진심으로 원하지 않는 한 그 돌을 없앨 수 없다고 설명했다.

28 "나는 그것을 더 이상 원하지 않아. 무슨 일이 있어도 일어나게 해!"

29 Doli는 그에게 그 돌을 땅에 던지고 집으로 돌아가라고 말했다.

30 Maibon은 Doli가 말한 대로 했다. 그가 집에 도착했을 때, Modrona는 그에게 달걀이 닭이 되고 소가 새끼를 낳았다는 좋은 소식을 말해 주었다.

31 그리고 Maibon은 아기의 입에 첫 이가 난 것을 보고 기뻐서 웃었다.

32 Maibon과 Modrona, 그리고 그들의 자녀들과 손주들은 오랫동안 살았다.

33 Maibon은 그의 흰 머리와 긴 수염을 자랑스러워했다.

※ 다음 문장을 우리말로 쓰시오.

1 One day, Maibon was driving down the road on his horse and cart when he saw an old man.
➡ _____

2 The old man looked very sick. Maibon began to worry about growing old.
➡ _____

3 Later that day, he saw a dwarf, Doli, in the field.
➡ _____

4 He was trying to get his leg out from under a log.
➡ _____

5 Maibon pulled the log away and freed the dwarf.
➡ _____

6 "You'll have your reward. What do you want?"
➡ _____

7 "I've heard that you have magic stones that can keep a man young. I want one."
➡ _____

8 "Oh, you humans have it all wrong. Those stones don't make you young again. They only keep you from getting older."
➡ _____

9 "Just as good!" Doli tried to explain the problem with the stones, but Maibon didn't listen.
➡ _____

10 So Doli handed him a magic stone and went away.
➡ _____

11 After a few days, Maibon saw that his beard didn't grow at all.
➡ _____

12 He became happy, but his wife, Modrona, got upset.
➡ _____

13 "The eggs don't change into chickens!" "Oh, the season's slow, that's all."
➡ _____

14 But she was not happy. "The cow doesn't give birth!" Maibon, then, told her about the stone, and she got very angry and told him to throw it away.
➡ _____

15 He didn't want to, but he listened to his wife and threw the stone out the window.
➡ _____

16 However, the next morning, he found the stone sitting by the window!
➡ _____

17 Maibon was worried about the animals, but he was glad that he was still young.

➡ _____

18 Now Maibon's baby was having trouble. No tooth was seen in his mouth.

➡ _____

19 His wife told him to throw away the stone and this time, Maibon put the stone under the ground.

➡ _____

20 But, the next day, the stone came back! Time went by and nothing grew or changed.

➡ _____

21 Maibon began to worry. "There's nothing to look forward to, nothing to show for my work."

➡ _____

22 Maibon tried to destroy the stone, but it kept coming back.

➡ _____

23 Maibon decided to throw away the stone far from his house.

➡ _____

24 On his way to the field, he saw the dwarf. Maibon got angry with him.

➡ _____

25 "Why didn't you warn me about the stone?"

➡ _____

26 "I tried to, but you wouldn't listen."

➡ _____

27 Doli explained that Maibon couldn't get rid of the stone unless he really wanted to.

➡ _____

28 "I want no more of it. Whatever may happen, let it happen!"

➡ _____

29 Doli told him to throw the stone onto the ground and go back home.

➡ _____

30 Maibon did as Doli said. When he arrived home, Modrona told him the good news — the eggs changed into chickens and the cow bore her baby.

➡ _____

_____

31 And Maibon laughed with delight when he saw the first tooth in his baby's mouth.

➡ _____

32 Maibon, Modrona and their children and grandchildren lived for many years.

➡ _____

33 Maibon was proud of his white hair and long beard.

➡ _____

※ 다음 괄호 안의 단어들을 우리말에 맞도록 바르게 배열하시오.

1 (day, / one / was / Maibon / driving / the / down / load / his / on / horse / and / when / cart / saw / he / old / an / man.)
➡ _____

2 (old / the / man / very / looked / sick. // Maibon / to / began / worry / growing / old. / about)
➡ _____

3 (that / later / day, / saw / he / dwarf, / a / Doli, / field. / the / in)
➡ _____

4 (was / he / trying / get / to / leg / his / from / out / log. / a / under)
➡ _____

5 (pulled / Maibon / log / the / and / away / the / freed / dwarf.)
➡ _____

6 (have / "you'll / reward. / your // do / what / want?" / you)
➡ _____

7 ("I've / that / heard / have / you / stones / magic / can / that / keep / a / young. / man // one." / want / I)
➡ _____

8 ("oh, / humans / you / it / have / wrong. / all // stones / those / make / don't / you / again. / young // only / they / keep / from / you / older." / getting)
➡ _____

9 (as / good!" / "just // tried / Doli / explain / to / problem / the / with / stones, / the / but / didn't / Maibon / listen.)
➡ _____

10 (Doli / so / him / handed / magic / a / stone / away. / and / went)
➡ _____

11 (a / after / days. / few / saw / Maibon / that / beard / his / grow / didn't / all. / at)
➡ _____

12 (became / he / happy, / but / wife, / his / got / Modrona, / upset.)
➡ _____

13 ("the / don't / eggs / chickens!" / into / change // "oh, / season's / the / slow, / all." / that's)
➡ _____

14 (she / but / not / happy. / was // "the / doesn't / cow / birth!" / give // then, / Maibon / her / told / the / about / stone, / and / got / she / angry / very / and / him / told / throw / to / away. / it)
➡ _____
_____
_____

15 (didn't / he / to, / want / but / listened / he / his / to / wife / and / the / threw / stone / the / out / window.)
➡ _____

16 (however, / the / morning, / next / found / he / stone / the / by / sitting / window! / the)
➡ _____

1 어느 날, Maibon이 한 노인을 보았을 때, 그는 마차를 타고 길을 내려가고 있던 중이었다.

2 그 노인은 매우 아파 보였다. Maibon은 늙어 가는 것이 걱정되기 시작했다.

3 그날 오후, 그는 들판에서 Doli라는 난쟁이를 보았다.

4 그는 통나무 아래에 깔린 그의 다리를 빼내려고 하고 있었다.

5 Maibon은 통나무를 잡아당겨서 난쟁이를 풀어주었다.

6 "너는 보상을 받게 될 거야. 원하는게 뭐니?"

7 "나는 네가 사람의 젊음을 유지해 주는 마법의 돌들을 가지고 있다고 들었어. 나는 그것을 원해."

8 "오, 너희 인간들은 잘못 알고 있어. 그 돌들은 너희들이 다시 젊어지게 해 주지 않아. 단지 더 늙지 않게 막아 줄 뿐이라고."

9 "그것대로 좋아!" Doli는 그 돌에 관한 문제를 설명하려고 했지만, Maibon은 듣지 않았다.

10 그래서 Doli는 그에게 마법의 돌을 건네고는 가버렸다.

11 며칠이 지나서, Maibon은 그의 수염이 전혀 자라지 않았음을 알았다.

12 그는 행복해졌지만, 그의 아내 Modrona는 화가 났다.

13 "달걀이 닭이 되지 않아요!" "아, 시기가 더딘 거예요. 그 뿐이에요."

14 하지만 그녀는 탐탁해하지 않았다. "소가 새끼를 낳지 않아요!" 그때 Maibon은 그 돌에 대해 그녀에게 이야기를 했고 그녀는 매우 화를 내며 그에게 그것을 버리라고 말했다.

15 그는 원하지 않았지만, 아내의 말을 듣고 창밖으로 돌을 던졌다.

16 그러나 다음날 아침 그는 창가에 그 돌이 있는 것을 발견했다!

17 (was / Maibon / worried / the / about / animals, / but / was / he / glad / that / was / he / young. / still)

➡ _____

18 (Maibon's / now / was / baby / trouble. / having // tooth / no / seen / was / mouth. / his / in)

➡ _____

19 (wife / his / him / told / throw / to / the / away / stone / and / time, / this / Maibon / the / put / under / stone / ground. / the)

➡ _____

20 (but, / next / the / day, / stone / the / back! / came // went / time / and / by / grew / nothing / changed. / or)

➡ _____

21 (began / Maibon / worry. / to // "there's / to / nothing / look / to, / forward / to / nothing / show / for / work." / my)

➡ _____

22 (tired / Maibon / destory / to / stone, / the / it / but / back. / coming / kept)

➡ _____

23 (decided / Maibon / throw / to / away / stone / the / from / far / house. / his)

➡ _____

24 (his / on / to / way / field, / the / saw / he / dwarf. / the // got / Maibon / him. / with / angry)

➡ _____

25 ("why / you / didn't / me / warm / about / stone?" / the)

➡ _____

26 ("I / to, / tried / you / but / listen." / wouldn't)

➡ _____

27 (Doli / that / explained / Maibon / get / couldn't / rid / the / of / unless / stone / he / to. / wanted / really)

➡ _____

28 ("I / no / want / of / more / it. // may / whatever / happen, / let / happen!" / it)

➡ _____

29 (told / Doli / him / throw / to / stone / the / onto / ground / the / and / back / home. / go)

➡ _____

30 (did / Maibon / Doli / as / said. // he / when / home, / arrived / Modrona / him / told / good / the / news / – / eggs / the / into / changed / chickens / the / and / bore / cow / baby. / her)

➡ _____

31 (Maibon / and / with / laughed / delight / with / when / saw / he / first / the / tooth / his / in / mouth. / baby's)

➡ _____

32 (Modrona / Maibon, / and / children / their / and / lived / grnadchildren / for / years. / many)

➡ _____

33 (was / Maibon / proud / of / white / his / hair / beard. / long / and)

➡ _____

17 Maibon은 동물들이 걱정되긴 했지만, 자신이 여전히 젊어서 기뻤다.

18 이제 Maibon의 아기에게 문제가 생겼다. 아기의 입에서 이가 보이지 않았다.

19 그의 아내는 그에게 그 돌을 버리라고 말했고 Maibon은 이번엔 그 돌을 땅속에 묻었다.

20 그런데 그 다음날 그 돌은 다시 돌아왔다! 시간이 흘렀고 어떤 것도 자라거나 변하지 않았다.

21 Maibon은 걱정이 되기 시작했다. "기대할 것도 내 일의 결과를 보여 줄 것도 아무것도 없어."

22 Maibon은 그 돌을 없애려고 노력했지만 돌은 계속 되돌아왔다.

23 Maibon은 그 돌을 그의 집에서 멀리 떨어진 곳에 버리기로 결심했다.

24 그는 들판으로 가는 길에 난쟁이를 보았다. Maibon은 그에게 화를 냈다.

25 "너는 왜 내게 그 돌에 대해 경고하지 않았어?"

26 "나는 하려고 했지만, 너는 들으려 하지 않았어."

27 Doli는 Maibon이 진심으로 원하지 않는 한 그 돌을 없앨 수 없다고 설명했다.

28 "나는 그것을 더 이상 원하지 않아. 무슨 일이 있어도 일어나게 해!"

29 Doli는 그에게 그 돌을 땅에 던지고 집으로 돌아가라고 말했다.

30 Maibon은 Doli가 말한 대로 했다. 그가 집에 도착했을 때, Modrona는 그에게 달걀이 닭이 되고 소가 새끼를 낳았다는 좋은 소식을 말해 주었다.

31 그리고 Maibon은 아기의 입에 첫 이가 난 것을 보고 기뻐서 웃었다.

32 Maibon과 Modrona, 그리고 그들의 자녀들과 손주들은 오랫동안 살았다.

33 Maibon은 그의 흰 머리와 긴 수염을 자랑스러워했다.

※ 다음 우리말을 영어로 쓰시오.

1 어느 날, Maibon이 한 노인을 보았을 때, 그는 마차를 타고 길을 내려가고 있던 중이었다.

➡ _____

2 그 노인은 매우 아파 보였다. Maibon은 늙어 가는 것이 걱정되기 시작했다.

➡ _____

3 그날 오후, 그는 들판에서 Doli라는 난쟁이를 보았다.

➡ _____

4 그는 통나무 아래에 깔린 그의 다리를 빼내려고 하고 있었다.

➡ _____

5 Maibon은 통나무를 잡아당겨서 난쟁이를 풀어 주었다.

➡ _____

6 "너는 보상을 받게 될 거야. 원하는 게 뭐니?"

➡ _____

7 "나는 네가 사람의 젊음을 유지해 주는 마법의 돌들을 가지고 있다고 들었어. 나는 그것을 원해."

➡ _____

8 오, 너희 인간들은 잘못 알고 있어. 그 돌들은 너희들이 다시 젊어지게 해 주지 않아. 단지 더 늙지 않게 막아 줄 뿐이라고."

➡ _____

9 "그것대로 좋아!" Doli는 그 돌에 관한 문제를 설명하려고 했지만, Maibon은 듣지 않았다.

➡ _____

10 그래서 Doli는 그에게 마법의 돌을 건네고는 가버렸다.

➡ _____

11 며칠이 지나서, Maibon은 그의 수염이 전혀 자라지 않았음을 알았다.

➡ _____

12 그는 행복해졌지만, 그의 아내 Modrona는 화가 났다.

➡ _____

13 "달걀이 닭이 되지 않아요!" "아, 시기가 더딘 거예요. 그 뿐이에요."

➡ _____

14 하지만 그녀는 탐탁해하지 않았다. "소가 새끼를 낳지 않아요!" 그때 Maibon은 그 돌에 대해 그녀에게 이야기를 했고 그녀는 매우 화를 내며 그에게 그것을 버리라고 말했다.

➡ _____

15 그는 원하지 않았지만, 아내의 말을 듣고 창밖으로 돌을 던졌다.

➡ _____

16 그러나 다음날 아침 그는 창가에 그 돌이 있는 것을 발견했다!

➡ _____

17 Maibon은 동물들이 걱정되긴 했지만, 자신이 여전히 젊어서 기뻤다.

➡ _____

18 이제 Maibon의 아기에게 문제가 생겼다. 아기의 입에서 이가 보이지 않았다.

➡ _____

19 그의 아내는 그에게 그 돌을 버리라고 말했고 Maibon은 이번엔 그 돌을 땅속에 묻었다.

➡ _____

20 그런데 그 다음날 그 돌은 다시 돌아왔다! 시간이 흘렀고 어떤 것도 자라거나 변하지 않았다.

➡ _____

21 Maibon은 걱정이 되기 시작했다. "기대할 것도 내 일의 결과를 보여 줄 것도 아무것도 없어."

➡ _____

22 Maibon은 그 돌을 없애려고 노력했지만 돌은 계속 되돌아왔다.

➡ _____

23 Maibon은 그 돌을 그의 집에서 멀리 떨어진 곳에 버리기로 결심했다.

➡ _____

24 그는 들판으로 가는 길에 난쟁이를 보았다. Maibon은 그에게 화를 냈다.

➡ _____

25 "너는 왜 내게 그 돌에 대해 경고하지 않았어?"

➡ _____

26 "나는 하려고 했지만, 너는 들으려 하지 않았어."

➡ _____

27 Doli는 Maibon이 진심으로 원하지 않는 한 그 돌을 없앨 수 없다고 설명했다.

➡ _____

28 "나는 그것을 더 이상 원하지 않아. 무슨 일이 있어도 일어나게 해!"

➡ _____

29 Doli는 그에게 그 돌을 땅에 던지고 집으로 돌아가라고 말했다.

➡ _____

30 Maibon은 Doli가 말한 대로 했다. 그가 집에 도착했을 때, Modrona는 그에게 달걀이 닭이 되고 소가 새끼를 낳았다는 좋은 소식을 말해 주었다.

➡ _____

_____

31 그리고 Maibon은 아기의 입에 첫 이가 난 것을 보고 기뻐서 웃었다.

➡ _____

32 Maibon과 Modrona, 그리고 그들의 자녀들과 손주들은 오랫동안 살았다.

➡ _____

33 Maibon은 그의 흰 머리와 긴 수염을 자랑스러워했다.

➡ _____

영어 기출 문제집

적중100

2학기

정답 및 해설

비상 | 김진완

중 2

영어 기출 문제집

적중100

2학기

정답 및 해설

비상 | 김진완

중 2

Lesson 7

Art around Us

06 (1) stay away from: ~을 가까이 하지 않다 (2) take a look at: ~을 보다 (3) right away: 즉시, 바로

교과서 Conversation

핵심 Check   p.10~11

1 (1) What kind of concert
  (2) movie do you want to see   (3) type
2 (1) Which do you prefer
  (2) taking photos, drawing pictures
  (3) I prefer dogs to cats

시험대비 실력평가   p.08

01 melt   02 ①   03 ⑤
04 (1) took   (2) glanced
   (3) artworks   (4) soap bubbles
05 (1) myth   (2) landscape   (3) details
   (4) wax   (5) wings
06 ①

01 주어진 단어의 관계는 반의어 관계이다. melt: 녹다, freeze: 얼다
02 특히 자연적이거나 역사적인 사건을 설명하기 위해 만들어진 고대의 이야기를 가리키는 말은 myth(신화)이다.
03 despite: ~에도 불구하고
04 (1) take a look at: ~을 보다 (2) glance at: ~을 힐끗 보다 (3) artwork: 미술 작품 (4) soap bubble: 비눗방울
06 주어진 문장에서 notice는 '알아차리다'라는 의미를 나타내며 이와 같은 의미로 쓰인 것은 ①번이다. 나머지는 모두 '통지, 공고'라는 의미로 쓰였다.

교과서 대화문 익히기

Check(√) True or False   p.12

1 T   2 F   3 T   4 T

서술형 시험대비   p.09

01 princess
02 (1) melts   (2) exhibition   (3) feathers
03 (1) landscape   (2) notice   (3) stick
   (4) promise   (5) seaside
04 (1) I wonder why he invited me to his party.
   (2) Production of new cars will start next month.
   (3) Nobody noticed me at first.
05 melt
06 (1) Stay away from windows during a storm.
   (2) May I take a look at your movie ticket?
   (3) I called the police right away.

01 prince: 왕자, princess: 공주
02 melt: 녹다, exhibition: 전시회, feather: 깃털
03 notice: 알아차리다, landscape: 풍경, stick: 내밀다, promise: 약속하다, seaside: 해안가
05 열을 가함으로써 고체에서 액체로 변하는 것을 가리키는 말은 melt(녹다)이다.

교과서 확인학습   p.14~15

Listen & Talk 1 A-1
going to play / almost every day / What kind of music / play songs

Listen & Talk 1 A-2
how to paint clean lines / What kind of brush / flat , better, Try

Listen & Talk 1 B
meeting, right / do you want to watch first / want to / Sounds, right / watching the play / the one

Listen & Talk 2 A-1
a story / of it, prefer, to / like, better / scenes, real

Listen & Talk 2 A-2
Have, listened / cool, part / dance version / I prefer the guitar version / matches

Listen & Talk 2 B
interesting painting / looks like / Which do you prefer / prefer, to / How about you / prefer, to / modern

Communication
so, find out, May, ask / What kind of performance / do, prefer / prefer rock to hip-hop / favorite musician / Thank, for

Can, help / various kinds, What kind of music / want to / should get

시험대비 기본평가　p.16

01 ①, ④　　02 What kind of brush were you using?
03 (A) *Life of Pi*　(B) the movie　　04 ④

01 (A)는 도움을 요청하는 표현이다.
04 ④ Minsu는 소설보다 영화를 더 선호한다.

시험대비 실력평가　p.17~18

01 ⑤　　02 (A) Jane's new song (= Girl Friend)
(B) a dance version　(C) the guitar version
03 ④　　04 ⑤　　05 (A) Jack　(B) Mina
(C) It has an interesting smile.　(D) His Mona Lisa is
cute, and it looks modern.　06 ③　　07 which
do you prefer 08 She likes rock better.　09 (C) →
(B) → (D) → (A)

03 ④ Tony는 Jane의 목소리가 기타 버전에 잘 어울린다고 생각한다.
04 ⑤ Steve가 '로미오와 줄리엣' 연극 볼 것을 왜 제안하는지는 알 수 없다.
08 Emily는 록을 더 좋아한다.
09 (C) 어떠한 종류의 음악을 연주하고 싶은지 질문→ (B) 대답 → (D) 기타 추천 → (A) 구매

서술형 시험대비　p.19

01 (A) ⓑ　(B) ⓒ　(C) ⓐ
02 They have listened to Girl Friend .
03 Because he thinks that the guitar version matches
Jane's voice better.
04 I prefer the movie to the novel.
05 It's about a boy and a tiger.
06 It's because he thinks that the scenes are very
beautiful and the tiger looks so real.

02 Tony와 Sue가 Jane의 앨범에서 들은 노래는 *Girl Friend* 이다.
03 Tony는 기타 버전이 Jane의 목소리와 더 잘 어울린다고 생각하기 때문이다.

04 prefer A to B: A를 B보다 선호하다
05 *Life of Pi* 는 소년과 호랑이에 관한 이야기이다.
06 민수가 소설보다 영화를 더 선호한 이유는 장면이 매우 아름답고 호랑이가 매우 진짜처럼 보이기 때문이다.

교과서
Grammar

핵심 Check　p.20~21

1 (1) me watch　(2) him use　(3) my dad come
2 (1) who she is　(2) why you study　(3) where you went

시험대비 기본평가　p.22

01 (1) to read → read
　(2) was the weather → the weather was
　(3) buying → buy
　(4) were you → you were
02 (1) Oliver wanted to ask if[whether] she was
　　satisfied with his service.
　(2) Can you tell me where we are going?
　(3) I'd like to know what you do during your free
　　time.
　(4) I wonder how often you water the plant.
03 (1) The boss made him stay in the office.
　(2) Did you let your friend borrow your bicycle?
　(3) We had him wear a straw hat.
　(4) Please let me see the answer.

01 (1), (3) 사역동사의 목적격 보어는 동사원형 형태이다. (2),
(4) 의문사가 이끄는 문장이 명사 역할을 할 때 '의문사+주어+
동사'의 어순임에 유의하자.
02 의문사가 없는 경우는 if나 whether를 사용하여 간접의문문을
만들
03 사역동사 make, have, let은 목적격 보어로 동사원형 형태를
사용한다. 이때 목적어와 목적격 보어의 관계는 주어와 서술어
의 관계가 성립하여 '목적어가 ~ 하도록 시키다'라고 해석한다.

시험대비 실력평가　p.23~25

01 ⑤　　02 ③　　03 ④　　04 ⑤
05 come　06 will　07 ③　08 ③
09 Who do you suppose broke the window?
10 ②　　11 ③

12 Why do you think she made you do it again?

13 I made him repair my watch.

| 14 ④ | 15 ④ | 16 ③ | 17 ③ |
| 18 ④ | 19 ⑤ | 20 ③ | 21 ④ |

22 what you do when you are free

23 ③　　　　24 ②

25 I want to know if[whether] she liked the present.

01 want는 목적격 보어로 to부정사를 취하는 동사이다.

02 '목적어가 ~하도록 시키다'라는 의미로 쓰이는 동사는 사역동사이다.

03 간접의문문의 의문사를 문두에 배치하는 동사는 추측동사로 think, imagine, guess, suppose, believe 등이 이에 속한다.

04 모두 목적격 보어로 동사원형 형태를 취할 수 있는 동사이지만, allow는 목적격 보어로 to부정사를 취하는 동사이다.

05 make는 사역동사이므로 목적격 보어로 동사원형 형태를 취한다.

06 주어진 문장을 영어로 옮기면 'I wonder when you will arrive here.'이다.

07 ⓑ when they will call me ⓒ let me wear라고 쓰는 것이 옳다.

08 간접의문문을 만드는 문제이다. 간접의문문의 어순은 '의문사+주어+동사'이다.

09 suppose가 있는 문장에서 간접의문문의 주어를 문두에 배치하는 것에 유의한다.

10 '누가 한글을 만들었는지'라는 의미이므로 who made Hanguel이라고 쓰는 것이 옳다.

11 사역동사의 목적격 보어는 동사원형의 형태를 취하며, '너의 부모님이 집에 없는 동안 너를 누가 돌볼 것인지를 말해 달라'는 것이므로 간접의문문을 이용하여 who will take care of you라고 쓰는 것이 옳다.

12 think가 있는 문장이므로 간접의문문의 의문사를 문두에 배치해야 한다.

13 '그가 내 시계를 고치게 했다'는 것은 사역동사를 이용하여 나타낼 수 있다.

14 주어진 말을 영어로 쓰면 What time do you think it is?이다.

15 allow는 목적격 보어로 to부정사를 취하는 동사이다. help는 목적격 보어로 to부정사나 동사원형 형태를 취한다.

16 간접의문문의 어순은 '의문사+주어+동사'임에 유의한다.

17 사역동사로 쓰인 make이므로 목적격 보어로 동사원형 형태를 쓴다.

18 3형식, 4형식, 5형식으로 모두 쓰이면서 목적격 보어로 동사원형 형태까지 취할 수 있는 것은 동사 make이다.

19 Who do you guess built the building?이라고 쓰는 것이 옳다.

20 대답으로 미루어 보아 몇 학년인지를 묻는 말이 들어가는 것이 가장 적절하다. 간접의문문의 어순인 '의문사+주어+동사'에 유의한다.

21 목적격 보어로 동사원형 형태를 취하는 동사는 사역동사이다.

22 답변으로 보아 여가 시간에 무엇을 하는지를 묻는 말이 들어가는 것이 적절하다.

23 think가 있는 문장이므로 Who do you think you are? 라고 쓰는 것이 옳다.

24 엄마가 내게 무언가를 하라고 말하는 것이므로 ②번이 내용상 가장 적절하다.

25 의문사가 없는 문장의 간접의문문은 if 혹은 whether를 써서 만든다.

01 Mom made me and my sister clean the house.

02 Who do you think stole the money?

03 Can you tell me when they let you go home?

04 (1) me drive his car

　　(2) him bring her

　　(3) me look at

05 Brad made me accept the job.

06 (1) I don't know where he lives.

　　(2) How old do you guess he is?

　　(3) Can you tell me why you were absent from school?

　　(4) I want to know when you met him for the first time.

　　(5) When do you think the concert starts?

　　(6) Why do you imagine the baby is crying?

　　(7) Do you know if(또는 whether) Charley was sleeping at that time?

07 I helped my cousin (to) do his homework.

08 (1) play　　(2) published　　(3) take

　　(4) work　　(5) will report

09 the oranges are / how many oranges he wants to buy

10 The woman lets the man drink water.

11 The suit makes me look fancy.

12 A: How do you think the movie was?

　　B: It made me feel sleepy.

13 Do you know who drove the car yesterday?

14 (1) Can you tell me when she wrote this book?

　　(2) You can lead a horse to water, but you can't make him drink.

　　(3) I wonder if(또는 whether) he is full or not.

01 make는 '목적어에게 ~하도록 시키다'라는 의미의 사역동사이다. 따라서 목적격 보어로 동사원형 형태를 써서 문장을 만든다.

02 think가 있는 문장에서는 간접의문문의 의문사를 문두로 배치한

다. 이 문장에서 who는 의문사이자 주어 역할을 동시에 하고 있음에 유의한다.

03 tell의 직접목적어로 간접의문문을 쓰며, '그들이 너를 집에 가게 했다'고 하였으므로 사역동사를 이용하여 문장을 만들 수 있다.

04 위 문장에서 let, make, have는 모두 사역동사로 쓰이고 있으므로 목적격 보어로 동사원형 형태를 쓰는 것에 유의한다.

05 force+목적어+to부정사: 목적어가 ~하도록 강요하다

06 의문사가 이끄는 문장이 절 내에서 주어, 목적어, 보어 역할을 할 때 이를 간접의문문이라고 한다. 간접의문문의 어순은 '의문사+주어+동사'의 어순이며 think, believe, suppose, imagine, guess와 같은 동사가 있을 때에는 의문사를 문두로 배치한다.

07 help는 목적격 보어로 to부정사나 동사원형 형태를 취한다.

08 (1), (3), (4) 사역동사의 목적격 보어는 동사원형의 형태를 취한다. (2) 작년에 이 책을 누가 출간했는지를 궁금해 하는 내용이므로 과거 시제를 쓴다. (5) 내일 무엇을 보고할 것이라고 생각하느냐는 문장이다. 내용에 맞게 미래 시제를 써서 나타낸다.

09 Andy는 오렌지 가격이 얼마인지 알고 싶어한다. 그래서 Paul은 Andy에게 얼마나 많은 오렌지를 사길 원하는지 묻는다.

10 사역동사 let은 목적격 보어로 동사원형 형태를 취한다.

11 정장이 나를 멋지게 보이도록 하는 것이므로 주어는 the suit, 목적어는 me로 하여 사역동사를 써서 문장을 완성할 수 있다.

12 Do you think?와 How was the movie?를 하나의 문장으로 만들어 How do you think the movie was?를 만들 수 있다.

13 who가 의문사와 주어 역할을 동시에 하고 있으므로 who drove the car의 어순으로 쓸 수 있다.

14 의문사가 있는 간접의문문은 '의문사+주어+동사'의 어순을 쓰고 의문사가 없는 경우 if나 whether를 써서 간접의문문을 나타낼 수 있다. 사역 동사는 목적격 보어로 동사원형 형태를 취한다.

교과서 Reading

확인문제 p.28

1 F 2 T 3 T 4 F 5 F

확인문제 p.29

1 F 2 T 3 T 4 T 5 T 6 F

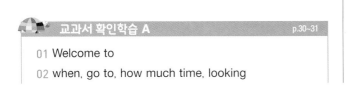

교과서 확인학습 A   p.30~31

01 Welcome to
02 when, go to, how much time, looking

03 glance at, for, a few, on
04 might miss, since, to notice them
05 look at, closely, help you see   06 at, first
07 seaside landscape, peaceful, isn't it
08 title, is   09 where Icarus is
10 are sticking out of the water
11 in the famous myth
12 made wings for him, to stay away from
13 However, listen   14 flew too close
15 melted, fell into   16 at, entire
17 Despite, going on with
18 still look peaceful
19 What do you think   20 move on to
21 see, behind   22 actually painted
23 Who do you think he is   24 Take
25 seems to be, because   26 title, painting
27 drawing, beside   28 Take
29 make you wonder
30 which direction the artist is
31 see, in the mirror, background
32 Who do you think he is

교과서 확인학습 B   p.32~33

1 Welcome to the World Art Museum tour.
2 When you go to an art museum, how much time do you spend looking at each painting?
3 Many visitors glance at one painting for only a few seconds before they move on.
4 But you might miss the important details of paintings since it is hard to notice them right away.
5 Today, we'll look at two paintings closely and I'll help you see interesting details.
6 Look at this painting first.
7 The seaside landscape is so peaceful and beautiful, isn't it?
8 The title of this painting is *Landscape with the Fall of Icarus*.
9 So, can you see where Icarus is?
10 Do you see two legs that are sticking out of the water near the ship?
11 This is Icarus in the famous myth in Greece.
12 In the myth, Icarus' father made wings for him with feathers and wax and told him to stay away from the sun.
13 However, Icarus didn't listen.
14 He flew too close to the sun.

5

15 So, the wax melted and he fell into the water.

16 Now, look at the entire painting again.

17 Despite the tragedy of Icarus, people are going on with their everyday activities.

18 Does the painting still look peaceful?

19 What do you think the artist is trying to tell us?

20 Now, let's move on to the next painting.

21 Do you see the artist behind the large canvas?

22 He is Diego Velázquez, and he actually painted this picture.

23 Who do you think he is painting?

24 Take a quick look.

25 The young princess seems to be the main person because she is in the center of the painting.

26 But the title of the painting is *The Maids of Honour*.

27 Then, is the artist drawing the two women beside the princess?

28 Take a close look.

29 It will make you wonder about the painting more.

30 Try to see which direction the artist is looking at.

31 Can you see the king and the queen in the mirror in the background of the painting?

32 Who do you think he is painting now?

시험대비 실력평가

p.34~37

01 ①　　　　02 notice　　　03 ③

04 We will look at two paintings closely.

05 Can you see where Icarus is?

06 ①　　　　07 ②

08 It is *Landscape with the Fall of Icarus*.

09 ③　　　　10 ④　　　　11 wonder　　　12 ③

13 The young princess seems to be the main person because she is in the center of the painting.

14 We can find him behind the large canvas.

15 ⑤　　　　16 ②

17 It takes them only a few seconds to see one painting.

18 ③　　　　19 ③　　　　20 ⑤　　　　21 ②

22 ⑤

23 He told Icarus to stay away from the sun.

24 ③　　　　25 ④　　　　26 ④

27 The young princess is in the middle of the painting.

28 ②

01 문장에서 since는 이유를 나타내는 접속사로 쓰였다. 따라서 ① 번이 옳다.

02 '무언가를 혹은 어떤 사람을 인식하게 되다'는 '알아차리다 (notice)'이다.

03 (B)는 진주어로 쓰인 to부정사이다. ① 명사적 용법 중 목적어 ② 부사적 용법 중 감정의 원인 ③ 명사적 용법 중 진주어 ④ 형용사적 용법 ⑤ 명사적 용법 중 보어

04 두 개의 그림을 자세히 살펴볼 것이라고 하였다.

05 간접의문문을 만드는 문제이다. '의문사+주어+동사'의 어순에 유의하여 문장을 만든다.

06 이카루스의 비극에도 불구하고 사람들은 일상의 활동을 계속하고 있다는 의미가 가장 자연스럽다. 따라서 despite와 같은 의미인 in spite of를 쓰는 것이 옳다.

07 이카루스의 아버지는 날개를 만들어 주며 태양에 가까이 가지 말라고 말했지만 이카루스는 그의 말을 듣지 않았다는 순서가 자연스러우며 ②번 이하의 문장은 주어진 문장의 결과 이다.

08 그림의 제목은 '추락하는 이카루스가 있는 풍경'이라고 하였다.

09 그림에서 이카루스는 물에 빠져서 두 다리만 보이는 상황이다. 따라서 ③번은 그림에서 찾아볼 수 없다.

10 이카루스의 날개는 그의 아버지가 만들어 준 것이다.

11 사역동사의 목적격 보어 자리이다. 따라서 동사원형 형태를 쓰는 것이 옳다.

12 (B)는 진행형을 만드는 현재분사이다. 모두 동명사이지만 ③번은 현재분사이다.

13 seem to부정사: ~인 것 같다

14 두 번째 그림의 화가는 커다란 캔버스 뒤에 있다고 하였다.

15 그림이 얼마나 큰지는 글을 읽고 알 수 없다.

16 (A) 시간은 셀 수 없으므로 how much (B) the important details of paintings를 가리키므로 복수 대명사 them (C) help는 목적격 보어로 to부정사나 동사원 형 형태를 취한다.

17 많은 방문객들은 이동하기 전에 하나의 그림을 몇 초간만 힐 끗 본다고 하였다. It takes+사람+시간+to V: 사람이 … 하는 데 ~만큼의 시간이 걸리다

18 두 개의 그림을 자세히 살펴보며 흥미로운 세부 사항들을 볼 수 있게 도와준다고 하였으므로 ③번이 가장 적절하다.

19 아버지가 태양에 가까이 가지 말라고 이야기했지만 이카루스 는 그의 말을 듣지 않고 태양에 가깝게 날았다는 내용이므로 However가 옳다.

20 이카루스가 어디에 보이는지 물음 - (C) 그림 속에서 이카루스 가 어디에 있는지 설명하며 이카루스는 그리스 신화에 나오는 인물임을 언급함 - (B) 그리스 신화에 나오는 이카루스의 이야 기 - (A) 아버지의 말을 듣지 않은 이카루스는 물에 빠짐

21 의문사가 이끄는 문장이 절 내에서 명사 역할을 하는 간접의문 문의 어순은 '의문사+주어+동사'의 어순이다.

22 이카루스는 아버지의 말을 듣지 않고 태양 가까이로 날았다가 밀랍이 녹아 물에 빠졌다고 하였다.

23 이카루스의 아버지는 그에게 태양에 가까이 가지 말라고 이야기 하였다.

24 make는 목적격 보어로 동사원형을 취하는 사역동사이며 feel은 형용사를 보어로 취하는 감각동사이다.

25 ④ David Myriam이 그의 작품에서 사용한 것은 모래라고 하였다.

26 추측동사 believe, think, guess, imagine, suppose가 있는 문장에서는 간접의문문의 의문사를 문두로 배치한다. know는 이러한 동사에 해당하지 않는다.

27 그림의 중앙에 있는 사람은 공주라고 하였다.

28 커다란 캔버스 뒤에 있는 화가가 Diego Velázquez이므로 그가 그림에 등장하지 않는다는 것은 글의 내용과 일치하지 않는다.

서술형 시험대비 p.38~39

01 how much time you spend looking at each painting.

02 the important details of paintings

03 I'll help you (to) see interesting details.

04 What do you think the artist is trying to tell us?

05 tragedy

06 He made wings for him.

07 melt

08 where Icarus is, are sticking out of the water

09 actually

10 Diego Velázquez painted the picture.

11 그림을 자세히 보는 것

12 They are the king and the queen.

13 I wonder who actually painted this picture.

14 what the artist used

15 Because a tree in the moon makes the writer feel calm.

01 간접의문문을 완성하는 문제이다. '의문사+주어+동사' 어순에 유의하여 답을 쓴다.

02 그림의 중요한 세부 사항들을 가리키는 말이다.

03 help는 목적격 보어로 to부정사나 동사원형을 모두 쓸 수 있는 준사역동사이다.

04 문장의 동사가 think인 경우 간접의문문의 의문사를 문두에 배치하는 것에 유의하여 답을 쓴다.

05 화가가 그림을 통해 말하려는 것은 우리는 타인의 비극을 알 수 없다는 것이다.

06 이카루스의 아버지는 그를 위하여 날개를 만들어 주었다고 하였다.

07 무엇이 밀랍을 녹게 만들었느냐는 질문을 쓰는 것이 옳다. 사역동사의 목적격 보어 자리이므로 동사원형 형태를 쓰는 것에 유의한다.

08 두 사람의 대화로 미루어 보아 A는 이카루스가 어디에 있는지 묻고 있으며 B가 알려주는 중임을 알 수 있다.

09 동사를 수식하므로 부사로 고쳐야 한다.

10 그림을 그린 사람은 Diego Velázquez라고 하였다.

11 It은 앞 문장 전체인 'Take a close look.'을 가리킨다.

12 그림의 배경에 있는 거울 속 사람들은 왕과 왕비라고 하였다.

13 간접의문문을 이용하여 문장을 만들 수 있다. 여기에서 who는 의문사와 주어 역할을 동시에 하는 것에 유의한다.

14 답변으로 미루어 보아 작가가 그림에 무엇을 사용했는지 묻는 말이 들어가는 것이 옳다.

15 글쓴이가 그 그림을 좋아하는 이유는 달에 있는 나무가 차분한 기분을 느끼게 해 주어서라고 하였다.

영역별 핵심문제 p.41~45

01 tragedy　　02 ⑤　　03 ④

04 (1) tourists　(2) stick　(3) novelist

05 (1) I prefer the novel to the poem.
　(2) My family will take a trip to the seaside.
　(3) The war was a tragedy for the whole world.

06 ②　　07 ①　　08 ⑤　　09 ③

10 What kind of performance do you want to watch first?

11 ⑤　　12 ③　　13 ③　　14 ⑤

15 She doesn't know how to paint clean lines.

16 She will use a flat brush.　17 ③　　18 ⑤

19 ④　　　　20 Where do you think she is now?

21 ②　　22 ③　　23 ⑤

24 help, do　25 ①

26 The monster made the children scream.

27 (1) I didn't hear what you said.
　(2) I'd like to know if you are friends with Jina.

28 ①, ②　　29 ③

30 They were made of feathers and wax.　31 ⑤

32 if the painting still looks peaceful

33 tragedy　　34 (A) looking　(B) a few　(C) closely

35 We might miss the important details of a painting.

36 ③

01 주어진 단어의 관계는 반의어 관계이다. comedy: 희극, tragedy: 비극

02 특히 죽음과 관련된 매우 슬픈 사건을 가리키는 말은 tragedy(비극)이다.

03 flat: 평평한

06 주어진 문장은 '내밀다'라는 뜻을 나타내며 이와 같은 의미로 쓰인 것은 ②번이다. ①, ④ ~을 붙이다, ③, ⑤ 막대기

07 direct: ~으로 향하다, (길을) 안내하다[알려주다], direct flight: 직행 항공편

08 주어진 문장은 소설을 더 좋아하는 이유로 적절하므로 (E)가 알맞다.

09 ③ Jean이 Sally와 함께 영화 *The Maze Runner* 를 보았다는 설명은 대화의 내용과 일치하지 않는다.

13 주어진 문장은 영화를 선호한다는 것으로 다음에 이유를 질문하는 문장에 자연스럽게 이어지므로 (C)가 적절하다.

14 대화를 통해 민수가 언제 영화를 봤는지 알 수 없다.

15 Sora는 선을 깔끔하게 그리는 방법을 모른다.

16 Sora는 선을 그릴 때 납작한 붓을 사용할 것이다.

17 파티에 초대한 주체가 who이므로 who invited you의 어순이 옳다.

18 조건절과 명사절을 동시에 이끌 수 있는 접속사는 if이다.

19 let은 사역동사로 목적격 보어로 동사원형 형태를 취한다. 따라서 use라고 쓰는 것이 옳다.

20 Do you think?와 Where is she now?를 하나로 만든 문장이다.

21 주어진 문장을 영어로 쓰면 I wonder who made you send me this flower.이다.

22 Who kicked the ball?에서 Who는 의문사이자 주어 역할을 동시에 하고 있으므로 ③번이 가장 적절하다.

23 tell은 목적격 보어로 to부정사를 취하는 동사이다.

24 help는 목적격 보어로 to부정사나 동사원형 형태를 모두 쓸 수 있는 동사이다.

25 ⓐ who you are talking with ⓑ have them go to school ⓓ what Jason does ⓔ if(또는 whether) you have brothers or sisters라고 쓰는 것이 옳다.

26 '아이들이 비명을 지르게 하는 것'이므로 사역동사를 이용하여 문장을 만들 수 있다. 사역동사의 목적격 보어는 동사원형 형태임에 유의한다.

27 (2)번은 if를 대신하여 whether를 써도 좋다.

28 의문사가 없는 의문문에는 whether나 if를 써서 간접의문문을 만든다.

29 모두 이카루스를 지칭하는 말이지만 ③번은 이카루스의 아버지를 가리키고 있다.

30 이카루스의 날개는 깃털과 밀랍으로 이루어졌다고 하였다. be made of: ~으로 이루어지다

31 밀랍과 깃털로 이루어진 날개를 달고 태양 가까이 날아간 것 때문에 이카루스는 물에 빠지게 되었다. 따라서 ⑤번은 옳지 않다.

32 의문사가 없는 문장의 간접의문문은 if나 whether를 써서 만든다.

33 '특히 죽음과 관련된 아주 슬픈 사건'은 '비극(tragedy)'이라고 한다.

34 (A) spend+시간+Ving: V하는 데에 시간을 쓰다 (B) 셀 수 있는 seconds를 수식하므로 a few (C) '자세히'라는 의미의 부사가 적절하므로 closely

35 하나의 그림을 몇 초간만 힐끗 보는 것의 문제는 그림의 중요한 세부 사항들을 놓칠 수 있다는 것이다.

36 ⓐ는 가주어로 쓰인 it이다. ① 비인칭 주어 ② 비인칭 주어 ③ 가주어 ④ 인칭대명사 ⑤ 인칭대명사

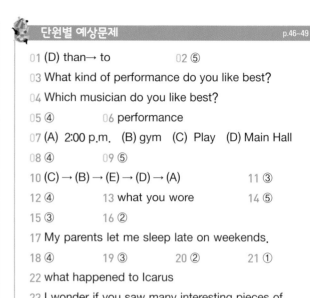

단원별 예상문제   p.46~49

01 (D) than→ to   02 ⑤

03 What kind of performance do you like best?

04 Which musician do you like best?

05 ④   06 performance

07 (A) 2:00 p.m.   (B) gym   (C) Play   (D) Main Hall

08 ④   09 ⑤

10 (C) → (B) → (E) → (D) → (A)   11 ③

12 ④   13 what you wore   14 ⑤

15 ③   16 ②

17 My parents let me sleep late on weekends.

18 ④   19 ③   20 ②   21 ①

22 what happened to Icarus

23 I wonder if you saw many interesting pieces of art.

24 ④

01 prefer A to B: A보다 B를 선호하다

02 Tony가 Girl Friend 의 댄스 버전에 대해 어떻게 생각하는지는 알 수 없다.

08 주어진 문장은 상대방의 의견을 물어보는 표현이므로 (D)가 적절하다.

09 왜 보테로의 '모나리자'가 현대적으로 보이는지는 알 수 없다.

10 (C) Jina가 무엇을 읽고 있는지 질문 → (B) 대답 → (E) 자신은 영화도 보았다며 소설보다 영화를 더 선호함을 말함 → (D) 이유 질문 → (A) 이유 대답

11 '누가 너에게 그 비밀을 말해 줬는지'이므로 who가 간접의문의 주어 역할을 하는 것이 옳다.

12 사역동사의 목적어와 목적격보어가 능동 관계일 경우 목적격보어로 동사원형 형태를 쓴다. drop by: ~에 들르다

13 간접의문문의 어순은 '의문사+주어+동사'이다. 과거시제를 사용하고 있으므로 what you wore라고 쓰는 것에 유의한다.

14 목적격보어로 동사원형 형태를 취할 수 있는 것은 사역동사와 help이다.

15 사역동사 let의 목적격 보어로 동사원형 형태를 쓰는 것이 옳다.

16 What kind of fruit do you like most?를 간접의문문으로 만든 것이므로 '의문사+주어+동사' 어순에 맞는 것을 답으로 고른다.

17 let은 목적격보어로 동사원형 형태를 취하는 사역동사이다.

18 화가가 그리려고 했던 대상이 그림의 중앙에 있는 공주처럼 보이지만 그림의 제목이 '시녀들'이라면 화가가 그리려던 대상이 공주 옆에 있는 두 여인일지 묻는 말로 이어지는 것이 가장 자연스럽다.

19 그림의 제목이 '시녀들'이라고 말하며 '그렇다면 화가는 공주 옆에 있는 두 여자를 그리고 있나요?'라고 하였으므로 시녀들은 두 명임을 알 수 있다.

20 그림에서 왕자는 등장하지 않는다.

21 태양으로 가까이 간 결과 밀랍이 녹아서 물에 빠졌다는 것이다. 따라서 결과를 이끄는 연결어가 나오는 것이 옳다.

22 간접의문문을 이용하여 답을 쓸 수 있다. 이때 what은 의문사와 주어 역할을 동시에 하는 것에 유의한다.

23 if를 대신하여 whether를 써도 무방하다.

서술형 실전문제 p.50~51

01 They will go to the arts festival.
02 They will watch it at the gym.
03 It is at 4. p.m. at the Main Hall.
04 (1) Tell me where Maria lives.
(2) I wonder if you are married.
(3) May I ask if he is alone?
(4) Can you tell me who drove your car?
05 Nothing will make me change my mind.
06 who opened the door
07 to know how many books you read last year
08 (A) melted   (B) fell into
09 What do you think the artist is trying to tell us?
10 near the ship, sticking out of the water
11 He couldn't make his son stay away from the sun.
12 flew, close, wax, melted
13 (D)–(A)–(C)–(B)
14 ⓐ on   ⓑ in

01 Anna와 Steve는 예술 축제에 갈 것이다.
02 Anna와 Steve는 체육관에서 힙합 댄스 공연을 볼 것이다.
03 로미오와 줄리엣은 4시에 Main Hall에서 공연한다.
04 (2), (3)번은 if를 대신하여 whether를 써도 무방하다.
05 make를 사역동사로 사용하고, 마음을 바꾸는 주체가 '나'이므로 이를 목적어로 사용하여 문장을 완성한다.
06 의문사가 주어 역할을 겸하고 있는 간접의문문이다. 이때 동사가 바로 이어져 나올 수 있다.
07 작년에 얼마나 많은 책을 읽었는지 알고 싶다는 문장을 완성 할 수 있다.
08 태양에 의해 밀랍이 녹아 물에 빠졌다고 하는 것이 적절하다.
09 think가 있는 문장에서는 간접의문문의 의문사를 문두로 보낸다.
10 이카루스는 배 가까이에 있으며 그의 두 다리가 물 밖으로 나와 있다고 하였다.
11 아들이 태양에서 멀리 떨어지도록 시키지 못했다는 것이므로 사역동사의 목적어로 his son, 목적격보어로 동사원형 형태를 써서 문장을 만들 수 있다.
12 이카루스는 태양에 너무 가깝게 날아서 날개의 밀랍이 녹았다.
13 주어진 글의 질문에 이어 (D)에서 Velázquez라고 답하고 누구를 그리려고 했는지 질문하고 (A)에서 공주가 주인공인 것처럼 보인다고 답하며 (C)에서 But으로 상반되는 제목을 소개하며 그림을

더 자세히 보라고 말하며 (B)에서 궁금하게 만들 것이라고 언급한 뒤. 화가가 보고 있는 방향 을 보라고 한 후 누구라고 생각하는지 묻는 것이 자연스럽다.
14 move on to: ~으로 옮기다, in the background of: ~ 의 배경에

창의사고력 서술형 문제 p.52

|모범답안|
01 (A) da Vinci's *Mona Lisa*   (B) Botero's
(C) an interesting smile   (D) Botero's *Mona Lisa*
02 what grade you are in / how often you go to a museum / what kind of museum you like to go to / how long you usually spend time in the museum

01 오늘 나는 미술책에서 재미있는 그림을 보았다. 그것은 다빈치의 '모나리자'처럼 보이는데 사실은 페르난도 보테로의 '모나리자'였다. 둘 중에, Jack은 보테로의 그림보다 페르난도의 '모나지라'를 더욱 좋아하였다. 왜냐하면 다빈치의 '모나리자'에 있는 흥미로운 미소 때문이었다. 그와 반대로, 나는 보테로의 '모나리자'가 훨씬 더욱 좋았다. 왜냐하면 그의 모나리자는 귀엽고 현대적으로 보였기 때문이었다.

단원별 모의고사 p.53~56

01 ⑤
02 (1) Melt   (2) Despite   (3) tourist
(4) direction   (5) wonder
03 Can you give me a hand?
04 What kind of music do you want to play?
05 ③   06 ②   07 ⑤
08 (C) → Which   09 ⑤   10 nearly
11 What kind of music are you going to play this year?
12 nineties   13 ⑤
14 Good music will make you feel better.
15 ⑤
16 (1) Do you remember where you found this bag?
(2) Can you tell me why Kelly wants to become a dancer?
17 ④   18 ③
19 They were just doing their everyday activities.
20 ②   21 why Icarus' wings melted
22 ②   23 ⑤   24 canvas   25 ⑤

01 brush: 붓; ~을 닦다
05 기타를 추천하고 구매하는 상황이므로 손님과 점원의 관계가 적

9

절하다.

06 (A) a few: 몇몇의, few: 거의 없는, (B) 이어지는 대답에서 가장 좋아하는 공연의 종류를 설명하고 있으므로 most, (C) 둘 중에 어느 것을 더 좋아하느냐고 묻고 있으므로 or(또는)가 적절하다.

07 위 대화에서 왜 Emily가 TJ를 가장 좋아하는지 알 수 없다.

08 '어느 것을 더 좋아하니?'라는 의미의 선호를 물어보는 질문이 적절하므로 'which'가 적절하다.

10 almost = nearly: 거의

12 ninety: 90, nineties: 90년대

13 라푼젤의 엄마는 라푼젤이 탑 안에 머물게 했다는 의미이다. make는 목적격보어로 동사원형 형태를 쓰는 사역동사이다.

14 '네가 기분이 더 좋아지도록 만들다'이므로 사역동사 make 를 활용하여 문장을 만들 수 있다. 기분이 좋아지는 주체는 you이므로 이를 목적어로 사용한다.

15 what made Tom upset이라고 쓰는 것이 옳다. 간접의문문에서 의문사가 주어 역할을 동시에 하는 경우에 유의한다.

16 간접의문문의 어순은 '의문사+주어+동사'임에 유의한다.

17 의문사가 주어인 경우이므로 who turned off the lights라고 쓰는 것이 옳다.

18 빈칸 (A)에는 전치사 from이 들어간다. ① listen to: ~을 듣다 ② take care of: ~을 돌보다 ③ suffer from: ~으로 고통받다 ④ turn off: ~을 끄다 ⑤ be satisfied with: ~에 만족하

19 They were going on with their everyday activities.'라고 써도 무방하다.

20 이카루스의 다리는 물 밖으로 나와 있다.

21 대답으로 미루어 보아 이카루스의 날개가 녹은 이유를 묻는 말이 들어가는 것이 옳다. 간접의문문을 이용하여 답을 쓸 수 있다.

22 화가가 누구를 그리고 있는지를 추측하는 내용이 이어지고 있으므로 ②번이 적절하다.

23 간접의문문이므로 '의문사+주어+동사' 어순으로 써야 한다. 따라서 which direction the artist is looking at이라고 쓰는 것이 옳다.

24 '그림을 그리기 위해서 미술가들에 의해 사용되는 두꺼운 헝겊 조각'은 '화폭, 캔버스(canvas)'이다.

25 '시녀들'의 작가는 그림의 배경에 있는 거울 속에 왕과 왕비를 그렸다고 하였다.

Lesson
8

Changes Ahead

시험대비 실력평가   p.60

01 disagree   02 ②   03 ⑤
04 (1) donate   (2) local   (3) hand-free
05 (1) We should know the importance of the environment.
    (2) I try to balance work and play.
    (3) My younger[little] brother works in downtown Seattle.
06 ②

01 주어진 관계는 반의어 관계를 나타낸다. agree: 동의하다, disagree: 반대하다

02 '누군가에게 그들이 해야 하는 것, 그들이 가야 하는 곳 등에 대해 당신의 생각을 말하다'를 가리키는 말은 suggest(제안하다)이다.

03 mixture: 혼합물

04 donate: 기부하다, local: 지역의, 현지의, hand-free: 손을 쓸 필요

05 importance: 중요성, balance: 균형을 잡다, downtown: 시내의

06 주어진 문장에서 'post'는 '게시하다'를 의미하며 이와 같은 의미로 쓰인 것은 ②번이다. ①: 직책, ③: 우편, ④: 우편물, ⑤: (우편물을) 발송하다

서술형 시험대비   p.61

01 unimportant
02 (1) throw away   (2) rely on
    (3) get attention   (4) Even though   (5) fall asleep
03 (1) Spend your time wisely.
    (2) We will post these pictures on the Internet.
    (3) The job needs some creative imagination.
04 bakery
03 (1) Some scientists say sugar-free drinks are bad for your teeth.
    (2) The little girl felt shy in the boy's presence.
    (3) My classmates threw a surprise party for me.
    (4) What do you think about my new dress?
    (5) The trip was one of the most exciting moments in my life.

01 주어진 관계는 반의어 관계를 나타낸다. important: 중요한, unimportant: 중요하지 않은

02 get attention: 주목을 받다, throw away: 버리다, rely on: ~에 의존하다, fall asleep: 잠들다, even though: 비록 ~할지라도

03 wisely: 현명하게, post: 올리다, 게시하다, creative: 창의적인

04 '빵과 케이크를 만들거나 파는 곳'을 가리키는 말은 bakery(빵집)이다.

05 sugar-free: 무가당의, presence: 존재, throw a party: 파티를 열다, What do you think about ~?: ~에 대해 어떻게 생각하니? moment: 순간

Conversation 교과서

핵심 Check   p.62~63

1 (1) What do you think about / fresh vegetables, greener

(2) do you feel about / I think it's good, for free

(3) What's / in need, healthy

2 (1) online, offline / with, on / I don't think so

(2) theater / not with you, effects

교과서 대화문 익히기

Check(√) True or False   p.64

1 F   2 T   3 F   4 F

교과서 확인학습   p.66~67

Listen & Talk 1 A-1

memory stick / saved, think, present / touching

Listen & Talk 1 A-2

what do you think about / sound effects / interesting / scared

Listen & Talk 1 B

heard / donates / what / creative, have fun, help out / try, out

Listen & Talk 2 A-1

better than before / get closer / with you on that, wait to watch

---

Listen & Talk 2 A-2

comments / comfortable / that, posts / not with you on that, share

Listen & Talk 2 B

help, order / press / How, pay for my order / bottom, pay / simple, counter / with you, saves, time, line

Communication

debate / What, think / trendy, price / on that, throw away / opinions, move on

Wrap Up 1

making the posting, What do you think about it / get attention, below / one, right / change / hope, find

---

시험대비 기본평가   p.68

01 ⓔ → try it out   02 ⑤   03 ②

04 He thinks that this singing contest helps the singers get closer to their dreams.

01 이어동사의 목적어가 인칭대명사일 때 대명사는 동사와 부사 사이에 위치한다.

03 I can't wait to ~: ~하기를 기대하다

04 Jack은 이 노래 경연 대회가 가수들이 그들의 꿈에 좀 더 가까워지도록 도와준다고 생각한다.

시험대비 실력평가   p.69~70

01 What do you think about the present?

02 (A) a family video clip   (B) the present   03 ⑤

04 ④   05 ⑤   06 (C)→ (B) → (A) → (D)

07 ⑤   08 ②, ⑤

09 (A) Choose your hog dog and drink.

(B) Pay for your order.

10 ③   11 ④

03 아빠가 Jane의 가족 동영상을 보았다는 설명은 대화에서 알 수 없다.

04 주어진 문장은 의견을 묻는 질문에 대한 대답이므로 (D)가 적절하다.

05 위 대화를 통해 Tony가 얼마나 많은 쌀을 배고픈 사람들에게 기부할지는 알 수 없다.

06 (C) 의견 질문 → (B) 좋아하지 않음과 이유 설명 → (A) 반대되는 의견 주장 → (D) 자신의 의견 설명

07 very는 비교급을 강조할 수 없다.

08 ⓐ는 도움을 요청하는 표현으로 ②, ⑤와 바꾸어 쓸 수 있다.

10 (A) finish는 목적어로 동명사를 취하므로 making, (B) 주어

가 the title "LOST CAT" in big letters로 단수이므로 is,

(C) get attention: 주의를 끌다. attentive: 주의 깊은

11 Alex는 제목 밑에 있는 사진들을 모두 버꾸는 것이 아니라 오른쪽에 있는 사진을 바꿀 것이다.

서술형 시험대비

p.71

01 She is talking about her mom's birthday gift with him.

02 She will give her mom a memory stick for a birthday gift.

03 She saved a family video clip on it.

04 (A) too many sound effects

(B) scared

(C) the sound effects

05 what do you think about the game?

06 (A) right   (B) donate

(C) help out hungry people

01 Jane과 그녀의 아빠는 엄마의 생일 선물에 대해 이야기하고 있다.

02 Jane은 생일 선물로 엄마에게 막대 기억 장치(메모리 스틱)를 줄 것이다.

03 Jane이 준비한 막대 기억 장치에는 Jane이 만든 가족 동영상이 있다.

04 오늘 나는 Mike와 새 온라인 만화 '무서운 밤'에 대해 이야기했다. 사실 나는 너무 많은 음향 효과 때문에 그것이 마음에 들지 않았다. 나는 너무 무서워서 이야기에 집중할 수 없었다. 반면에 Mike는 내게 음향 효과가 이야기를 더 흥미진진하게 만들었다고 말했다.

06 정답을 맞혀 쌀을 기부하자. 당신은 재미있게 놀면서 배고픈 사람들을 도와줄 수 있다.

교과서

Grammar

핵심 Check

p.72~73

1 (1) so young that, can't work / too young to work

(2) so tired that, couldn't / too tired to

2 (1) singing   (2) written   (3) writing

시험대비 기본평가

p.74

01 (1) so big → too big   (2) can't → couldn't

(3) excited → exciting   (4) thrown → throwing

02 (1) to take   (2) burning   (3) to attract

(4) named   (5) talking

03 (1) Olivia felt so cold that she couldn't fall asleep.

(2) The house is warm enough to live in.

(3) I looked at the falling leaves.

(4) A spectator is someone watching a game or a play.

01 (1) to부정사가 이어지고 있으므로 'too ~ to V'구문을 쓰는 것이 적절하다. (2) 주절이 과거시제 이므로 종속절의 시제를 일치시켜 couldn't라고 써야 한다. (3) bowling game이 흥분을 유발 하는 것이므로 exciting을 써야 한다. (4) 소년은 공을 던지는 주체이므로 현재분사로 수식하는 것이 적절하다.

02 (1) 'too+부사+to V'로 '너무 ~해서 …할 수 없다'는 의미이다. (2) 무언가가 '타고 있는' 것이므로 현재분사로 수식한다. (3) '형용사+enough+to V'는 '~하기에 충분히 …한'이라는 의미이다. (4) '~라고 이름 지어진'이라는 의미이므로 과거분사로 수식한다. (5) 로봇이 말하는 주체가 되므로 현재분사로 수식한다.

03 (1) 'so+형용사+that+주어+can't+동사원형'은 '너무 ~해서 …할 수 없다'라는 의미이다. (2) '살기에 충분히 따뜻해'라고 하였으므로 warm enough to live in'이라고 쓰는 것이 적절하다. (3) '떨어지는 낙엽'이므로 falling leaves라고 쓴다. (4) someone이 지켜보는 주체가 되므로 현재분사가 someone을 수식하도록 문장을 만든다.

시험대비 실력평가

p.75~77

01 ④   02 ③   03 ②

04 is too hot for me to drink   05 ⑤

06 ③   07 ⑤

08 (1) This wallet was too big to put in my pocket.

(2) This wallet was so big that I couldn't put it in my pocket.

09 ④   10 ④   11 ⑤

12 We like to walk on fallen leaves.

13 ④   14 ②, ⑤   15 so, can't

16 dancing boy   17 ⑤   18 ③

19 He hit the flying ball.

20 sleeping, so cute that I can't

21 ④   22 ③

23 surprising news made me excited

24 too fast, to catch

01 'too ~ to V'는 '너무 ~해서 V할 수 없는'이라는 의미로, 'to+동사원형'을 쓴다.

02 '책을 읽는' 소녀이므로 현재분사로, '깨진 유리창'이므로 과거분사로 각각 수식하는 것이 적절하다.

03 'too+형용사+to V'로 '너무 ~해서 …할 수 없다'는 의미로 'so+형용사+that+주어+can't+동사원형'과 같다.

04 우유가 너무 뜨거워서 마실 수 없다는 의미이므로 'too+형용사+to V'를 사용하여 같은 의미의 문장을 만들 수 있다.

05 '너무 ~해서 …할 수 없는'은 'too ~ to V'로 나타낼 수 있다.

06 주어진 문장의 밑줄 친 부분은 '~하는 것'이라고 해석되는 동명사이다. ③번은 '당황스러운 순간'이라는 의미로 embarrass를 유발하는 순간을 의미한다. embarrass: 당황스럽게 만들다

07 too high to climb 혹은 so high that we couldn't climb이라고 쓰는 것이 적절하다.

08 'too ~ to V'는 'so ~ that 주어 can't'와 같으며 '너무 ~해서 …할 수 없는'이라고 해석된다.

09 '너무 ~해서 …할 수 없는'은 'too ~ to V'와 'so ~ that 주어 can't'로 표현할 수 있다.

10 '사진이 찍히도록 하는 것'이므로 had our picture taken이라고 쓰는 것이 적절하다.

11 영화가 감동을 유발하는 것이므로 moving이라고 쓰는 것이 적절하다.

12 낙엽은 떨어진 잎을 말하는 것이므로 'fallen leaves'라고 쓸 수 있다.

13 너무 멀리 있어서 듣지 못했다는 의미이므로 'too far away to hear' 혹은 'so far away that I couldn't hear'라고 쓰는 것이 적절하다.

14 목적격 보어로 과거분사를 취할 수 없는 동사는 want와 appear이다.

15 주어진 문장을 지시에 맞게 영어로 쓰면 He is so lazy that he can't do the job.이다.

16 '춤추는 소년'이므로 현재분사 dancing이 소년을 수식하도록 문장을 완성한다.

17 '너무 ~해서 …할 수 없는'은 'too ~ to V'나 'so ~ that 주어 can't'로 표현할 수 있다. he couldn't say hello라고 쓰는 것이 적절하다.

18 이어지는 문장으로 보아 첫 번째 빈칸에는 너무 늦어서 회의에 참석할 수 없었다는 것이 들어가야 하고, 두 번째 빈칸에는 차를 살 만큼 부자지만 차를 사지 않았다는 말이 들어가는 것이 적절하다.

19 '날아오는 공'이므로 현재분사로 ball을 수식하도록 문장을 만든다.

20 '잠자는 고양이'이므로 현재분사 sleeping으로 cat을 수식하도록 해야 하고, '너무 ~해서 …할 수 없다'는 'so ~ that 주어 can't 동사원형'이다.

21 '구워진 생선'이란 의미로 baked fish를 쓰는 것이 적절하다.

22 영화에 지루함을 느낀 것이므로 'bored'라고 쓰는 것이 적절하다.

23 '놀라운 뉴스'이므로 surprise를 현재분사형으로 만들어 news를 수식하게 만들고, 내가 흥분을 느끼는 것이므로 과거분사 excited로 me를 설명하는 목적격 보어를 만들어준다.

24 'too ~ to V'는 'so ~ that 주어 can't'와 같으며 to부정사의 의미상의 주어는 'for+목적격'으로 나타낸다.

서술형 시험대비

p.78~79

01 (1) The table was too heavy to move.
   (2) The table was so heavy that nobody could move it.

02 Show me the broken chair.

03 Her family was so poor that they couldn't buy the house.

04 too young to stay / so young that he can't stay

05 (1) playing (2) exciting (3) repaired
   (4) amazing (5) hit

06 (1) 해석: Jane은 얇게 썰어진 치즈를 좋아한다.
   (2) 해석: Jane은 치즈를 얇게 써는 것을 좋아한다.
   (3) 어법상 차이: sliced는 '썰어진 (치즈)'라는 의미의 과거분사로 cheese를 수식하고, slicing은 '(치즈를) 써는 것'이라는 의미로 동명사로 쓰였다

07 The room is so small that you can't invite all the friends to your party.

08 hidden

09 The news is so good that it can't be true.

10 Santa Claus checks his phone so often that he can't focus on his work.

11 annoyed / remaining

12 (1) I was too tired to open my eyes.
   (2) I was so tired that I couldn't open my eyes.

13 (1) Daisy was so nervous that she couldn't speak in front of many people.
   (2) Christopher is tall enough to be a model.
   (3) Jamie is so scared that he can't be alone at home.
   (4) Amelia was so rich that she could throw a big party for her friend.

14 It sounds like an exciting game.

15 (1) He has too much work to sleep.
   (2) He has so much work that he can't sleep.

01 'too ~ to V'는 'so ~ that 주어 can't'와 같으며 '너무 ~해서 …할 수 없는'이라고 해석된다. 주절의 시제에 맞추어 couldn't를 쓰는 것에 주의한다.

02 '부서진 의자'라고 하였으므로 과거분사로 chair를 수식하도록 문장을 만든다.

03 '너무 ~해서 …할 수 없다'는 'so ~ that 주어 can't 동사원형'으

로 표현할 수 있다.

05 (1) 배드민턴을 치고 있는 소녀는 나의 여동생이다. (2) 나는 너에게 해 줄 흥미진진한 이야기가 있어. (3) 우리는 그 차가 Potter와 Parker에 의해 수리되게 하였다. (4) Jina는 놀라운 농구 선수이다. (5) 너는 그 건물이 덤프 트럭에 부딪친 것을 보았니?

06 like는 동명사를 목적어로 취할 수 있는 동사이며, 위 문장에서 치즈는 slice의 주체가 될 수 없으므로 slicing이 현재 분사라고 볼 수 없다.

07 방이 너무 작아서 모든 친구들을 초대할 수 없다는 말이다. 'so ~ that 주어 can't 동사원형'으로 표현할 수 있다.

08 '숨겨진 보물'이므로 과거분사 hidden으로 treasure를 수식하는 것이 적절하다.

09 'too ~ to V'는 'so ~ that 주어 can't'와 같으며 '너무 ~ 해서 … 할 수 없는'이라는 의미이다.

10 '너무 ~해서 …할 수 없다'는 'so ~ that 주어 can't'이다.

11 내가 성가심을 느끼는 것이므로 첫 번째 빈칸에는 과거분사를 쓰는 것이 옳고, '남아 있는 날들 동안'이라는 의미이므로 두 번째 빈칸에는 현재분사를 쓰는 것이 적절하다.

12 '너무 ~해서 …할 수 없는'은 'too ~ to V'와 'so ~ that 주어 can't'로 표현할 수 있다.

13 'too ~ to V'는 'so ~ that 주어 can't 동사원형'과 같고, '~ enough to V'는 'so ~ that 주어 can 동사원형'과 같다.

14 게임이 신나는 감정을 유발하는 것이므로 현재분사 exciting으로 game을 수식하도록 문장을 만든다.

15 주어진 문장은 '그는 많은 일을 가지고 있기 때문에 잠을 잘 수 없다'는 의미이다. 따라서 'too ~ to V'와 'so ~ that 주어 can't 동사원형'을 사용하여 문장을 만들 수 있다

교과서
Reading

확인문제   p.80

1 T   2 T   3 F   4 F

확인문제   p.81

1 T   2 F   3 F   4 F   5 T

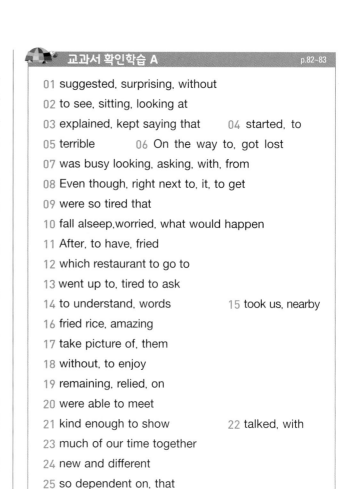

교과서 확인학습 A   p.82~83

01 suggested, surprising, without
02 to see, sitting, looking at
03 explained, kept saying that   04 started, to
05 terrible   06 On the way to, got lost
07 was busy looking, asking, with, from
08 Even though, right next to, it, to get
09 were so tired that
10 fall alseep, worried, what would happen
11 After, to have, fried
12 which restaurant to go to
13 went up to, tired to ask
14 to understand, words   15 took us, nearby
16 fried rice, amazing
17 take picture of, them
18 without, to enjoy
19 remaining, relied, on
20 were able to meet
21 kind enough to show   22 talked, with
23 much of our time together
24 new and different
25 so dependent on, that
26 that, without it
27 From, have learned, balanced use
28 would I travel   29 try to use it

교과서 확인학습 B   p.84~85

1 Last summer, my father suggested a surprising event: a family trip without smartphones!

2 He said, "I hate to see you sitting together and only looking at your smartphones."

3 My sister and I explained the need for smartphones, but he kept saying that we could not fully enjoy the trip with them.

4 So we started a technology-free trip to a new city, Barcelona, Spain.

5 Our first day was terrible.

6 On the way to our guesthouse around Plaza Reial, we got lost in downtown Barcelona.

7 Dad was busy looking at the map and asking for directions with a few Spanish words he got from a tour guidebook.

8 Even though our guesthouse was right next to the Plaza, it took us about two hours to get there.

9 We were so tired that we could not go out for dinner.

10 I went to bed but couldn't fall asleep because I was worried about what would happen the next day.

11 After looking around Gaudi's Park Guell, we decided to have seafood fried rice for lunch.

12 However, we didn't know which restaurant to go to.

13 We needed help, so Mom went up to an elderly lady and tried to ask for directions to a popular seafood restaurant.

14 Luckily, she seemed to understand Mom's few Spanish words.

15 She took us to a small local restaurant nearby.

16 The seafood fried rice was amazing.

17 I really wanted to take pictures of the food and post them on my blog.

18 But without my phone, I just decided to enjoy the moment.

19 During the remaining days, we relied more and more on the locals.

20 We were able to meet and talk with various people on the streets, in the bakeries, and in the parks.

21 They were always kind enough to show us different sides of Barcelona with a smile.

22 Also, our family talked a lot with each other.

23 We spent much of our time together on the Spanish train, on the bus, and at the restaurants.

24 Our technology-free trip was a new and different experience.

25 Before the trip, I was so dependent on my smartphone that I couldn't do anything without it.

26 But now I see that I can enjoy the moment without it.

27 From the experience, I have learned the importance of a balanced use of the smartphone.

28 So, next time, would I travel without a smartphone?

29 Probably not. But I will try to use it more wisely.

시험대비 실력평가
p.86~89

01 ②　　　　　02 saying
03 They went to Barcelona, Spain.　　　04 ⑤
05 ④　　　　06 ⑤　　　07 It was terrible.
08 ③　　　09 ③　　　10 ⑤
11 balance
12 The writer learned the importance of a balanced

use of the smartphone.　　13 ③　　　14 ④
15 (to) our guesthouse
16 He suggested a family trip without smartphones.
17 ③　　　18 ③　　　19 ⑤
20 He wanted to take pictures of the food and post them on his blog.
21 ⑤　　　22 our technology-free trip
23 ④　　　24 ③　　　25 ⑤
26 He will try to use his smartphone more wisely.

01 글쓴이와 여동생이 스마트폰의 필요성을 설명했지만 아버지는 계속해서 주장을 굽히지 않으셨다는 의미이다. 따라서 대조의 문장을 이끄는 접속사 but이 가장 적절하다.

02 keep+Ving: 계속해서 V하다

03 그들은 가족 여행으로 스페인의 바르셀로나로 갔다.

04 글쓴이의 아버지는 글쓴이와 동생이 함께 앉아 있는 것을 보기 싫어한 것이 아니라 함께 앉아 스마트폰만 쳐다보고 있는 것을 보기 싫다고 하셨다.

05 '광장 바로 옆에'라는 의미이다.

06 레이알 광장이 얼마나 큰지는 위 글을 읽고 알 수 없다.

07 글쓴이는 여행 첫 날은 엉망이었다고 하였다

08 점심으로 해산물 볶음밥을 먹기로 했지만 어느 식당으로가야 할지 몰랐다는 의미이다. 따라서 However가 가장 적절하다.

09 엄마가 한 노부인에게 길을 물었는데 다행히도 그녀가 엄마의 말을 알아들어 식당으로 안내했다는 순서가 자연스럽다.

10 스마트폰이 없어서 사진을 찍지 못했다고 하였으므로 Frank는 글을 잘못 이해하였다.

11 한 쪽으로 넘어지지 않고 꾸준한 위치를 유지하는 것은 '균형을 잡다(balance)'이다.

12 글쓴이는 여행을 통해 스마트폰을 균형 있게 사용하는 것의 중요성을 배웠다고 하였다.

13 글쓴이의 가족은 '첨단 과학 기술이 없는' 여행을 하였다.

14 (A) 의미상 sitting과 연결되므로 looking, (B) '길을 잃었다'는 수동이므로 'got lost', (C) It takes 시간 to V: V하는 데 ~ 만큼의 시간이 걸리다

15 글쓴이 가족의 여행자 숙소를 가리킨다.

16 아빠는 스마트폰이 없는 가족 여행을 제안하였다.

17 길을 잃었고, 너무 피곤해서 저녁도 먹을 수 없었지만 다음날 이 걱정되어 잠을 잘 수도 없었다고 하였으므로 ③번이 가장 적절하다. anxious: 걱정스러운 embarrassed: 당황한

18 너무 피곤해서 저녁을 먹을 수 없었다고 하였다. 따라서 ③번은 글을 읽고 답할 수 없다.

19 점심으로 해산물 볶음밥을 먹기로 함 - (C) 그러나 어느 식당으로 가야 할지 몰라 한 노부인에게 물어 봄 - (B) 다행히 노부인이 엄마의 말을 이해하고 식당으로 데려다 줌 - (A) 해산물 볶음밥이 맛있었음

20 글쓴이는 스마트폰으로 음식 사진을 찍어 블로그에 올리고 싶었다고 하였다.

21 노부인은 글쓴이의 가족을 식당으로 직접 데려다 주었다.

22 글쓴이가 경험한 것은 '첨단 과학 기술 없는 여행'이다.

23 바르셀로나의 다양한 면을 보여준 것은 현지 주민들이었다.

24 각각 ① dependent, ② different, ④ new, ⑤ more의 반의어이다. sensibly는 '분별력 있게, 현명하게'라는 의미로 wisely와 유의어이다.

25 글쓴이는 스마트폰 없이 여행을 하게 되지는 않을 것 같다고 하였다.

26 여행 후에 글쓴이는 스마트폰을 좀 더 현명하게 사용하기 위해 노력할 것이라고 하였다.

---

01 It is a trip without smartphones.

02 He explained the need for smartphones with his sister.

03 We were too tired to go out for dinner.

04 He got them from a tour guidebook.

05 enjoy the trip, without smartphones

06 It was right next to the Plaza.

07 It's because they didn't know which restaurant to go to.

08 enough to take   09 pictures of the food

10 ⑤번 → without   11 balanced

12 met and talked, talked a lot

13 No, it wasn't, was a new and different experience

14 travel without a smartphone

15 They depended on the locals.

---

01 '첨단 과학 기술 없는 여행'이란 스마트폰을 사용하지 않는 여행이다.

02 아빠의 제안을 들은 글쓴이는 여동생과 함께 스마트폰이 필요하다고 설명했다.

03 'so ~ that 주어 can't 동사원형'은 'too ~ to V'와 같다.

04 아빠는 여행안내 책자에서 스페인어를 배웠다고 하였다.

05 여행을 완전히 즐기기 위해서, 우리는 스마트폰 없이 여행해야 해.

06 가족의 숙소는 광장 바로 옆에 있었다.

07 도움이 필요했던 이유는 어떤 식당으로 가야 할지 몰라서이다.

08 식구들을 근처에 있는 작은 현지 식당으로 데려다 줄 만큼 친절했다는 의미이다.

09 음식의 사진을 가리키는 말이다.

10 음식 사진을 찍어 블로그에 올리고 싶었지만 스마트폰이 없었기 때문에 그 순간을 즐기기로 한 것이 자연스럽다.

11 '균형 잡힌 사용'이라는 의미이므로 과거분사로 use를 수식하는 것이 적절하다.

12 가족들은 바르셀로나에서 다양한 사람들을 만나 이야기했을 뿐

만 아니라 서로 많은 대화를 나누었다. not only A but also B: A뿐만 아니라 B도

13 '첨단 기술 없는 여행'은 글쓴이에게 새롭고 색다른 경험이었다고 하였다.

14 아마도 나는 스마트폰 없이 여행을 하지 않을 것이지만, 나는 그것을 좀 더 현명하게 사용하기 위해 노력할 것이다.

15 남아 있는 날들 동안 글쓴이의 가족은 현지 사람들에게 의존하였다.

---

01 present   02 fry   03 ③

04 (1) wait to (2) keep going (3) pay for   05 ④

06 (1) importance (2) side (3) thought (4) effect

07 ⑤   08 ①

09 He thought they made the story more interesting.

10 She was too scared.

11 ⑤   12 ②   13 ③   14 ⑤

15 ③   16 ④   17 ③

18 My room is so dirty that I can't invite my friends.

19 ④   20 ⑤   21 ③   22 ⑤

23 ④   24 I was too upset to hear the news.

25 ③   26 ③   27 ④

28 he hated to see the writer and his sister sitting together and only looking at their smartphones

29 ④   30 ⑤번 → post   31 ④

32 ⑤

---

01 주어진 관계는 반의어 관계를 나타낸다. present: 출석한, absent: 결석한

02 '뜨거운 기름으로 무언가를 요리하다'를 가리키는 말은 fry(튀기다)이다.

03 suggest: 제안하다, beneficial: 유익한

04 can't wait to: ~하기를 기대하다, keep -ing: 계속해서 ~하다, pay for: 지불하다

05 experience: (동) 경험하다, (명) 경험

06 importance: 중요성, thought: 생각, side: 측면, effect: 영향, 효과, scared: 무서워하는, 겁먹은

07 주어진 문장과 나머지는 모두 '계산대'를 뜻하지만 ⑤번은 '반대의'를 의미한다.

08 terrified: 무서운, 겁에 질린, terrific: 멋진, brilliant: 똑똑한, pleased: 기쁜

09 Mike는 Scary Night의 음향 효과가 이야기를 더 흥미진진하게 만들어 주었다고 생각했다.

10 Jenny는 Scary Night을 보면서 너무 무서웠다.

11 ⑤번을 제외하고 (A)와 나머지는 상대방의 의견에 이의를 나타낸다.

12 Lisa는 게시물 공유에 관해 Steve와 다른 의견을 갖고 있다.

13 Wendy가 James의 의견에 반대되는 주장을 설명하고 있으므로 주어진 문장은 (C)가 적절하다.

14 대화를 통해 Wendy가 무엇을 자주 버렸는지는 알 수 없다.

15 have는 목적어와 목적격 보어의 관계가 수동인 경우 목적격 보어로 과거분사를 사용하는 사역동사이다. 신발에 광이 나게 한다는 의미이므로 과거분사를 쓰는 것이 적절하다.

16 2형식 동사의 보어가 필요하므로 빈칸에는 형용사가 들어가야 한다.

17 첫 번째 빈칸에는 I를 설명하는 보어가 필요하므로 형용사를 쓰는 것이 옳으며, 두 번째 빈칸에는 '할인된 가격'이라는 의미이므로 과거분사로 수식하는 것이 적절하다.

18 '너무 ~해서 …할 수 없다'는 'so ~ that 주어 can't 동사원형'이다.

19 kind enough to take care of ~라고 쓰는 것이 적절하다.

20 만족을 느끼는 것이므로 satisfied라고 쓰는 것이 적절하다.

21 주어진 문장의 밑줄 친 부분은 동명사이다. 따라서 '~하는 중인'이라는 의미의 현재분사로 쓰인 ③번이 답이다.

22 '~ enough to V' 혹은 'so ~ that 주어 can 동사원형'을 써서 문장을 완성할 수 있다.

23 ①, ②, ③ '~을 사용하는'이라는 의미의 현재분사, ⑤ 동명사, ④번에는 과거분사 used가 쓰여 '중고차'라는 의미를 만든다.

24 '너무 ~해서 …할 수 없는'은 'too ~ to V'로 표현한다.

25 숙소가 광장 바로 옆에 있었지만 가는 데 약 2시간이 걸렸다는 의미이다. 따라서 내용상 반대되는 문장을 이끄는 접속사 Although가 적절하다.

26 '스마트폰이 있으면 여행을 충분히 즐길 수 없다'고 말하는 것이 자연스럽다. 따라서 with them이라고 쓰는 것이 적절하다.

27 (B)와 ④의 take는 '(~ 만큼의 시간이) 걸리다'라는 의미로 쓰였다. ① ~로 안내하다, 데려가다 ② 가져가다 ③ 선택하다, 사다 ⑤ (~을) 타다

28 아빠가 스마트폰 없는 여행을 제안한 이유는 필자와 그의 여동생이 함께 앉아 각자의 스마트폰만 보고 있는 걸 보는 것이 싫어서이다.

29 지도를 보느라 바빴던 것은 글쓴이의 아버지이다.

30 사진을 찍어 블로그에 올리기를 원한 것이므로 to take와 병렬 연결되어 (to) post라고 쓰는 것이 적절하다. posted라고 쓸 경우 '사진을 찍기를 원했고 블로그에 올렸'라는 의미가 된다.

31 공원 근처에 있는 현지 식당이다. 따라서 ④번은 not far from 이라고 쓰는 것이 적절하다.

32 해산물 식당이 얼마나 인기 있는지는 위 글을 읽고 알 수 없다.

🐾 단원별 예상문제   p.98~101

01 (A) the new online comic Scary Night
   (B) many sound effects

02 ③   03 I can donate rice.

04 She thinks it's a creative game.

05 He will try it out this weekend.   06 ⑤

07 I'm looking forward to watching their next performances.

08 They are debating the fast fashion.

09 Because he thinks that we can wear trendy clothes at a cheaper price.

10 She thinks that it makes us spend too much money and throw away clothes too often.

11 ④   12 ①

13 The walking robot is my favorite toy.

14 ②   15 ⑤

16 so busy that she couldn't

17 writing, written

18 (C) → (B) → (A)   19 ③

20 They met and talked with various people on the streets, in the bakeries, and in the parks.

21 ③   22 ③   23 ②   24 ④

25 ⑤

02 Mike와 Jenny의 Scary Night에 대한 의견이 같다는 설명은 대화의 내용과 일치하지 않는다.

03 당신은 '퀴즈와 쌀' 게임에서 정답을 맞히면 쌀을 기부할 수 있다.

04 Julie는 '퀴즈와 쌀' 게임이 창의적인 게임이라고 생각한다.

05 Tony는 '퀴즈와 쌀' 게임을 이번 주말에 해보려 한다.

06 ⑤번을 제외한 나머지는 모두 상대방의 의견과 같음을 표현하고 있다.

07 can't wait to = look forward to ~ing: ~하기를 기대 하다, 고대하다

08 학생들은 패스트 패션에 대해 토론하고 있다.

09 James는 우리가 보다 저렴한 가격으로 최신 유행의 옷들을 입을 수 있기 때문에 패스트 패션이 좋다고 생각한다.

10 Wendy는 패스트 패션이 우리가 너무 많은 돈을 쓰고 너무 자주 옷을 버리게 한다고 생각한다.

11 첫 번째 빈칸에는 'too ~ to V', 두 번째 빈칸에는 'enough to V', 마지막 빈칸에는 '놀라움을 주는 선물'이라 는 의미이므로 현재분사를 쓰는 것이 적절하다.

12 'too ~ to V'와 'so ~ that 주어 can't'는 '너무 ~해서 …할 수 없다'는 의미이다. 절을 이끄는 that이 쓰이고 있으므로 too가 아닌 so를 쓰는 것이 적절하다.

13 '걷고 있는 로봇'이라고 하였으므로 walk를 현재분사형으로 만들어 robot을 수식하게 만든다.

14 @와 ⓒ는 '~하는'이라고 해석되거나 '~한 감정을 유발하는'이라고 해석되는 현재분사이고, ⓑ와 ⓓ는 '~하는 것'이라고 해석되는 동명사이다.

15 나무는 심어지는 것이므로 planted in the garden이라고 쓰는 것이 적절하다.

16 'too ~ to V'는 'so ~ that 주어 can't 동사원형'과 같다.

17 '~을 쓰고 있는 소년'이라는 의미이므로 현재분사로 the boy를

17

수식하고, '한국어로 쓰여진'이라는 의미이므로 과거 분사로 a letter를 수식하는 것이 적절하다.

18 현지인들에 의존함 - (C) 다양한 현지인들을 만나고 대화함 - (B) 그들은 친절했음 - (A) 또한 가족들과 많은 대화를 나눔

19 글쓴이는 스마트폰 없이 순간을 즐길 수 있다는 사실을 안다고 하였다.

20 그들은 다양한 현지인들을 길거리에서, 빵집에서, 공원에서 만나 이야기할 수 있었다고 하였다.

21 가족들이 현지인들을 만난 곳은 길거리, 빵집, 공원이었다. 식당에서는 가족들 간에 함께 시간을 보냈다.

22 '3분 동안'이라는 의미이므로 전치사 for가 적절하다.

23 잘라진 사과 조각을 의미하므로 과거분사로 수식하는 것이 적절하다.

24 식빵 위에 올릴 사과 소는 약한 불에서 조린 것을 올리는 것이므로 혜준이 글의 내용을 잘못 이해하였다.

25 잘라진 사과 조각들을 약한 불에서 얼마나 조리하는지는 위 글에 나와 있지 않다.

서술형 실전문제
p.102~103

01 I'm not with you on that.

02 He thinks (that) it's great.

03 She wants to share them with her close friends.

04 (C) → (B) → (D) → (A)

05 encouraging, encouraged

06 (1) cheering   (2) sliced

07 (1) She is tall enough to reach the top shelf.
   (2) She is so tall that she can reach the top shelf.

08 the dog was so hungry that he couldn't bark at a stranger

09 He asked for directions with a few Spanish words he got from a tour guidebook.

10 Because he was worried about what would happen the next day.

11 They got lost in downtown Barcelona.

12 He was too sleepy to focus during class.

13 He felt moved.

14 I was so moved that I couldn't say anything.

02 Steve는 많은 사람들과 게시물들을 공유하는 것에 대해 좋다고 생각한다.

03 Lisa는 친한 친구들과 게시물들을 공유하고 싶어 한다.

04 (C) 엄마의 생일 선물 보여 줌 → (B) 질문 → (D) 대답 및 선물 설명 → (A) 반응

05 '격려하는 말'이라는 의미이므로 현재분사로 words를 수식하고, 이 말에 내가 용기와 격려를 느낀 것이므로 과거분사를 써서 문장을 완성할 수 있다.

06 (1) 능동의 의미이므로 현재분사 (2) 수동의 의미이므로 과거 분사

07 '~할 만큼 …한'은 '~ enough to V' 혹은 'so ~ that 주어 can 동사원형'을 써서 표현할 수 있다.

08 '너무 배가 고파서 낯선 사람을 보고 짖을 수 없었다'는 말이 들어가는 것이 타당하다.

09 아빠는 여행 안내 책자에서 배운 스페인어 몇 마디로 길을 물었다고 하였다.

10 글쓴이가 잠들 수 없었던 이유는 내일 무슨 일이 일어날지 걱정되어서라고 하였다.

11 그들이 길을 잃은 곳은 바르셀로나 시내라고 하였다.

12 너무 졸려서 수업에 집중할 수 없었다고 하였다. 'so ~ that 주어 couldn't 동사원형'이 쓰이고 있으므로 'too ~ to부정사'로 나타낼 수 있다.

13 Jesse는 감동하였다.

14 'too ~ to부정사'는 'so ~ that 주어 can't 동사원형'과 같다.

창의사고력 서술형 문제
p.104

|모범답안|

01 (A) find   (B) big letters   (C) two photos
   (D) it didn't show Leon's face well

02 (1) The man was too shocked to say anything.
   (2) The book was too difficult to be read easily.
   (3) The dog was too hungry to bark at a stranger.
   (4) She was too frightened to phone us.

02 'so ~ that 주어 can't 동사원형'은 'too ~ to V'과 같다. 이때 주절의 시제가 과거인 경우 couldn't를 쓰는 것에 유의한다.

단원별 모의고사
p.105~108

01 ⑤   02 (1) Even though   (2) get, attention

03 (1) guidebook   (2) handwritten   (3) guesthouse
   (4) elderly   (5) local

04 (1) I was busy cleaning my room.
   (2) I couldn't fall asleep after drinking a cup of coffee.
   (3) Young people rely on technology too much.

05 She should touch the Done button at the bottom.

06 He thinks (that) it really saves a lot of time when there's a long line.

07 debate   08 ⓒ → throw

09 ③   10 ⑤   11 ⑤

12 I think shopping online is better than shopping at the stores.

13 She will be disappointed with the shocking news.

14 ①, ⑤   15 ④   16 ④   17 ⑤

18 They spent their time together on the Spainish train, on the bus, and at the restaurants.

19 They were always kind enough to show them different sides of Barcelona with a smile.

20 ③   21 so late that I couldn't   22 ⑤

23 ②

01 thought: (명) 생각, (동) think의 과거, 과거분사

02 even though: 비록 ~ 할지라도, get one's attention: ~의 관심을 얻다

03 elderly: 나이가 지긋한, handwritten: 손으로 쓴, guidebook: (여행) 안내서, local: 지역의, 현지의, guesthouse: 숙소, 여관 organic: 유기농의

04 be busy -ing: ~하느라 바쁘다, fall asleep: 잠들다, rely on: 의존하다

05 Emma는 주문한 것을 결제하기 전에 맨 아래에 있는 '완료' 버튼을 눌러야 한다.

06 Tom은 줄이 길 때, 기계가 정말 많은 시간을 절약해 준다고 생각한다.

07 '다른 의견들을 표현하는 논쟁 또는 토론'을 나타내는 말은 debate(토론, 토의)이다.

08 ⓒ는 spend와 병렬 구조로 throw가 적절하다.

09 Wendy는 James와 패스트 패션에 대해 다른 의견을 갖고 있다. pros and cons: 장단점

10 주어진 문장은 상대방의 의견에 동의를 나타내고 있으므로 (E)가 적절하다.

13 실망을 느끼는 것이므로 과거분사를, 충격을 유발하는 소식이므로 현재분사를 써서 문장을 만든다.

14 수프가 너무 뜨거워서 먹을 수 없다는 의미이다.

15 주절이 과거 동사이므로 종속절 역시 과거 동사를 쓰는 것이 적절하다. 따라서 couldn't라고 써야 한다.

16 각각 ① moment ② post ③ elderly ④ guidebook ⑤ bakery를 풀이한 말이다.

17 구엘 공원에서 식당까지 얼마나 멀었는지는 알 수 없다.

18 그들은 스페인의 기차에서, 버스에서, 그리고 식당에서 많은 시간을 함께 보냈다고 하였다.

19 현지 사람들은 항상 웃으면서 너무나 친절히도 바르셀로나의 다양한 면을 보여주었다고 하였다.

20 너무 들떠서 잠을 제대로 자지 못할 정도였지만 생일의 시작이 좋지 않았다는 연결이 자연스럽다. 따라서 However가 적절하다.

21 너무 늦게 일어나서 생일상을 받을 수 없었다고 하였다. 'too ~ to부정사'는 'so ~ that 주어 can't 동사원형'과 같다.

22 깜짝 파티를 예상치 못한 일이라고 말했으므로 ⑤번은 그의 내용과 일치하지 않는다.

23 (B) 여행 전에는 스마트폰에 의존적이었음 - (A) 그러나 여행 후에는 스마트폰을 균형 있게 사용하는 것이 중요함을 배움 - (C) 다음번 여행에 스마트폰 없이 여행을 하게 되지는 않겠지만 현명하게 사용하려고 노력할 것임

Lesson
S

The Stone

교과서
Reading

확인문제   p.112

1 F   2 T   3 T   4 T

확인문제   p.113

1 F   2 F   3 T

교과서 확인학습 A   p.114~115

01 driving down, when

02 looked, sick, to worry about   03 Later that day

04 to get, out from

05 pulled, away, freed   06 reward

07 that, young

08 it all wrong, young again, keep from

09 to explain, listen   10 handed him

11 a few, grow at all

12 become, got upset

13 change into, slow

14 give birth, got, angry, to throw it away

15 listen to, threw, out   16 found, sitting

17 worried about, glad that

18 having trouble, seen

19 to throw away, put, under

20 came back, went by, grew, changed

21 to worry, nothing to look forward to

22 to destroy, coming back

23 to throw away, far from

24 On, to, got angry

25 didn't you warn   26 listen

27 explained, get rid of, unless

28 no more of, Whatever, let, happen

29 to throw, onto

30 did, said, arrived, changed into, bore

31 laughed with delight

32 lived for   33 was proud of

1 One day, Maibon was driving down the road on his horse and cart when he saw an old man.

2 The old man looked very sick. Maibon began to worry about growing old.

3 Later that day, he saw a dwarf, Doli, in the field.

4 He was trying to get his leg out from under a log.

5 Maibon pulled the log away and freed the dwarf.

6 "You'll have your reward. What do you want?"

7 "I've heard that you have magic stones that can keep a man young. I want one."

8 "Oh, you humans have it all wrong. Those stones don't make you young again. They only keep you from getting older."

9 "Just as good!" Doli tried to explain the problem with the stones, but Maibon didn't listen.

10 So Doli handed him a magic stone and went away.

11 After a few days, Maibon saw that his beard didn't grow at all.

12 He became happy, but his wife, Modrona, got upset.

13 "The eggs don't change into chickens!" "Oh, the season's slow, that's all."

14 But she was not happy. "The cow doesn't give birth!" Maibon, then, told her about the stone, and she got very angry and told him to throw it away.

15 He didn't want to, but he listened to his wife and threw the stone out the window.

16 However, the next morning, he found the stone sitting by the window!

17 Maibon was worried about the animals, but he was glad that he was still young.

18 Now Maibon's baby was having trouble. No tooth was seen in his mouth.

19 His wife told him to throw away the stone and this time, Maibon put the stone under the ground.

20 But, the next day, the stone came back! Time went by and nothing grew or changed.

21 Maibon began to worry. "There's nothing to look forward to, nothing to show for my work."

22 Maibon tried to destroy the stone, but it kept coming back.

23 Maibon decided to throw away the stone far from his house.

24 On his way to the field, he saw the dwarf. Maibon got angry with him.

25 "Why didn't you warn me about the stone?"

26 "I tried to, but you wouldn't listen."

27 Doli explained that Maibon couldn't get rid of the stone unless he really wanted to.

28 "I want no more of it. Whatever may happen, let it happen!"

29 Doli told him to throw the stone onto the ground and go back home.

30 Maibon did as Doli said. When he arrived home, Modrona told him the good news — the eggs changed into chickens and the cow bore her baby.

31 And Maibon laughed with delight when he saw the first tooth in his baby's mouth.

32 Maibon, Modrona and their children and grandchildren lived for many years.

33 Maibon was proud of his white hair and long beard.

서술형 실전문제   p.118~119

01 (1) bore   (2) beard   (3) field   (4) logs

02 (1) goes by   (2) went away   (3) Throw away
    (4) worry about   (4) change into

03 (1) I try to get rid of my bad habits.
    (2) My teacher keeps us from using cell phones in school.
    (3) My aunt gave birth to a cute baby.

04 (1) They told us not to use the computer.
    (2) I plan to visit my uncle this weekend.

05 (1) My car was repaired by David yesterday.
    (2) A car hit the man on the street.

06 (D)–(A)–(C)–(E)–(B)

07 He looked very sick.

08 He worried about growing old.

09 It is Doli.

10 사람의 젊음을 유지해 주는 마법의 돌

11 She is Maibon's wife

12 He didn't want to throw it away

13 He found the stone sitting by the window.

---

01 bear: 아이를 낳다, beard: 수염, filed: 들판, log: 통나무

02 throw away: 버리다, change into: ~으로 바꾸다, worry about: ~에 대해 걱정하다, go by: 흐르다, 지나가다, go away: 떠나가다

03 get rid of ~을 없애다, keep ~ from -ing ~가 -하지 못 하게 하다, give birth (아기를[새끼를]) 낳다

04 tell은 to부정사를 목적격 보어로 취하는 동사이며, to부정사의 부정은 not to V으로 표기한다. plan은 to부정사를 목적어로 취하는 동사이다.

05 (1) 목적어가 my car이므로 이를 주어로 하고, 과거시제이므로 동사는 was repaired를 써서 수동태를 만들 수 있다. (2) 수동태의 행위 주체를 능동태의 주어로 하여 능동태를 만들 수 있다.

06 (D) 난쟁이 Doli가 통나무 아래에 깔린 다리를 빼내려 함 - (A) Maibon은 통나무를 잡아당겨 난쟁이를 풀어 주자 이에 난쟁이는 보상으로 무엇을 원하는지 물음 - (C) 젊음을 유지해 주는 마법의 돌을 요구함 - (E) 다시 젊어지게 해 주는 것이 아니라 늙지 않게 해 주는 돌이라 말함 - (B) 그것대로 좋다고 말함

07 그 노인은 아파 보였다고 하였다.

08 Maibon은 늙어가는 것이 걱정되었다.

09 난쟁이의 이름은 Doli이다.

10 magic stones 중 하나를 의미하는 말이다.

11 Modrona는 Maibon의 아내이다.

12 앞선 문장의 to부정사 이하를 생략한 문장이다. 따라서 to throw it away를 써서 나타낼 수 있다.

13 그는 창가에 돌이 있는 것을 발견했다.

 단원별 예상문제 p.120~124

01 ⑤　　　　02 ①
03 (1) warn　(2) hand　(3) reward　(4) trouble　(5) glad
04 ①
05 (1) I don't need this chair. Let's throw it away.
　(2) My hometown is not far from Seoul.
　(3) I'm looking forward to visiting Hong Kong.
　(4) On my way to school, I met a foreigner.
　(5) As years go by, the work becomes more
　　difficult.
06 ④
07 Paul met a woman who knew Ann's best friend.
08 ③　　　　09 ④　　　　10 ⑤
11 She kept talking about her life.
12 (1) to drink　(2) to say
13 (1) handed me two flowers　(2) bought us pizza
14 ③　　　　15 ⑤　　　　16 He went away.
17 He was driving down the road on his horse and
　cart.
18 ④
19 No, it can only keep people from getting older
20 He tried to explain the problem with the stones.
21 ②　　　　22 ③　　　　23 coming back
24 ③, ⑤　　　　25 No tooth was seen in his mouth.
26 He tried to explain the problem with the stones.
27 It's because he was still young.
28 No, he tried to, but he failed to destroy it.

29 ⑤　　　　30 ②　　　　31 ④
32 He told Maibon to throw the stone onto the
　ground and go back home.
33 Because he didn't really want to.
34 Because he saw the first tooth in his baby's
　mouth.
35 He was proud of his white hair and long beard.

01 free: 풀어 주다
02 bear: (동) 참다, 아이를 낳다, (명) 곰
03 reward: 보상, 보답, trouble: 문제, 골칫거리, warn: 경고하다, glad: 기쁜, hand: 건네주다, chore: 집안일
04 남자 얼굴의 턱과 뺨에 자라는 털을 가리키는 말은 beard(수염)이다.
05 throw away: 버리다, look forward to: ~을 기대하다, on one's way to: ~로 가는 길에, go by: 흐르다, 지나 가다
06 목적격 보어로 쓰일 수 있는 것은 부사가 아닌 형용사이다.
07 주격 관계대명사 who를 대신하여 that을 써도 좋다.
08 목적격 보어로 원형부정사를 취하는 동사는 help와 사역동사 make, let, have이다. tell은 목적격 보어로 to부정사를 받는 동사이다.
09 모두 명사로 쓰인 to부정사이지만 ④번은 형용사로 쓰인 to부정사이다.
10 주어진 문장의 that은 완전한 절을 이끄는 명사절 접속사이다. ⑤번은 관계대명사로 불완전한 절을 이끈다.
11 keep Ving: 계속 V하다
12 형용사적 용법의 to부정사이다.
13 hand와 buy는 모두 4형식 동사로, '사람+사물' 어순으로 간접목적어와 직접목적어를 취한다.
14 통나무 아래에 깔린 다리를 빼내는 것을 돕기 위해 통나무를 잡아당겨서 난쟁이를 풀어 준 것이다.
15 Doli가 들판으로 간 이유는 알 수 없다.
16 마법의 돌을 보상으로 준 Doli는 돌을 건넨 후 가버렸다.
17 Maibon이 한 노인을 보았을 때 그는 마차를 타고 길을 내려가고 있던 중이었다.
18 보상을 주고자 한 것은 난쟁이였다. 난쟁이가 Maibon에게 보상을 주겠다고 하였다.
19 사람들을 젊어지게 해 주는 것이 아니라 더 늙지 않게 막아 주는 돌이다.
20 Doli는 돌에 관한 문제를 설명하려고 애썼다.
21 아내의 말대로 창 밖으로 돌을 버렸지만 다음날 아침 돌이 창가에 있었다고 하였으므로 '그러나'가 가장 적절하다.
22 go by: 흐르다, 지나가다, by: ~ 옆에
23 돌이 계속해서 되돌아왔다는 의미이다. keep Ving는 '계속 해서 V하다'는 뜻으로 쓰인다.
24 아기에게 문제가 생기자 Maibon은 돌을 버렸고, 두 번째로 돌을

버리려고 했을 때에는 땅 속에 돌을 묻었다고 하였다.

25 아기의 입에서 이가 보이지 않는 문제가 생겼다.

26 Doli는 돌에 관한 문제를 설명하려고 애썼다.

27 자신이 여전히 젊었으므로 기뻤다고 하였다.

28 Maibon은 돌을 없애려고 노력했지만 돌이 계속해서 되돌아와 결국 실패하였다.

29 decide는 to부정사를 목적어로 취하는 동사이며, 사역동사 let 은 목적격 보어로 동사원형을 취한다.

30 ②번은 난쟁이를 가리키는 대명사이다.

31 난쟁이에게 화가 났지만, 난쟁이의 조언을 받아들인 후 그는 기뻐하였다. relieved: 안도한

32 Doli는 Maibon에게 돌을 땅에 던지고 집으로 돌아가라고 말했다.

33 진정으로 돌을 없애길 원하지 않았기 때문에 돌을 없앨 수 없었음을 알 수 있다.

34 아기의 입에 첫 이가 난 것을 보고 기뻐서 웃었다고 하였다.

35 그의 흰 머리와 긴 수염을 자랑스러워했다고 하였다.

교과서 파헤치기

Lesson 7

01 왕자	02 클래식의	03 녹다
04 생산하다	05 방향	06 전시하다
07 깃털	08 예술가, 미술가	09 약속하다
10 붓	11 풍경	12 소설
13 ~에도 불구하고	14 예술 작품	15 십 대
16 미로	17 생산	18 ~을 알아차리다
19 궁금해하다	20 납작한	21 해변, 바닷가
22 세부 사항	23 비극	24 더 좋아하다
25 날개	26 현대의	27 왕비, 여왕
28 록 음악	29 진짜의, 현실적인	30 소설가
31 ~ 때문에, ~이므로		32 신화
33 관광객	34 (어떤 것의) 변형	35 밀랍, 왁스
36 화폭, 캔버스	37 A를 B보다 더 좋아하다	
38 ~을 보다	39 ~을 힐끗 보다	
40 ~을 가까이하지 않다		41 즉시, 바로
42 ~을 보다	43 ~로 이동하다, 넘어가다	

01 melt	02 produce	03 feather
04 wing	05 direction	06 queen
07 artist	08 brush	09 prince
10 exhibit	11 frog	12 maze
13 promise	14 novel	15 despite
16 modern	17 flat	18 teen
19 notice	20 landscape	21 art work
22 version	23 detail	24 myth
25 production	26 tragedy	27 prefer
28 wonder	29 real	30 canvas
31 tourist	32 wax	33 rock
34 novelist	35 comedy	36 since
37 seaside	38 move on	39 prefer A to B
40 glance at	41 take a look[look at]	
42 stay away from		43 right away

1 feather, 깃털 2 seaside, 해변, 바닷가 3 melt, 녹다
4 tragedy, 비극 5 direction, 방향 6 wonder, 궁금해하다
7 landscape, 풍경 8 notice, 알아차리다 9 stick, 내밀다
10 artist, 예술가 11 wing, 날개 12 detail, 세부 사항
13 exhibit, 전시하다 14 rock, 록 음악

15 canvas, 화폭, 캔버스 16 myth, 신화

Listen & Talk 1 A-1

going to play / practicing almost every day / What kind of music / play songs, nineties

Listen & Talk 1 A-2

how to paint clean lines / What kind of brush, using / round brush / When, paint, flat, better, Try

Listen & Talk 1 B

meeting, right / performance do you want to watch first / want to, performance / Sounds, right / about watching the play / the one, near

Listen & Talk 2 A-1

are, reading / a story / seen, of it, too, prefer, to / Why, like, better / scenes, looks, real

Listen & Talk 2 A-2

Have, listened / cool, part, great / dance version / listened to, I prefer the guitar version, matches, better

Listen & Talk 2 B

interesting painting, Look at / looks like / Which do you prefer / prefer, to / smile, How about you / prefer, to / looks modern

Communication

are planning, so, fine out, May, ask, a few questions / What kind of performance / performances best / do, prefer / prefer rock to hip-hop / favorite musician / favorite musicia / Thank, for

Wrap Up 1

Can, help, to buy / various kinds, What kind of music, to play / want to / should get / take, classical guitar

Listen & Talk 1 A-1

W: Brian, is your band going to play at the Teen Music Festival?

M: Yes, we're practicing almost every day.

W: What kind of music are you going to play this year?

M: Rock music. We'll play songs from the nineties.

Listen & Talk 1 A-2

W: Can you help me? I don't know how to paint clean lines.

M: What kind of brush were you using?

W: This round brush.

M: When you paint lines, a flat brush is better. Try this one.

W: Okay, thank you.

Listen & Talk 1 B

W: (*ringing*) Hello, Steve.

M: Hi, Anna. We're meeting at the arts festival tomorrow at 1:30, right?

W: Right. What kind of performance do you want to watch first?

M: I want to watch the hip-hop dance performance first.

W: Sounds good. It's at 2 p.m. at the gym, right?

M: Yeah, and how about watching the play, Romeo and Juliet, at 4 p.m.?

W: Oh, the one at the Main Hall near the gym? Sure!

Listen & Talk 2 A-1

M: What are you reading, Jina?

W: The novel, Life of Pi. It's a story of a boy and a tiger.

M: It's a great book. I've seen the movie of it, too. I prefer the movie to the novel.

W: Why do you like it better?

M: The scenes are very beautiful. And the tiger looks so real.

Listen & Talk 2 A-2

W: Have you listened to Jane's new song, Girl Friend ?

M: Yeah, it's really cool. The guitar part is great.

W: There is also a dance version of the song on the album.

M: I've listened to it, but I prefer the guitar version to the dance version. It matches her voice better.

Listen & Talk 2 B

W: I saw an interesting painting in an art book. Look at this.

M: Wow, it looks like da Vinci's Mona Lisa .

W: Actually, it's Mona Lisa by Fernando Botero. Which do you prefer?

M: I prefer da Vinci's to Botero's. Da Vinci's Mona Lisa has an interesting smile. How about you?

W: Well, I prefer Botero's to da Vinci's. His Mona Lisa is cute, and it looks modern.

Communication

M: Hi, we are planning a school festival, so we want to find out students' favorite types of performances. May I ask you a few questions?

W: Sure.

M: What kind of performance do you like best?

W: I like music performances best.

M: Okay. Then, which do you prefer, rock or hip-hop?

W: I prefer rock to hip-hop.

M: Who's your favorite musician?

W: My favorite musician is TJ.

M: Great. Thank you for your answers.

Wrap Up 1

M: Can you help me? I want to buy a guitar.

W: There are various kinds of guitars. What kind of music do you want to play?

M: I want to play pop songs.

W: Then you should get a classical guitar.

M: Okay, I will take a classical guitar.

본문 TEST Step 1   p.09~10

01 Welcome to, tour

02 when, much, looking, each

03 glance, for, few, on

04 might miss, since, notice

05 at, closely, help, see   06 Look at, first

07 seaside, peaceful, isn't it   08 title, is, with

09 where Icarus is

10 that, sticking out, near

11 in, famous myth

12 wings, feathers, stay away

13 However, didn't listen   14 flew, close to

15 melted, fell into   16 look at, entire

17 Despite, going on, everyday

18 still look peaceful

19 What, think, trying   20 move on to

21 see, behind, large

22 actually painted

23 Who, think he is   24 Take, look

25 seems to, main, because   26 title, painting

27 drawing, beside, princess   28 Take, close

29 make you wonder

30 Try, which direction

31 see, in, mirror, background   32 Who, think, is

본문 TEST Step 2   p.11~12

01 Welcome to, tour

02 when, go to, how much time, spend looking at

03 glance at, for, a few, move on

04 might miss, since, to notice them

05 look at, closely, help you see, details

06 Look at, first

07 seaside landscape, peaceful, isn't it

08 title of, is　　09 where Icarus is

10 are sticking out of the water near

11 in the famous myth

12 made wings for him with feathers, to stay away from

13 However, didn't listen　　14 flew too close

15 melted, fell into　　16 look at, entire

17 Despite, going on with, everyday activities

18 still look peaceful

19 What do you think, trying to　　20 move on to

21 see, behind　　22 actually painted

23 Who do you think he is

24 Take, quick look

25 seems to be, because, in the center

26 title, painting

27 drawing, beside

28 Take, close look

29 make you wonder

30 Try to, which direction the artist is

31 see, in the mirror, background

32 Who do you think he is

---

16 이제, 그림 전체를 다시 보세요.

17 이카루스의 비극에도 불구하고 사람들은 일상의 활동을 계속하고 있습니다.

18 그림이 여전히 평화로워 보이나요?

19 화가가 우리에게 무엇을 말하려 한다고 생각하나요?

20 이제, 다음 그림으로 넘어갑시다.

21 커다란 캔버스 뒤에 있는 화가가 보이나요?

22 그는 Diego Vel②zquez이고, 그가 실제로 이 그림을 그렸습니다.

23 그가 누구를 그리고 있다고 생각하나요?

24 재빨리 봅시다.

25 어린 공주가 그림의 중앙에 있기 때문에 주인공처럼 보입니다.

26 하지만 그림의 제목은 '시녀들'입니다.

27 그렇다면 화가는 공주 옆에 있는 두 여인을 그리고 있나요?

28 자세히 보세요.

29 그림에 대해 더 궁금하게 될 겁니다.

30 화가가 바라보고 있는 방향을 보려고 노력해 보세요.

31 그림의 배경에 있는 거울 속 왕과 왕비가 보이나요?

32 이제 여러분은 그가 누구를 그리고 있다고 생각하나요?

---

1 세계 미술관(the World Art Museum)에 오신 것을 환영합니다.

2 미술관에 갈 때 여러분은 각각의 그림을 보는 데 얼마나 많은 시간을 보내나요?

3 많은 방문객들은 이동하기 전에 하나의 그림을 몇 초간만 힐끗 봅니다.

4 하지만 그림의 중요한 세부 사항들을 즉시 알아채는 것은 어렵기 때문에 여러분들은 그것들을 놓칠 수 있습니다.

5 오늘 우리는 두 개의 그림을 자세히 살펴볼 것이고, 여러분이 흥미로운 세부 사항들을 볼 수 있도록 제가 도와드리겠습니다.

6 먼저 이 그림을 보세요.

7 바닷가 풍경이 매우 평화롭고 아름답죠, 그렇지 않나요?

8 이 그림의 제목은 '추락하는 이카루스가 있는 풍경'입니다.

9 그러면 이카루스가 어디에 있는지 보이나요?

10 배 근처에 물 밖으로 나와 있는 두 다리가 보이죠?

11 이것이 그리스의 유명한 신화에 나오는 이카루스입니다.

12 신화에서 이카루스의 아버지는 그를 위해 깃털과 밀랍으로 날개를 만들어 주었고 그에게 태양을 가까이 하지 말라고 말했습니다.

13 하지만 이카루스는 듣지 않았습니다.

14 그는 태양에 너무 가깝게 날았습니다.

15 그래서 밀랍이 녹았고 그는 물에 빠졌습니다.

---

1 Welcome to the World Art Museum tour.

2 When you go to an art museum, how much time do you spend looking at each painting?

3 Many visitors glance at one painting for only a few seconds before they move on.

4 But you might miss the important details of paintings since it is hard to notice them right away.

5 Today, we'll look at two paintings closely and I'll help you see interesting details.

6 Look at this painting first.

7 The seaside landscape is so peaceful and beautiful, isn't it?

8 The title of this painting is *Landscape with the Fall of Icarus*.

9 So, can you see where Icarus is?

10 Do you see two legs that are sticking out of the water near the ship?

11 This is Icarus in the famous myth in Greece.

12 In the myth, Icarus' father made wings for him with feathers and wax and told him to stay away from the sun.

13 However, Icarus didn't listen.

14 He flew too close to the sun.

15 So, the wax melted and he fell into the water.

16 Now, look at the entire painting again.

17 Despite the tragedy of Icarus, people are going on with their everyday activities.

18 Does the painting still look peaceful?

19 What do you think the artist is trying to tell us?

20 Now, let's move on to the next painting.

21 Do you see the artist behind the large canvas?

22 He is Diego Velázquez, and he actually painted this picture.

23 Who do you think he is painting?

24 Take a quick look.

25 The young princess seems to be the main person because she is in the center of the painting.

26 But the title of the painting is *The Maids of Honour*.

27 Then, is the artist drawing the two women beside the princess?

28 Take a close look.

29 It will make you wonder about the painting more.

30 Try to see which direction the artist is looking at.

31 Can you see the king and the queen in the mirror in the background of the painting?

32 Who do you think he is painting now?

Listen & Talk

1. are, reading
2. reading, who, in a maze
3. seen, too, prefer, to
4. Why, like, better
5. various stories, show, important parts

Grammar in Real Life

1. let, in
2. Who, you
3. promised me, let you enter, be
4. serve you, cookies, tea
5. Never let, in
6. worry, make the princess keep

Think and Write C

1. Amazing Art exhibition
2. interesting pieces of art
3. Among, called
4. was made by
5. Interestingly, was used
6. because, makes me feel calm
7. can be used to
8. Anything, possible

Listen & Talk

1. M: What are you reading, Sally?
2. W: I'm reading *The Maze Runner*. It's about boys who are put in a maze.
3. M: It's a great story. I've seen the movie of it, too. I prefer the novel to the movie.
4. W: Why do you like it better?
5. M: The novel has various stories. But the movie didn't show some important parts of the story.

Grammar in Real Life

1. Princess, please let me in.
2. Who are you?
3. The princess promised me, "If you help me, I'll let you enter the palace and be my friend."
4. Come here. I'll have people serve you some cookies and tea.
5. No! Never let him in. I don't like him.
6. Don't worry, Frog. I'll make the princess keep her promise.

Think and Write C

1. Today, I went to the Amazing Art exhibition.
2. At the exhibition, I saw many interesting pieces of art.
3. Among them, I liked the piece called Moon Tree.
4. It was made by French artist, David Myriam.
5. Interestingly, sand was used in this painting.
6. I like it because a tree in the moon makes me feel calm.
7. Now I know that anything can be used to make art.
8. Anything is possible!

단어 TEST Step 1 p.21

01 균형을 잡다　02 계산대, 판매대　03 혼합물, 혼합
04 무가당의　05 전달하다, 배달하다
06 생각　07 효과　08 (여행) 안내서
09 손으로 쓴　10 튀기다　11 빵집, 제과점
12 존재　13 백, 100　14 제안하다
15 중요함　16 의존, 의지
17 (웹 사이트에 정보, 사진을) 올리다
18 지역의, 현지의; 주민, 현지인　19 기계
20 경험　21 순간　22 근처에
23 최신 유행의　24 의견　25 시내의
26 창의적인　27 토론, 논의　28 가격
29 남아 있다, 남다　30 무서워하는, 겁먹은
31 나이가 지긋한　32 기부하다　33 (과학) 기술
34 현명하게　35 ~을 버리다　36 ~하기를 기대하다
37 ~에 의존하다　38 비록 ~할지라도　39 주목을 받다
40 대금을 지불하다　41 잠들다　42 계속해서 ~하다
43 ~하느라 바쁘다

단어 TEST Step 2 p.22

01 counter　02 technology　03 suggest
04 debate　05 machine　06 donate
07 downtown　08 effect　09 sugar-free
10 experience　11 fry　12 presence
13 price　14 handwritten　15 balance
16 hundred　17 importance　18 thought
19 local　20 creative　21 deliver
22 nearby　23 trendy　24 opinion
25 post　26 mixture　27 agree
28 remain　29 dependence　30 wisely
31 moment　32 scared　33 guesthouse
34 elderly　35 keep -ing　36 pay for
37 be busy -ing　38 throw away　39 rely on
40 even though　41 fall asleep　42 get attention
43 get lost

단어 TEST Step 3 p.23

1 fry, 튀기다　2 guidebook, (여행) 안내서
3 local, 지역의, 현지의　4 bakery, 빵집, 제과점
5 remain, 남아 있다, 남다　6 moment, 순간
7 balance, 균형을 잡다　8 experience, 경험

9 post, (웹사이트에 정보, 사진을) 올리다
10 wisely, 현명하게　11 downtown, 시내의, 도심지의
12 guesthouse, (여행자 등의) 숙소, 여관
13 donate, 기부하다　14 technology, (과학) 기술
15 suggest, 제안하다　16 dependence, 의지, 의존

대화문 TEST Step 1 p.24~25

Listen & Talk 1 A-1

birthday gift / giving, memory stick / video clip, saved, think, present / touching

Listen & Talk 1 A-2

what do you think about / thought, sound effects / made, interesting / couldn't focus, scared

Listen & Talk 1 B

Have, heard / donates, right answer / what, think about / creative, have fun, help out, Have, played / going to try, out

Listen & Talk 2 A-1

better than before / singing contest, get closer / with you on that, wait to watch, next performances

Listen & Talk 2 A-2

comments / comfortable to share / that, posts / not with you on that, share, close friends

Listen & Talk 2 B

help, order / press, choose / How, pay for my order / bottom, pay / simple, much faster than, counter / with you, saves, time, when, line

Communication

debate, first topic What, think / trendy, at a cheaper price / with, on that, spend, throw away / opinions, move on

Wrap Up 1

finished making the posting, What do you think about it / get attention, How about, below / one, right / change / hope, find

대화문 TEST Step 2 p.26~27

Listen & Talk 1 A-1

Jane: Look, Dad. This is Mom's birthday gift.
Dad: Oh, you're giving her a memory stick?
Jane: Yeah, I've made a family video clip for Mom and saved it on this stick. What do you think about the present?
Dad: I think it's really touching. She'll love it.

Listen & Talk 1 A-2

Mike: Jenny, what do you think about the new online comic Scary Night?

Jenny: I didn't like it. I thought it had too many sound effects.

Mike: Really? I thought they made the story more interesting.

Jenny: Not me. I couldn't focus because I was too scared.

Listen & Talk 1 B

Tony: Hey, Julie! Have you heard about the Quiz & Rice game?

Julie: Yeah, isn't it the one that donates rice when you get a right answer?

Tony: Yeah, what do you think about the game?

Julie: I think it's a creative game. You can have fun and help out hungry people. Have you played it yet?

Tony: No, but I'm going to try it out this weekend.

Listen & Talk 2 A-1

Jack: Sally, did you watch Super Voice's Top 10 finalists yesterday?

Sally: Yeah. They all sang much better than before.

Jack: Yeah, they did. I think this singing contest helps them get closer to their dreams.

Sally: I'm with you on that. I can't wait to watch their next performances.

Listen & Talk 2 A-2

Steve: Hey, Lisa. I've got over a hundred comments on my SNS posts.

Lisa: Oh, I wouldn't feel comfortable to share my posts with so many people.

Steve: Really? I think it's great that a lot of people see my posts.

Lisa: I'm not with you on that. I only want to share my posts with my close friends.

Listen & Talk 2 B

Emma: Excuse me. Can you help me order with this machine?

Tom: Sure. First, press the Hot Dog button and choose your hot dog and drink.

Emma: Okay. How do I pay for my order?

Tom: Touch the Done button at the bottom and pay for them.

Emma: Wow, it's so simple. This machine is much faster than ordering at the counter.

Tom: I'm with you on that. It really saves a lot of time when there's a long line.

Communication

Sujin: Now, we will start the three-minute debate. Today's first topic is fast fashion. What do you think about it? Please, begin, James.

James: I think fast fashion is good. We can wear trendy clothes at a cheaper price.

Wendy: I'm not with you on that. It makes us spend too much money and throw away clothes too often.

Sujin: It looks like the two of you have different opinions on the first topic. Now, let's move on to the second topic.

Wrap Up 1

Alex: I've just finished making the posting for Leon, Mom. What do you think about it?

Mom: Oh, the title "LOST CAT" in big letters at the top is easy to see.

Alex: Yeah, I did it to get attention. How about these photos below the title?

Mom: Hmm... the one on the right doesn't show Leon's face well.

Alex: Okay, I'll change the photo.

Mom: Oh, I hope we can find Leon.

본문 TEST Step 1   p.28~29

01 suggested, surprising, without
02 to, sitting, looking at
03 explained, kept saying, fully   04 started, trip to
05 first, terrible   06 way, around, lost, downtown
07 busy looking, asking, few, from
08 Even though, right, get
09 so tired that, out
10 fall alseep, worried, happen
11 looking around, have, fried
12 However, which, to
13 up, elderly, tired, directions
14 seemed, understand, words
15 took, local, nearby
16 fried rice, amazing
17 take, post, blog
18 without, decided, enjoy, moment
19 remaining, relied, on
20 able, various, on, streets
21 kind enough, sides
22 talked, with, other
23 much, together on

24 trip, different experience

25 dependent on, that, without

26 that, moment without

27 From, learned, importance, balanced

28 So, would, travel

29 Probalby, try, wisely

---

01 suggested, surprising, family trip without

02 hate to see, sitting together, looking at

03 explained, kept saying that, not fully enjoy

04 started, trip to

05 first day, terrible

06 On the way to, around, got lost in downtown

07 was busy looking, asking for, with a few, from

08 Even though, right next to, it took, to get

09 were so tired that, could not go out

10 went to bed, fall alseep, worried, what would happen

11 After looking around, to have, fried

12 which restaurant to go to

13 went up to, tired to ask for directions

14 seemed to understand, words   15 took us, nearby

16 fried rice, amazing

17 take picture of, post them

18 without, decided to enjoy

19 During, remaining, relied, on

20 were able to meet, talk with

21 kind enough to show, with a smile

22 talked, with each other

23 much of our time together

24 new and different experience

25 so dependent on, that, couldn't, without

26 that, without it

27 From, have learned, importance, balanced use

28 would I travel   29 try to use it, wisely

---

1 지난여름, 아빠가 깜짝 놀랄 만한 이벤트로 스마트폰 없는 가족 여행을 제안하셨다!

2 아빠는 "나는 우리 가족이 함께 앉아서 각자의 스마트폰만 보고 있는 걸 보는 게 참 싫구나."라고 말씀하셨다.

3 여동생과 내가 스마트폰이 필요하다고 설명했지만, 아빠는 스마트폰이 있으면 여행을 충분히 즐길 수 없을 거라고 계속해서 말씀하셨다.

---

4 그래서 우리는 새로운 도시인 스페인의 바르셀로나로 '첨단 과학 기술 없는 여행'을 시작했다.

5 우리의 첫째 날은 엉망이었다.

6 레이알 광장 주변에 있는 여행자 숙소로 가는 길에 우리는 바르셀로나 시내에서 길을 잃었다.

7 아빠는 지도를 보며 여행안내 책자에서 배운 스페인어 몇 마디로 길을 묻느라 분주하셨다.

8 우리의 숙소가 광장 바로 옆에 있었음에도 불구하고, 우리가 그곳에 도착하는 데는 거의 두 시간이 걸렸다.

9 우리는 너무 피곤해서 저녁을 먹으러 나갈 수가 없었다.

10 나는 잠자리에 들었지만 내일 무슨 일이 일어날지 걱정이 되어서 잠들 수가 없었다.

11 가우디가 지은 구엘 공원을 둘러본 후, 우리는 점심으로 해산물 볶음밥을 먹기로 했다.

12 그러나 우리는 어떤 식당으로 가야 할지 몰랐다.

13 우리는 도움이 필요해서, 엄마가 한 노부인에게 가서 인기 있는 해산물 식당으로 가는 길을 물어보려고 애쓰셨다.

14 운이 좋게도 그녀는 몇 마디 안 되는 엄마의 스페인어를 이해하는 듯했다.

15 그녀는 우리를 근처에 있는 작은 현지 식당으로 데려다 주었다.

16 그 해산물 볶음밥은 놀랍도록 맛있었다.

17 나는 음식 사진을 찍어 그것을 내 블로그에 올리고 싶은 마음이 정말 간절했다.

18 그러나 스마트폰이 없었기 때문에 나는 그냥 그 순간을 즐기기로 했다.

19 (여행의) 남아 있는 날들 동안, 우리는 점점 더 현지 사람들에게 의존하게 되었다.

20 우리는 거리에서, 빵집에서, 공원에서 다양한 사람들을 만나 이야기할 수 있었다.

21 그들은 항상 웃으면서 너무나 친절히도 바르셀로나의 다양한 면을 우리에게 보여 주었다.

22 또한 우리 가족은 서로 많은 대화를 나누었다.

23 우리는 스페인의 기차에서, 버스에서, 그리고 식당에서 많은 시간을 함께 보냈다.

24 우리의 '첨단 과학 기술 없는' 여행은 새롭고 색다른 경험이었다.

25 여행 전에 나는 내 스마트폰에 너무 의존해서 그것 없이는 아무것도 할 수 없었다.

26 하지만 지금은 내가 스마트폰 없이도 그 순간을 즐길 수 있음을 알고 있다.

27 그 경험을 통해, 나는 스마트폰을 균형 있게 사용하는 것이 중요함을 배우게 되었다.

28 그러면, 다음번에 나는 스마트폰 없이 여행을 하게 될까?

29 아마도 그렇지는 않을 것이다. 하지만 나는 그것을 좀 더 현명하게 사용하기 위해 노력할 것이다.

1 Last summer, my father suggested a surprising event: a family trip without smartphones!

2 He said, "I hate to see you sitting together and only looking at your smartphones."

3 My sister and I explained the need for smartphones, but he kept saying that we could not fully enjoy the trip with them.

4 So we started a technology-free trip to a new city, Barcelona, Spain.

5 Our first day was terrible.

6 On the way to our guesthouse around Plaza Reial, we got lost in downtown Barcelona.

7 Dad was busy looking at the map and asking for directions with a few Spanish words he got from a tour guidebook.

8 Even though our guesthouse was right next to the Plaza, it took us about two hours to get there.

9 We were so tired that we could not go out for dinner.

10 I went to bed but couldn't fall asleep because I was worried about what would happen the next day.

11 After looking around Gaudi's Park Guell, we decided to have seafood fried rice for lunch.

12 However, we didn't know which restaurant to go to.

13 We needed help, so Mom went up to an elderly lady and tried to ask for directions to a popular seafood restaurant.

14 Luckily, she seemed to understand Mom's few Spanish words.

15 She took us to a small local restaurant nearby.

16 The seafood fried rice was amazing.

17 I really wanted to take pictures of the food and post them on my blog.

18 But without my phone, I just decided to enjoy the moment.

19 During the remaining days, we relied more and more on the locals.

20 We were able to meet and talk with various people on the streets, in the bakeries, and in the parks.

21 They were always kind enough to show us different sides of Barcelona with a smile.

22 Also, our family talked a lot with each other.

23 We spent much of our time together on the Spanish train, on the bus, and at the restaurants.

24 Our technology-free trip was a new and different experience.

25 Before the trip, I was so dependent on my smartphone that I couldn't do anything without it.

26 But now I see that I can enjoy the moment without it.

27 From the experience, I have learned the importance of a balanced use of the smartphone.

28 So, next time, would I travel without a smartphone?

29 Probably not. But I will try to use it more wisely.

Read and Think

1. Technology-Free Trip

2. new, different experience, without

3. Troubles

4. On, on our way to

5. take pictures of, post, on

6. Joys

7. enjoyed, around

8. a lot, all the time

9. after

10. thoughts, using

11. couldn't do anything

12. importance, balanced use

Grammar in Real Life B

1. Wash, running, cut, into, pieces

2. cut, with, low, heat

3. Add, to make, mixture

4. Roll, out, put, filling

5. rolled bread, take it out, bake, minutes

6. Decorate, remaining apple filling

Read and Think

1. Technology-Free Trip to Barcelona

2. Last summer, I had a new and different experience: a family trip without smartphones.

3. Troubles

4. On the first day, we got lost on our way to the guesthouse.

5. I couldn't take pictures of the food and post them on my blog.

6. Joys

7. I enjoyed the places and the people around me.

8. I talked a lot with my family all the time and everywhere.

9. Changes after the Trip

10. My thoughts on using a smartphone

11. Before: I couldn't do anything without it.

12. Now: I understand the importance of a balanced use of it.

Grammar in Real Life B

1. Wash one apple under running water and cut it into small pieces.

2. Cook the cut apple pieces with brown sugar on low heat.

3. Add salt, milk, and a beaten egg to make the egg mixture.

4. Roll the bread out and put the cooked apple filling on it.

5. Put the rolled bread in the egg mixture and take it out quickly. Then bake it for 3 minutes .

6. Decorate a dish with the bread rolls and the remaining apple filling.

Lesson 5

단어 TEST Step 1   p.40

01 수염	02 수레, 우마차	03 손주
04 아내, 부인	05 땅, 지면	06 돌
07 문제	08 파괴하다, 없애다	09 기쁜
10 건네주다	11 도착하다	12 (새끼를) 낳다
13 경고하다	14 통나무	15 마술의
16 소, 암소	17 기쁨	18 아무것도 ~아닌 것
19 보상, 보답	20 빼내다, 풀어 주다; 자유로운	
21 결심하다, 결정하다		22 계절
23 난쟁이	24 설명하다	25 들판, 밭
26 이, 치아	27 ~하지 않는 한	28 흐르다, 지나가다
29 ~을 기대하다, ~을 고대하다		30 ~을 없애다
31 ~을 버리다	32 ~을 자랑스러워하다	
33 ~으로 바꾸다	34 ~에서 멀리	35 ~하려고 노력하다
36 새끼를 낳다, 출산하다		37 떠나가다
38 ~가 …하지 못하게 하다		39 ~로 가는 길에
40 ~에 대해 걱정하다		41 계속 ~하다

단어 TEST Step 2   p.41

01 arrive	02 season	03 delight
04 free	05 ground	06 decide
07 warn	08 explain	09 unless
10 field	11 beard	12 wife
13 glad	14 hand	15 log
16 magic	17 destroy	18 tooth
19 grandchild	20 nothing	21 cart
22 stone	23 bear	24 cow
25 reward	26 dwarf	27 trouble
28 far from	29 be proud of	
30 keep ~ from -ing		31 try to
32 get rid of	33 go away	34 change into
35 keep ~ing	36 look forward to	
37 on one's way to		38 go by
39 throw away	40 worry about	41 give birth

단어 TEST Step 3   p.42

1 stone, 돌멩이   2 hand, 건네주다

3 bear, (아이나 새끼를) 낳다   4 grandchild, 손주

5 beard, 수염   6 wife, 아내, 부인   7 arrive, 도착하다

8 destroy, 파괴하다   9 log, 통나무   10 cow, 소, 암소

31

11 season, 계절　12 field, 들판　13 cart, 수레, 우마차
14 reward, 보상　15 warn, 경고하다
16 free, 빼내다, 풀어 주다

본문 TEST Step 1　p.43~44

01 One, driving down, when
02 looked, sick, worry about
03 Later, saw, field
04 get, out, under
05 pulled, away, freed
06 have, reward, want
07 heard, that, keep, young
08 humans, wrong, keep from
09 tried, explain, with, listen
10 handed, went away
11 a few, grow, all
12 became, got upset
13 change into, slow
14 birth, got, throw, away
15 listen to, threw, out
16 found, sitting by
17 worried about, that, still
18 having trouble, tooth, seen
19 throw away, put, under
20 back, went by, grew
21 worry, look forward, nothing
22 destroy, kept, back
23 throw away, far from
24 On, way, got angry
25 didn't, warn, about
26 tried, wouldn't listen
27 explained, rid of, unless
28 more, Whatever, let, happen
29 throw, onto, back
30 as, arrived, changed, bore
31 with delight, tooth, mouth
32 their, lived for, years
33 proud of, beard

본문 TEST Step 2　p.45~46

01 driving down, on his horse, when
02 looked, sick, to worry about growing old
03 Later that day, dwarf
04 trying to get, out from
05 pulled, away, freed

06 reward, do, want
07 heard, that, keep, young
08 it all wrong, young again, keep, from getting older
09 tried to explain, didn't listen　10 handed him
11 a few days, grow at all
12 became, got upset
13 change into chickens, slow
14 give birth, got, angry, to throw it away
15 listen to, threw, out
16 However, found, sitting by
17 worried about, glad that, still young
18 having trouble, No tooth, seen
19 to throw away, put, under the ground
20 came back, went by, nothing grew, changed
21 to worry, nothing to look forward to
22 tried to destroy, kept coming back
23 decided to throw away, far from
24 On his way to, got angry
25 didn't you warn　26 tried to, listen
27 explained, get rid of, unless, wanted to
28 no more of, Whatever, let, happen
29 to throw, onto, go back home
30 did, said, arrived, changed into, bore
31 laughed with delight, his baby's mouth
32 lived for many years　33 was proud of

본문 TEST Step 3　p.47~48

1 어느 날, Maibon이 한 노인을 보았을 때, 그는 마차를 타고 길을 내려가고 있던 중이었다.
2 그 노인은 매우 아파 보였다. Maibon은 늙어 가는 것이 걱정되기 시작했다.
3 그날 오후, 그는 들판에서 Doli라는 난쟁이를 보았다.
4 그는 통나무 아래에 깔린 그의 다리를 빼내려고 하고 있었다.
5 Maibon은 통나무를 잡아당겨서 난쟁이를 풀어 주었다.
6 "너는 보상을 받게 될 거야. 원하는 게 뭐니?"
7 "나는 네가 사람의 젊음을 유지해 주는 마법의 돌들을 가지고 있다고 들었어. 나는 그것을 원해."
8 오, 너희 인간들은 잘못 알고 있어. 그 돌들은 너희들이 다시 젊어지게 해 주지 않아. 단지 더 늙지 않게 막아 줄 뿐이라고."
9 "그것대로 좋아!" Doli는 그 돌에 관한 문제를 설명하려고 했지만, Maibon은 듣지 않았다.
10 그래서 Doli는 그에게 마법의 돌을 건네고는 가버렸다.
11 며칠이 지나서, Maibon은 그의 수염이 전혀 자라지 않았음을 알았다.
12 그는 행복해졌지만, 그의 아내 Modrona는 화가 났다.
13 "달걀이 닭이 되지 않아요!" "아, 시기가 더딘 거예요. 그 뿐이에요."

14 하지만 그녀는 탐탁해하지 않았다. "소가 새끼를 낳지 않아요!" 그때 Maibon은 그 돌에 대해 그녀에게 이야기를 했고 그녀는 매우 화를 내며 그에게 그것을 버리라고 말했다.

15 그는 원하지 않았지만, 아내의 말을 듣고 창밖으로 돌을 던졌다.

16 그러나 다음날 아침 그는 창가에 그 돌이 있는 것을 발견했다!

17 Maibon은 동물들이 걱정되긴 했지만, 자신이 여전히 젊어서 기뻤다.

18 이제 Maibon의 아기에게 문제가 생겼다. 아기의 입에서 이가 보이지 않았다.

19 그의 아내는 그에게 그 돌을 버리라고 말했고 Maibon은 이번엔 그 돌을 땅속에 묻었다.

20 그런데 그 다음날 그 돌은 다시 돌아왔다! 시간이 흘렀고 어떤 것도 자라거나 변하지 않았다.

21 Maibon은 걱정이 되기 시작했다. "기대할 것도 내 일의 결과를 보여 줄 것도 아무것도 없어."

22 Maibon은 그 돌을 없애려고 노력했지만 돌은 계속 되돌아왔다.

23 Maibon은 그 돌을 그의 집에서 멀리 떨어진 곳에 버리기로 결심했다.

24 그는 들판으로 가는 길에 난쟁이를 보았다. Maibon은 그에게 화를 냈다.

25 "너는 왜 내게 그 돌에 대해 경고하지 않았어?"

26 "나는 하려고 했지만, 너는 들으려 하지 않았어."

27 Doli는 Maibon이 진심으로 원하지 않는 한 그 돌을 없앨 수 없다고 설명했다.

28 "나는 그것을 더 이상 원하지 않아. 무슨 일이 있어도 일어나게 해!"

29 Doli는 그에게 그 돌을 땅에 던지고 집으로 돌아가라고 말했다.

30 Maibon은 Doli가 말한 대로 했다. 그가 집에 도착했을 때, Modrona는 그에게 달걀이 닭이 되고 소가 새끼를 낳았다는 좋은 소식을 말해 주었다.

31 그리고 Maibon은 아기의 입에 첫 이가 난 것을 보고 기뻐서 웃었다.

32 Maibon과 Modrona, 그리고 그들의 자녀들과 손주들은 오랫동안 살았다.

33 Maibon은 그의 흰 머리와 긴 수염을 자랑스러워했다.

본문 TEST Step 4·Step 5　　　　　　p.49~52

1 One day, Maibon was driving down the road on his horse and cart when he saw an old man.

2 The old man looked very sick. Maibon began to worry about growing old.

3 Later that day, he saw a dwarf, Doli, in the field.

4 He was trying to get his leg out from under a log.

5 Maibon pulled the log away and freed the dwarf.

6 "You'll have your reward. What do you want?"

7 "I've heard that you have magic stones that can

keep a man young. I want one."

8 "Oh, you humans have it all wrong. Those stones don't make you young again. They only keep you from getting older."

9 "Just as good!" Doli tried to explain the problem with the stones, but Maibon didn't listen.

10 So Doli handed him a magic stone and went away.

11 After a few days, Maibon saw that his beard didn't grow at all.

12 He became happy, but his wife, Modrona, got upset.

13 "The eggs don't change into chickens!" "Oh, the season's slow, that's all."

14 But she was not happy. "The cow doesn't give birth!" Maibon, then, told her about the stone, and she got very angry and told him to throw it away.

15 He didn't want to, but he listened to his wife and threw the stone out the window.

16 However, the next morning, he found the stone sitting by the window!

17 Maibon was worried about the animals, but he was glad that he was still young.

18 Now Maibon's baby was having trouble. No tooth was seen in his mouth.

19 His wife told him to throw away the stone and this time, Maibon put the stone under the ground.

20 But, the next day, the stone came back! Time went by and nothing grew or changed.

21 Maibon began to worry. "There's nothing to look forward to, nothing to show for my work."

22 Maibon tried to destroy the stone, but it kept coming back.

23 Maibon decided to throw away the stone far from his house.

24 On his way to the field, he saw the dwarf. Maibon got angry with him.

25 "Why didn't you warn me about the stone?"

26 "I tried to, but you wouldn't listen."

27 Doli explained that Maibon couldn't get rid of the stone unless he really wanted to.

28 "I want no more of it. Whatever may happen, let it happen!"

29 Doli told him to throw the stone onto the ground and go back home.

30 Maibon did as Doli said. When he arrived home, Modrona told him the good news — the eggs

changed into chickens and the cow bore her baby.

31 And Maibon laughed with delight when he saw the first tooth in his baby's mouth.

32 Maibon, Modrona and their children and grandchildren lived for many years.

33 Maibon was proud of his white hair and long beard.

MEMO

MEMO

적중100

영어 기출 문제집

정답 및 해설

비상 | 김진완